The politics of corporate taxation in the European Union

The European Union is facing a political dilemma between avoiding the centralisation of corporate tax policy, or avoiding the undesirable consequences of unbridled tax competition and international double taxation. The political response has been haphazard, with the emergence of an embryonic European Union corporate tax policy regime, and an endemic reluctance to co-ordinate tax policy in Europe.

Although minimal, the existence of a European policy regime in this area defies the conventional idea that states will never surrender their tax sovereignty to the institutions of the European Union. This study explores the formation of the European Union's corporate tax policy and asks why member states did not raise objections to it. Claudio Radaelli's analysis is enriched by two further levels of inquiry. First, he examines the 'Europeanisation' of domestic tax policy in Italy and the UK, asking how domestic policy has changed and what is meant by 'Europeanisation'. Second, he puts the European Union tax policy in the wider context of tax globalisation. Will the liberalisation of capital movement, tax havens and the flexibility of multinationals in managing their taxable incomes wreck the European Union's fragile tax policies?

In addressing these issues the study finds that knowledge is one of the most important resources in the European corporate tax process. It highlights the political problems raised by the search for rules, principles and appropriate levels of tax co-ordination and concludes that the European Union should re-consider its tax policy with new arguments and new strategic perspectives.

Claudio M. Radaelli is Lecturer in European Public Policy, University of Bradford.

ROUTLEDGE RESEARCH IN EUROPEAN PUBLIC POLICY

Edited by Jeremy Richardson

1 **The Politics of Corporate Taxation in the European Union**
Knowledge and International Policy Agendas
Claudio M. Radaelli

The politics of corporate taxation in the European Union

Knowledge and international policy agendas

Claudio M. Radaelli

ROUTLEDGE

London and New York

First published 1997
by Routledge
11 New Fetter Lane, London EC4P 4EE

Simultaneously published in the USA and Canada
by Routledge
29 West 35th Street, New York, NY 10001

Typeset in Times by Routledge
Printed and bound in Great Britain by T.J. International Ltd, Padstow, Cornwall

British Library Cataloguing in Publication Data
A catalogue record for this book is available from the British Library

Library of Congress Cataloguing in Publication Data
Radaelli, Claudio M. (Claudio Maria), 1960–
The politics of corporate taxation in the European Union: knowledge and international policy agendas / Claudio M. Radaelli.
p. cm.
Includes bibliographical references.
1.Corporations–Taxation–European Union countries. I. Title.
HD2753.E8R33 1997
336.24′3′096–dc21 97-9647
CIP

ISBN 0–415–14999–1

Contents

Illustrations

FIGURE

TABLES

Series editor's preface

One of the enduring debates concerning the development of the European Union is the extent to which the erosion of national sovereignty takes place differentially across policy areas. Thus, some policy areas have long since exhibited a very high degree of 'Europeanisation' whilst others have remained firmly anchored at the national level. Conventional wisdom has it that certain policy areas, such as defence, healthcare, education and, above all, taxation, will be the most resistant to moves to shift the locus of power to the supranational level. Thus, control over central features of nation states, such as welfare policies and taxation policy, is usually thought unlikely to be subject to the pooling of sovereignty. Yet, Claudio Radaelli's perceptive study of corporate taxation policy suggests that at least some areas of taxation policy might not be immune to the process of Europeanisation.

The extent to which this policy area has been subject to a degree of Europeanisation and the potential for a much more significant shift constitute the empirical focus of this volume. Corporate taxation policy is seen as interesting because the Union faces a political dilemma between the centralisation of corporate tax policy and the undesirable consequences of tax competition and international double taxation. For example, the German government is in the process of launching a campaign against tax competition in an effort to persuade fellow member states not to use 'unfair' fiscal practices to attract companies and savers. With French support, it seems that, as the *Financial Times* put it in January 1997, European fiscal policy may be emerging from a long period of 'hibernation' in response, particularly, to the so-called 'beggar-thy-neighbour' tax policies of the member states. The OECD has also become interested in the possible effects of tax competition. Moreover, the effects of monetary union are likely to give greater impetus to the so-called fiscal federalism debate.

Thus, Claudio Radaelli's study is important if only because he analyses a policy area which now seems set to achieve greater political salience within the EU. However, his study is of much wider significance than this. He makes an important contribution to our general understanding of the policy process. In particular, he looks at the cognitive dimension of the policy process. As he argues, it is important to understand when, how and why knowledge is transmitted into policy choices. The so-called 'knowledge dimension' underpins his analysis of the corporate taxation policy process. A central thesis is that knowledge has less to do with specific actors than with the structure within which actors act. Actors operate within the knowledge structure of the policy process using shared paradigms. Yet their actions also modify the cognitive resources available in the policy process. The cognitive structure of the policy process in turn provides interpretations of events and learning opportunities. The learning process can then change the cognitive structure and so on.

The study also links features of the learning process – concepts, ideas and policy paradigms – developed in the EU policy process, to Europeanisation of domestic policy. Europeanisation can take place when national policy makers begin to see domestic issues within a European 'frame' and adjust their national policies to a European paradigm, even though there is no compulsion to do so. Preferences are defined and modified through social interaction, not just by force or power. Hence, he argues, endogenous elements are important sources of policy change as well as more commonly recognised exogenous factors.

Finally, his study turns to the wider context of the globalisation of tax policy and its possible impact on what he terms the 'fragile tax bastions' erected around the European Union. Here, again, Claudio Radaelli is raising central issues in European policy making, beyond the confines of the particular policy area under scrutiny. In so doing, he draws upon a wide range of theoretical literature, from political science and policy analysis to sociology, to fashion a study which exhibits a finely crafted mixture of empirical research and theoretical analysis.

Jeremy Richardson
Essex University

Acknowledgements

This study was originally undertaken as part of my doctoral research at the University of Florence and was later substantially developed thanks to a post-doctoral Human Capital Mobility grant of the European Commission. The grant enabled me to spend a year at the University of Warwick where I had the opportunity to assist Jeremy Richardson in chairing the 1994 session of the 'public policy workshop'. Another grant, this time from the British Council, enabled me to spend ten days at the International Bureau of Fiscal Documentation in Amsterdam (September 1996). The IBFD provided an ideal forum of discussion and library research and I am grateful to Anna Bardadin, librarian at the IBFD, for her assistance in searching sources and documents.

Parts of the book were originally presented elsewhere and discussed in conferences. A slightly different version of Chapter 2 was published in the *Journal of European Public Policy*, vol. 2, no. 2, June 1995, 159–183; a draft of Chapter 5 was discussed at the Political Science Association annual conference (Glasgow, April 1996) and published with the title 'Harmonising What, Why, and to What Effect? The Politics of Problem Definition in EU Direct Corporate Tax Harmonisation', in I. Hampsher-Monk and J. Stanyer (eds) *Contemporary Political Studies*, vol. 2, PSA, 1996, 751–760; Chapter 6 was published (albeit in a different version) by the *Journal of Public Policy*, vol. 15, no. 2, 1995, 43–71; parts of Chapter 7 were included in a paper given to the *8ème Colloque International de la Revue Politiques et Management Public* on the Europeanisation of public policies (Paris, June 1996); slightly different versions of Chapter 7 have now been published in *Comparative Political Studies* (vol. 30, October 1997), and *Revue 'Politiques et Management Public'* (vol. 15, no. 2, June 1997); Chapter 8 was originally presented as a paper given to the annual meeting of the *Societa' Italiana di Scienza Politica* (Urbino, June

1996); and finally, an earlier version of Chapter 10 was originally presented at the 10th Conference of Europeanists (Chicago, March 1996) and parts of it appeared in the *Journal of European Public Policy* vol. 3, no. 3, 1996, 402–420. I am grateful to the above mentioned journals for permission to use this material.

I am much indebted to a number of people who encouraged and sustained my project with their friendship and intellectual generosity, most notably Jeremy Richardson, who helped me in organising some initial, vague thoughts on tax policy into a research plan that could be undertaken professionally and delivered. My *maestro* Bruno Dente, who taught me the 'art and craft' of public policy analysis, and my doctoral supervisor Gloria Regonini, were immensely helpful in providing advice and thorough discussion of my ideas. Other academics and experts were involved at some stage of the book: amongst the many, I would like to express my gratitude to Julian Alworth, John Chown, Kenneth Dyson, Geoffrey Dudley, Silvia Giannini, Wyn Grant, Maurizio Ferrera, Malcolm Gammie, Margaret Lamb, Giuseppe Marino, Andrew Moravcsik, Lorenzo Ornaghi, Vincenzo Russo, and Daniel Wincott. The Department of European Studies at the University of Bradford provided a formidable organisation of my teaching time in 1995–1996, thus assisting the completion of this book. Finally, the warmest acknowledgement goes to the many interviewees who agreed to comment upon my hypotheses and to discuss their involvement in the policy process; their names are listed in the appendix. The usual disclaimer applies.

This book is dedicated to my parents Luisa and Fausto, from whom I learned that dreams can come true, and to my dearest love and inspiration, Alison.

Delph Cottage, Keelham, January 1997

1 Introduction

International tax complexity as a political problem

The politics of international taxation is one of the less explored aspects of globalisation. Lawyers[1] have documented the growing complexity of tax laws affecting the cross-border activity of transnational corporations and individuals, and economists[2] have measured tax-induced distortions of economic activity, but the analysis of actors, principles, norms, rules, models of behaviour, and organisations dealing with the *international tax order* has barely emerged (Bird 1988; Tanzi 1995) and therefore deserves more in-depth analysis. There are several reasons for analysing international taxation from the perspective of political science. First, the liberalisation of capital movement (Sinn 1990) and the increasing mobility of skilled labour (Tanzi 1995) represent an objective threat to the link between taxation and representation. In the most extreme scenario, capital income taxes will be lowered, perhaps to zero, by the dynamics of tax competition and governments will be obliged to impose an increasing tax burden on unskilled labour and landowners, which are the only two immobile factors in a deeply integrated economy.

As a consequence, highly-skilled or wealthy citizens will have the option of paying low taxes (or no taxes at all) in countries other than those in which they are resident. This is tantamount to saying that a political time-bomb has been placed at the core of the welfare state by deep economic integration (Sinn 1990): redistributive policies would no longer be feasible. Conflicts are bound to be rife in political systems that would place the whole tax burden on certain segments of their populations, particularly low-skilled labour. Economic resources for welfare states, currently provided by wealthy citizens, would flow elsewhere should a state seek to impose more than zero-rate (or merely virtual) taxes. The fundamental link between taxation and representation would be relevant for some citizens, but not for others. A departure point of this book is that the internationalisation of taxation is not limited to the problems created by wealthy individuals who can hide their income abroad. Quite the contrary, the essential problem of the international tax system concerns sophisticated tax payers such as transnational enterprises. One of the characteristics of deep internationalisation (Tanzi 1995) is that a number of activities of transnational enterprises have now become mobile: examples are provided by head offices, central services, offshore banking centres, and captive insurance companies (OECD 1996b: 9). A recent OECD report explains that 'the introduction of new technologies and advanced communication networks combined with the removal of non-tax barriers, has given multinational enterprises a wide discretion in locating these central services' (OECD 1996b: 9). Accordingly, countries compete to attract activities which need not be location-specific. The competition for capital income and mobile activities of transnational enterprises has already generated important transformation in the structure of domestic corporate tax systems because countries cannot afford to tax companies without considering what other countries are doing. Corporate tax policy is thus made in a strategic context. As a consequence, the idea of sovereignty has been severely limited in corporate tax policy. Deep internationalisation of taxation (i.e. tax globalisation) hence contributes to the fragmentation of the state. Accordingly, analysing international taxation is part of the conceptual effort to understand and explain the transformation of the state.

Second, international taxation is a policy in search of institutionalisation. Although the challenge of setting up an international tax order was addressed by the League of Nations in 1928, with a report by four 'wise men' on international tax issues (Picciotto 1992: Chapter 1), there still remains a fundamental difficulty in building legitimacy around policy solutions and organisations. The uncertainty about 'what can be done?' is a radical form of uncertainty as it implies the question 'which institutions for which problems?' And indeed formal institutions capable of governing international taxation have not as yet emerged. Political scientists, whose professional remit is to explain the emergence of political order, are potentially qualified for studying this fascinating aspect of globalisation. Yet the study of international direct tax policy is a field characteristically free of political scientists[3].

A third reason for investigating the political aspects of international taxation is the political trade-off between tax competition and tax co-ordination (Edwards and Keen 1996; Frey and Eichenberger 1996). Given the current entropy of the international tax system, both solutions are available to policy-makers. In general terms, tax competition, as shown by the theory of fiscal federalism and by the school of public choice, curbs political distortions, whilst tax co-ordination has the advantage of mitigating tax-induced economic distortions. Why should tax competition be preferred to tax co-operation? Essentially, because politicians and political parties may pursue goals that deviate from citizens' preferences (Brennan and Buchanan 1980). In this classic public choice scenario, politicians and political parties form a cartel against voters. High and uniform taxes across jurisdictions – the argument goes on – will restrict the 'exit' option and citizens will face high costs in raising their voices against centralised governments (Frey and Eichenberger 1996; see Hirschman 1970 for the concepts of exit and voice). In addition, in the case of the European Union, citizens do not even have the right to sanction the government by not re-electing it. Tax competition is therefore advocated.

However, if tax competition works reasonably well in mature federations, in which there is a democratically elected federal government, a single currency, and appropriate stabilisation mechanisms for absorbing asymmetric shocks that hit certain areas of a federation, the dynamics of tax competition in the global economy can be far from optimal. As mentioned earlier, tax competition for portfolio investment can indeed trigger an unbridled competition for attracting capital. This phenomenon of tax degradation has raised the question of whether capital income taxes can be sustained at all in a world of capital movement liberalisation (Gordon 1992). Even regional integration, such as a uniform tax regime for capital income in the European Union, can become an idol with feet of clay if aggressive tax havens (Doggart 1993) are prepared to lure portfolio investment (Razin and Sadka 1989). Not only does tax globalisation affect portfolio investment, but foreign direct investment of transnational corporations is also sensitive to differences in tax regimes. Accordingly, economic theory has explored the possibilities for strategic use of corporate taxation by countries that want to attract investment and retain the most valuable functions of their transnational corporations (such as R&D and headquarters) at home (Bond and Samuelson 1989; Hamada 1966; Janeba 1995). A general result of this theory is that non-co-operative games between nations who engage in strategic use of corporate taxation produce a non-efficient equilibrium: capital stock is inefficiently allocated in a non-co-operative tax world. This is why a measure of co-ordination can be advocated.

The concrete specification of tax co-ordination is puzzling. What should be co-ordinated and for solving which problems? An extreme measure of co-ordination such as the harmonisation of tax systems, tax rates, and tax bases raises immense political and administrative costs. In addition, how could a tax rate (or a range of tax rates) be chosen? The different rates that countries have chosen reflect alternative conceptions of public policy and the welfare state that have been legitimated by democratic elections (Tanzi 1995: 119). Moreover, there is no tax rate that could be considered an optimal 'anchor' around which national tax systems ought to converge (Tanzi and Bovenberg 1990). Economic theory cannot help in selecting a widely agreed 'objective' reference point for harmonisation, and predicts that full harmonisation is bound to decrease the world welfare.

The political trade-off between co-ordination (i.e. the limitation of economic distortions) and competition (i.e. the mitigation of political distortions) can only be tackled politically. Of course, economic theory suggests that the two extremes of unbridled tax competition and full harmonisation should be eschewed. However, economic criteria do not provide a socially optimal position on the possibility frontier relating economic and political distortions, and economists such as Frey and Eichenberger (1996: 336) have therefore contended that an 'inward shift' of the possibility frontier can be achieved by manipulating 'institutional conditions' and the 'rules of the game'. Here is where political science is most obviously needed. Can international regimes improve the trade-off between competition and co-ordination and, if so, how do they emerge? How do political conflict and consensus shape the struggle for creating tax rules in supranational polities such as the European Union and in international policy fora such as the Organisation for Economic Cooperation and Development? Will European institutions play the role of a 'Stackelberg' leader[4] capable of curbing the most dangerous consequences of the prisoner's dilemma triggered by competition for capital? These are the questions that economists and, most crucially, policy-makers, interest groups and citizens address to political science.

The political trade-off between tax co-ordination and tax competition faced by policy-makers is compounded by another trade-off relating to the preferences of the business community. Indeed, firms' preferences are inherently ambiguous. On the one hand, an international tax order provides stability and mitigation of double taxation, two aspects that firms appreciate. On the other, however, a certain degree of entropy offers huge opportunities for tax arbitrage and tax avoidance. As a consequence, there is a trade-off between the benefits of co-ordination and the advantage of tax planning. The latter has its own cost, of course, but when tax planning can be exploited widely there is a *prima facie* suspicion that firms could prefer tax entropy to tax order. Thus the following questions arise: do firms seek a level playing field in international business taxation? With reference to the European Union, do business groups advocate tax co-ordination as an indispensable element of the single market, or, alternatively, do they prefer to rely on the exploitation of tax loopholes, special tax regimes, conduit companies, tax arbitrage with third countries outside the European Union, and all the *paraphernalia* of tax planning?

A final reason for analysing the politics of tax globalisation relates to the European Union. At the outset of the single market project, most notably in the widely quoted Cecchini report (Cecchini 1988), optimistic predictions were formulated on the advent of a single market in which people, goods, firms and capital could move completely freely. The 1993 deadline has passed and the progress of the single market bears witness to many achievements, such as capital movement liberalisation. Yet the phenomena of double taxation and other distortions still existing in business taxation show that the single market project has not been completed. Four years after the 1993 deadline expired, the European Commissioner for tax policy, Mario Monti, argued – see Agence Europe No. 6905, 1 February 1997 – that 'in tax matters the European Union has now reached a point where competition between the different national systems and schemes produces destructive effects, both on the functioning of the internal market and on the fiscal revenue of member states' (also see Commission 1996). Why did tax co-ordination evolve so slowly in the European Union? What are the political constraints hampering the consolidation of a neutral (in the sense of not distorting economic choice) tax regime in Europe which could be so beneficial to the single market? And finally, looking ahead at the new challenge of the European Union, i.e. the single currency, can European countries really enter a monetary union with complete neglect of tax issues?

Moreover, tax competition can compound the problem of sustaining national welfare states which already have been hit hard by the strict economic policies necessary for achieving a single currency before the end of the century (Scharpf 1996a, 1997; Sinn 1990). The European Union is capable of effective action in the area of negative integration (i.e. removing barriers to the single market), but is much less effective in taking decisions in the area of positive integration (i.e. the capability to Europeanise the conditions under which markets work, including welfare regimes). The result could be a degree of tax competition for attracting mobile factors – induced by positive integration – which would erode revenue resources that currently sustain welfare policies at the national level, without any accompanying measure of positive integration at the European level. In this scenario, a degree of tax co-ordination in the European Union, instead of being a mere complement to the single market, could become a key policy in the attempt to bridge the gap between positive and negative integration (Scharpf 1996a, 1997: 34). Will tax harmonisation 'rescue' the welfare state in Europe?

The questions raised above can sustain a long-term research agenda in which many contributions are needed before the politics of tax globalisation could be clarified and explained. At the same time, a strong case can be made for introducing political science into this new field of international taxation. Accordingly, one of the objectives of this book is to take the risk of pioneering into a new area and set the train of political science reflection on tax complexity in motion. The analysis of international taxation offered here proceeds along three different lines of enquiry. To begin with, the main empirical object of analysis is corporate tax co-ordination in the European Union (EU). The EU dimension of corporate tax policy is not considered in isolation but within the contexts of domestic tax policy and tax globalisation. The investigation of the EU corporate tax policy process is therefore supplemented by two further levels of analysis: first, the Europeanisation of domestic tax policy in Italy and the UK and, second, the wider context of tax globalisation in which the European policy regime represents a case of regional policy integration. Indeed, any analysis of EU corporate tax policy cannot be limited to European tax directives or other EU tax measures, but may be assessed only in conjunction with the consideration of domestic tax designs: to what extent have they become 'Europeanised'?

Symmetrically, the political litmus of EU tax initiatives revolves around the embedment of European policy within the global tax order. This leads to three fundamental questions tackled by the research presented in this book: how did the European dimension of corporate taxation emerge? Using the UK and Italy as case studies, what impact did this EU dimension have on domestic tax policy? And finally, is EU corporate tax policy part of a major drive towards a global tax order, or, alternatively, is it part of a poorly institutionalised and essentially entropic tax policy world?

The conclusions will provide answers to these three questions. At this stage it is useful instead to focus upon the theoretical background employed for tackling questions and reaching conclusions. In the case of this study, the theoretical underpinnings are to be found in the literature on the cognitive dimension of politics. The literature on the politics of tax reform and the literature on European integration provide additional useful hypotheses for empirical research. Consequently, Part I of the book considers the intersections between these three bodies of literature which are usually considered somewhat independent and distinct. The organisation of the theoretical underpinnings proceeds as follows: Chapter 2 examines the literature on the role of knowledge in the policy process; Chapter 3 considers the politics of policy-making in the European Union and Chapter 4 the politics of tax reform. The critical examination of the three literatures has two aims: one, as previously mentioned, is to illustrate the theoretical underpinnings of this research, and the other is to build hypotheses for empirical research. Indeed, the reader can consider Part I of this book as a hypothesis-building exercise.

Part II of the book contains the empirical research. Chapter 5 has a preliminary and interlocutory role, to explain the politics of problem definition in the EU corporate tax policy process. This chapter is not directly concerned with empirical analysis but prepares the groundwork for the elaboration of arguments which are developed at length in the remainder of the book. In Chapter 6 the European Union corporate tax policy process is analysed, stressing the need to use this policy process for controlling hypotheses developed in Part I. The main arguments raised by this chapter refer to the role of knowledge in EU tax policy change, the regulatory nature of European tax policy, and the characteristics of policy change in European taxation. Chapter 7 develops the analysis of Europeanisation of tax policy by investigating the transformation of corporate tax policy in Italy and the United Kingdom. In this chapter it is argued that the very meaning of 'Europeanisation' needs to be discussed. Indeed, instead of assuming that Europeanisation revolves around the 'top-down' effect of directives approved in Brussels, it makes sense to investigate if and to what extent the domestic taxation of international income is influenced by European paradigms and European policy. This corresponds to a shift in theoretical focus from 'top-down' to 'bottom-up' approaches in the study of Europeanisation.

Whilst in Chapter 7 EU corporate taxation is projected into the dynamics of domestic tax policy, in Chapter 8 the symmetrical exercise of putting European taxation into the wider, global context is undertaken. When the international tax order is taken into account, the EU becomes only one of the actors involved in the construction of rules, principles, agreements and codes of behaviour for coping with international tax problems. It will be argued that the EU is not a particularly influential actor in the international tax arena. The latter is dominated by policy choices of 'big' national players, most notably the USA.

These choices make political sense in national political systems, but when projected into the wider international tax arena they are the cause of major tax entropy. Thus in the global tax game, not only is the EU a non-starter, but the game finds it difficult to develop its own rules and problem-solving devices. Basically, the institutionalisation of international taxation remains poor.

Part III comprises two chapters, differently related to concluding remarks. Chapter 9 discusses international tax policy as a policy in search of institutionalisation and the problematic role of the EU tax policy regime therein. This chapter also offers the opportunity to comment upon three themes – i.e. the political role of knowledge, the theory of policy change, and the process of institutionalisation – that emerge throughout the research. The major aim in Chapter 9 is to bring arguments based on these three themes and developed in previous chapters to their conclusion. Finally, in Chapter 10 an interpretation of scenarios for future policy development is suggested. To be precise, the future of European direct corporate taxation is examined, taking into consideration the role of arguments drawn from fiscal federalism in tax policy development. This chapter appears after the conclusions because it presents policy recommendations and conjectures about the possible future of EU corporate tax policy.

Part I

Theoretical underpinnings

2 The role of knowledge in the policy process

> The ideas of economists and political philosophers, both when they are right and when they are wrong, are more powerful than is commonly understood.
>
> (J. M. Keynes)

> Ideas, unless outward circumstances conspire with them, have in general no very rapid or immediate efficacy in human affairs.
>
> (J. S. Mill)

> Knowledge is a deadly friend, when no one sets the rules.
>
> (King Crimson 1969)

INTRODUCTION: KNOWLEDGE VERSUS POWER? A FALSE ALTERNATIVE

The first part of this book assesses the development of theoretical reflection in three fields. In this chapter the literature on the cognitive dimension of policy-making is considered, whilst in the subsequent chapters two other fields will be examined, namely policy-formation in the European Union and the politics of tax reform. The role of knowledge in the policy process, public policy in the European Union, and tax reform represent distinct – although partly overlapping – analytical areas. However, the object of this study is situated precisely at the cross-roads of these three bodies of literature. Accordingly, it is useful to analyse first the three literatures separately, and then, in Part II of the book, weld them together when the construction of specific hypotheses for this study and the consequent empirical analysis are undertaken.

This chapter elucidates a theoretical perspective on the policy process which is relatively new, i.e. a perspective that analyses knowledge as an autonomous element of the policy process.[1] Indeed, as in other domains of the social sciences, the interest in the cognitive dimension of politics is more representative of rediscovery than of absolute novelty. If conceptualised in a broader sense, the cognitive dimension of politics is comprised of well-known, even classic, features of political studies. This is shown in the abundant literature developed in the following areas: incrementalism (Lindblom 1959), bounded rationality (Simon 1957), the cognitive maps of political elites (Axelrod 1976), the view of governance and politics as learning (Deutsch 1966: 80; Heclo 1972), the role of knowledge as a basis of elites' power (Wright Mills 1956), the function of technical expertise in the so-called 'military-industrial complex' (Rosen 1973), and the discussion on the dangers of technocracy for the democratic idea (Fischer 1990). Why then 'rediscover' the political role of knowledge? More precisely, what really is new arising from the bulk of studies which, both within public policy analysis (Hall 1989; 1993; Jobert 1989; Kingdon 1984; Sabatier and Jenkins-Smith 1993) and international relations (Goldstein 1993; Goldstein and Keohane 1993; Haas 1992; see Jacobsen 1995 for a review article), advocate the consideration of cognitive factors in policy choices? Finally, and most crucially, what are the costs and benefits of adopting a 'knowledge perspective'? This is the question of primary concern here – although the other questions will also be considered – because the aim in this first part of the book is to flesh out and ultimately choose theoretical perspectives which can orient empirical research on a specific public policy, in our case international taxation. But theoretical perspectives can be adopted only after having assessed their pros and cons.

There are few doubts that the costs of a unilateral perspective are huge: relying solely either on the Keynesian quotation or on Mill's scepticism, quoted above, is not to be recommended. As suggested by the third quote,[2] cognitive factors do not much matter if they are not embedded in a structure of rules;[3] and rule-making is ultimately an act of power. Therefore one contention here is to sketch a tentative agenda for the analysis of the policy process by attempting to outline the building blocks of a framework which goes beyond the quotations from Mill and Keynes. Indeed, the theoretical challenge is not to select an ultimate answer about the relative weight of power – the traditional 'core' of political science – and knowledge, but, rather, to develop an analytical treatment of such questions as *when and how knowledge matters in the policy process*. The quotations from Keynes and Mill are of course selected in order to illustrate two extreme poles. Indeed, Keynes knew perfectly well that 'ideas' often have no immediate effectiveness, as hinted by his famous description of the policy-makers as victims of dead economists! More recently, scholars have emphasised the role of knowledge and in so doing treat the concepts of 'power' and 'knowledge' as opposites, in order to outline different approaches to the study of the policy process. In practice the outcome of the debate is the complementary nature of these concepts.

Two preliminary remarks seem essential: first, since the analysis of the policy process in terms of 'power variables' is well known, this chapter attempts to explore the lesser-known face of the policy process – namely the role that knowledge can play. Second, the main focus is concerned with social science knowledge rather than the impact of scientific knowledge on policy-making (see Barker and Peters 1993).

The chapter is divided into four sections: the first introduces the main concepts; the second examines the different approaches which constitute a 'knowledge perspective' on the policy process; the third section analyses the general tendencies underlined by the approaches reviewed; and the final one reflects upon knowledge as part of a political process.

PUBLIC POLICY AND KNOWLEDGE

At the outset it is important to address briefly the notion of 'public policy'. Political scientists have traditionally regarded public policy as the 'output' of the political system. Analytical efforts have been consequently targeted towards 'inputs', i.e. political demands and the articulation of interests. Some policy scholars have changed this view considerably, establishing public policies as the unit of analysis. Work by Heclo (1972; 1974), Lindblom (1990), Majone (1989), and, from an organisational perspective, Crozier and Friedberg (1977), relates to the dynamic aspects of the policy process. This introduces a perspective which views policy in terms of learning and networks of interaction. In this context, learning should not be seen as necessarily positive and beneficial,[4] but rather as a concept emphasising collective decisions as an unending enquiry. As a consequence, the study of policies ought to take account of both time and learning. The analyst is expected to study a process, in which actors, problems, and solutions may change.

However, having identified public policy as the dependent variable, there is still the difficult task of selecting the independent variable. Conventional wisdom in political science is to focus on power as the most important independent variable explaining policy. Yet, at least since the work of James March (1966), we have been aware of the existence of a class of social choice models – the 'process models' in March's terminology – in which power is not a significant phenomenon. Moreover, Heclo (1974), Heclo and Wildavsky (1974), and King (1973) have produced analyses in which knowledge is a highly significant variable in the investigation of the policy process.

In selecting knowledge as a variable that cannot be reduced to power, we do need, however, to clarify the ways in which the term 'knowledge' will be used here. Clearly, knowledge includes both lay and professional knowledge, and the latter should not necessarily be considered as playing a pivotal or superior role: in fact there is a reciprocal influence between the two, with social science as an aid, refiner, extender or tester of lay knowledge (Lindblom and Cohen 1979; Lindblom 1990: 177, 216–217). According to Lindblom (ibid.: 123), knowledge is a 'well-probed belief, whether empirical or evaluative'. A different, and stricter, notion of 'policy-relevant knowledge' is introduced by Knott and Wildavsky (1980):

> By information we understand data arrayed to make a difference as to whether a decision is made and what shape it takes. . . . Knowledge specifies the relationship between variables and consequences; information relates variables to effects but the relationship remains hypothetical, untested by the results of actual decision. Knowledge is, therefore, a definitive statement of what will happen; information is an educated guess.
>
> (Knott and Wildavsky 1980: 548)

This notion seems so demanding that social science rarely qualifies as knowledge. Taking account of what we know about the real conditions in which policy decisions are shaped, it is easy to argue, following Lindquist (1990), that the main empirical focus ought to be on information, as only on rare occasions is there room for real knowledge utilisation, in the sense formulated by Knott and Wildavsky. Hence, it is more practicable to rely on Lindblom's notion in our general discussion, with knowledge in the Knott and Wildavsky formulation as a specific form of knowledge.

Knott and Wildavsky are, of course, also concerned with decisions, thus raising the question of knowledge utilisation. In fact, different authors define the concept of knowledge utilisation in different ways: for some, utilisation means specific actions taken on the basis of knowledge (*instrumental use*). For others there is a more diffuse and indirect form of utilisation (*conceptual use*). When the definition of utilisation varies so much, it is not surprising that the empirical analyses of knowledge utilisation are inconclusive. It is for this reason that Rich and Oh (1994: 2) recommend multiple dimensions and multiple measures of knowledge utilisation. Knowledge utilisation is more a process than a discrete event taking place at a specific time. Thus,

> information influences decision-making without necessarily being actively used. . . . Use of information needs to be investigated methodologically as an independent or intervening variable (i.e. use for what) rather than as a dependent variable (i.e. use as the end of information processing in decision-making).
>
> (Rich and Oh 1994: 85)

Moreover, the literature on organisational behaviour identifies various organisational processes associated with knowledge utilisation, namely the following ones: information processing, related to cognitions which define the particular elements of organisational environment; affective bounding, that is, the process of placing values and feelings on different alternatives of choice; strategy formulation and control, i.e. choices which integrate cognitions and feelings by making a selection between alternatives; and action generation, i.e. the attempt to implement choices (Beyer and Trice 1982; cf. Argyris and Schön 1978). Accordingly, it would be a mistake to consider knowledge utilisation only as 'action generation'. Action generation itself includes at least three sets of behaviour: decision-makers use knowledge to make choices, to implement decisions, and to develop standard operating procedures as part of a process of institutionalisation.

The study of organisations sheds light upon the *symbolic use* of information. The acts of producing and using information in organisational decision-making have the symbolic value of expressing the perceived rational foundations of choices. People in organisations are perceived as rational and competent when they show a certain command of information sources. Accordingly, 'individuals and organisations will consistently gather more information that can be justified' by real decision needs (Feldman and March 1981: 178). Justifying a decision in terms of information is a way in which a decision process is symbolised as legitimate.

Finally, if we consider the specific case of the utilisation of social science, knowledge can be conceived as 'social science information', 'ideas' (conclusions 'in good currency' and 'policy slogans', drawn from previous research, but stretched beyond the methodology and the findings of the original studies), or 'argument' (a package of evidence built with the aim of supporting an advocacy position). The analyses of Kingdon (1984), Majone (1989) and Weiss (1986; 1990) clearly support this classification of social science knowledge. Social science information in turn may be further subdivided into 'data' (the process of data generation, usually institutionalised through governmental and international data providers), and 'research' (the study of policy issues over a substantial amount of time. This goes beyond data generation in that it includes interpretation and some modelling of the main relations between variables), and 'policy-oriented analysis', which suggests some course of action, thus creating a type of information easily convertible into ideas in good currency or argument (Lindquist 1990: 32–33).

THE POWER OF KNOWLEDGE: CONVERGING PERSPECTIVES

In this section various fields of policy studies are discussed, namely knowledge utilisation and evaluation research; epistemic communities; policy paradigms and policy frameworks; agenda setting; and policy change. Some approaches (e.g. agenda setting and evaluation research) deal with stages of the policy process, while others stress political structures and institutions. It is not being argued here that we should analyse the policy process using 'stages' as an analytical device; in fact there is more than one reason for scepticism about stages or other 'linear' views of the policy process (Sabatier and Jenkins-Smith 1993: 1–4). It will become clear, as discussion proceeds, that the interest in agenda and evaluation has nothing to do with linear views of the policy process, but is oriented towards the investigation of concepts and hypotheses about the role of knowledge. This is the reason why evaluation, an area that in the 'stage model' ought to stay towards the end of the discussion, is introduced first.

Knowledge utilisation and evaluation research

A good deal of the knowledge utilisation literature emanates from scholars dealing with evaluation research. At the onset it must be clarified what type of knowledge is provided by evaluation research. Evaluation is a method of assessing policy effectiveness (i.e. evaluation essentially measures policy impacts), without a detailed causal analysis: even in the absence of information about the causal links at work, there is room for a 'pragmatic decision', in Peters and Barker's terms (1993).[5] This means that there is some relevant knowledge about the effectiveness of the policies, even if the causal structure of the mechanisms at work is unknown.

Indeed, the history of evaluation studies can be seen as a case study of the use and misuse of ideas, starting with the heroic dreams of

Donald Campbell (1969), the pioneer of a society in which reforms would be guided by social experiments generated by evaluation research, and ending with the theory of the policy process outlined by such sophisticated evaluators as Carol Weiss and Lee Cronbach (Shadish, Cook and Leviton 1992). The main divide within evaluation research is related to the treatment of knowledge: whilst some authors do not treat knowledge as an element in the policy process analysis, knowledge becomes an endogenous element in more elaborated conceptions of evaluations. Evaluation research can thus be divided into two periods (Radaelli and Dente 1996). The former period was dominated by a view of knowledge as exogenous to the policy process. The latter, 'modern' period, represented by authors such as Weiss and Cronbach, sees knowledge as endogenous to the policy process. In addition, Weiss is inclined to suggest an 'enlightenment' role for policy analysis. This role relies on path-breaking studies able gradually to change the policy vocabulary and the interpretative frames of policy-makers, rather than studies oriented to short-term 'solutions' and political consultancy. Thus the very issue of the role of knowledge in the policy process ought to be assessed in the longer term.

What, then, can one conclude about the impact of knowledge in the policy process, given the insights provided by the development of evaluation research? First, according to evaluators and policy theorists such as Cronbach *et al.* (1980), Lindblom and Cohen (1979), Majone (1989; 1993), Weiss (1979; 1986; 1987), Wittrock (1982), social research and ideas are only one component of the policy process. Consequently, they do not believe in a simple 'knowledge-driven model', that assumes some 'rational' progression as follows:

basic research → applied research → development → application.

Similarly, they reject the 'problem-solving model', in which a problem exists, information is lacking and research generates a solution, and the information deficit is removed. Interestingly, Lee Cronbach employs the term 'policy-shaping community', instead of 'policy-making community', with the aim of emphasising the 'garbage-can' features of decisions and the loose relationships between actors and policy problems. A second feature arising out of evaluations research is the broad meaning of knowledge: not only expert opinions and social research, but also the transformation of expert ideas into knowledge actually used by political actors; a knowledge in which research, information held by public administration bureaux, and even opinions expressed by the mass media, are all intertwined. This is consistent with Weiss' classification of knowledge in terms of data, ideas, and argument (Weiss 1986). Social research creeps or is absorbed into the policy processes via indirect, cumulative and diffuse processes (mainly through ideas and argument), and in combination with lay knowledge. The process of policy 'enlightenment' is diffuse, thus mirroring diffuse aspects (i.e. multiple decision-makers, multiple interests at stake, gradual adjustment of positions) of the policy-making process itself.

Finally, a third lesson to draw from the evolution of evaluation research is that the impact of knowledge is contingent upon the concrete structuration of specific policy processes (Radaelli and Dente 1996). Arguably, strategies for evaluation research that are feasible in a policy area dominated by a close policy community (as defined in Richardson and Jordan 1979) might not work in the context of a policy process characterised by a loose, open issue network (as defined in Heclo 1978). Evaluation, indeed, does not substitute for the decision-making process. The impact of evaluation (and, more generally, the impact of knowledge) is therefore contingent upon the characteristics of the policy process: who are the actors active in a certain policy process? What resources do they possess? How does conflict over a certain policy area evolve (for example, is there conflict between alternative coalitions?) and with what implications for decision-making? It is with these questions in mind that we now turn to studies dealing with the characteristics of the policy process, starting with an examination of actors endowed with considerable expertise.

Epistemic communities

The study of epistemic communities has a very different dependent variable (i.e. international policy co-ordination), but, like evaluation research, stresses 'a process that has to do more with politics than with science, turning the study of political process into a question about who learns what, when, to whose benefit, and why' (Adler and Haas 1992: 370). The term 'epistemic community' defines 'a network of professionals with recognised expertise and competence in a particular domain and an authoritative claim to policy-relevant knowledge' within that domain or issue-area (Haas 1992: 3). This approach is particularly interested in explaining the complex relations between epistemic communities and the behaviour of states in international policy co-ordination. The approach can also be used for explaining policy transfer (Dolowitz and Marsh 1996: 346), that is, the process of imitation and lesson-drawing (Rose 1991) from one country to another.

For our purposes, the approach suggested by Peter Haas deserves attention because knowledge is the key variable defining epistemic communities. More importantly, it introduces three characteristics of the policy process: uncertainty, interpretation and institutionalisation of ideas. When there is uncertainty – Haas argues – there is not a clear perception of what the interest of the actor is: accordingly, an epistemic community is able to generate a definition of interests by illuminating certain dimensions of an issue, from which an actor can deduce her/his interests. Interests therefore become a dynamic 'dependent' variable, framed by knowledge. Thus, Haas argues:

> many of the conditions facilitating a focus on power are absent. It is difficult for leaders to identify their potential political allies. Neither power nor institutional cues to behaviour will be available, and new patterns of action may ensue.
>
> (Haas 1992: 14)

This model considers the policy process as a process of policy evolution, consisting of four stages: innovation, diffusion, selection, and persistence. Diffusion is a very delicate process, as either an epistemic community acquires bureaucratic power (for instance, through the implementation of international advisory committees) or the diffusion of policy paradigms is seriously hampered and the consensual knowledge promoted by the community will not be effective. The policy selection step is also an important analytical tool, in that it avoids a naive model of knowledge utilisation (i.e. a community produces knowledge, and states 'abide' to the epistemic policy paradigm). In practice, epistemic communities 'create reality, but not as they wish' (Adler and Haas 1992: 381). To be effective, an epistemic community must act under conditions of uncertainty, in which case the community benefits from the absence of a mainstream view of an issue and from the impossibility of calculating the expected outcomes of different courses of action.

The main results of this approach are the international dimension of the role of experts in political life, the role of consultation rights and legal resources (Haas employs the term 'bureaucratic power') in bringing epistemic communities into the core of policy choice, and the possibility of bringing broad unorganised interests into policy choices, overcoming the Olsonian paradox of collective action. In addition, it is worth noting the implications of the evolutionary metaphor used by Haas and taken from developmental biology. According to the latter, evolutionary changes to structures, once in place, are largely irreversible, and these changes virtually determine the array of subsequent choices available to the species (Adler and Haas 1992: 372). Similarly, the policy process might be analysed via the new science of chaos. The chaos perspective illustrates the high dependency of phenomena on initial conditions (path dependency), but, at the same time, indicates that these phenomena are dynamic. Indeed, when they move away from the equilibrium point they reach 'bifurcations', i.e. transformations that cannot be reversed (Dobuzinskis 1992).

Economic orthodoxies, discourse structuration and frames

Epistemic communities advocate policy solutions which are consistent with the evolution of paradigms in the social sciences. It is therefore necessary to examine how orthodoxies and paradigms influence the policy process. Uncertainty, institutionalisation of ideas, and path-dependency features of the policy process – i.e. three features of the epistemic community approach – are also present in the study of economic policy paradigms. Historians and political scientists have produced an impressive *corpus* of research on Keynesism, the most important economic orthodoxy of this century (Furner and Supple 1990; Gourevitch 1984; Hall 1989; Weir and Skocpol 1985). Recently, scholars have also examined other cases, such as, for example, trade policy paradigms (Goldstein 1993), monetary policy paradigms (Dyson 1994), and the political economy of the new right (Thompson 1990). These studies suggest an important conclusion: that the transmission of ideas is more important than their 'production'. Yet two questions arise: first, why and how is knowledge transmitted into the policy process? Second, why do interests not provide the necessary and sufficient conditions upon which political action can proceed? Goldstein's answers to these questions are useful here as she shows the independent role played by knowledge without denying the importance of interests in political life. Usually – Goldstein avers – there is more than one policy choice consistent with a set of interests, but the selection of a specific choice cannot generally be made in terms of the calculations assumed by the interest-driven model of the policy process (Goldstein 1993: 9–11, 252–254). Thus, even if the perception of the various conflicting interests at stake is clear and interests are well defined, there is a range of indeterminacy in the choice of a particular decision. Under these conditions, shared causal beliefs about economic variables behave like switches (or 'road maps') that funnel interests down specific policy directions (Goldstein 1993). Economic paradigms are not merely pegs on which interests can hang their case; rather, they are filters, focal points, or lenses providing policy-makers with strategies. Of course, in order to be transmitted into policy choices, an economic paradigm must be consistent with social values and normative patterns prevailing in a given society. Also, its chances of selection improve dramatically if it can be translated easily and 'sold' in the political market in the form of 'ideas in good currency'. Alternatively, the paradigm can be manipulated into 'causal stories' (Stone 1989). Keynesism is a good case in point: the conversion of the *General Theory* into the simple IS-LM model and the 'causal Keynesian story' of the origins of unemployment are two important ingredients of the astonishing success of Keynesian solutions after the end of the Second World War.

Hall deals with the problem of Keynesian paradigm diffusion across the nations by highlighting the importance of more traditional macro variables, such as state structures. In doing so, Hall blends the analysis of knowledge with a variety of institutional analysis which assigns priority to state structures and their political capacities (see Jacobsen 1995: 294–295; Weir and Skocpol 1985). His main ideas can be summarised by a two-part model (Hall 1989: 361–391). The first is more or less a 'gatekeeping' analysis, or an interpretation of how ideas are judged. Ideas are judged in a three-dimensional 'space' – the three dimensions being economic, political and administrative viability. The second part, relating to the adoption of ideas, takes into account both political (the orientation of the governing party) and administrative factors (in particular, three features of a state structure: permeability of the administration, power of the central bank, and concentration of macroeconomic management) and the structure of the 'political discourse' (on this concept see Hall 1989: 383–386 and below).

Once accepted by policy-makers, an economic paradigm undergoes a *process of institutionalisation*. As shown by Goldstein (1993), the institutionalisation of knowledge affects both actors (i.e. institutions generate networks which are functionally linked to them) and the actors' perceptions of future economic change. A paradigm encased in institutions is not only a set of rules for tackling a current problem; rather, this process implies an institutionalisation of meaning (March and Olsen 1989). Through institutionalisation, a policy paradigm is interpreted 'in relation to the structures of meaning that every culture generates' (Furner and Supple 1990: 33). The acceptance of economic ideas into cognitive and political structures is in turn the major cause of the persistence of institutionalised policy paradigms. Thus, policies are capable of outliving their usefulness. Hence the focus on knowledge also sheds light upon institutions. More generally, the 'institutional approach to the study of the policy process', as Guy Peters suggests, explains why policy change is so difficult. It is not easy to change the shared causal beliefs encased in institutions. Nevertheless, once the beliefs are eventually changed, major policy change can occur and 'the ability to interpret both change and persistence appears one of the most important features of the institutionalist approach' (Peters 1992a: 178).

The notion of policy paradigm is obviously reminiscent of Kuhn's theory of scientific revolution. A question therefore arises: can political science borrow the notion of paradigm from Kuhnian epistemology, which – it must be stressed – does not deal with social sciences? Jobert (1989: 379) has objected that 'the purpose of politics is not – as in Kuhn's paradigms – to resolve enigmas but to limit the impact of conflict on social cohesion'. Accordingly, Jobert opts for the notion of 'policy frameworks' or 'frames of references', stressing that, given 'the fundamental ambiguity of politics' (Jobert 1989: 379), a policy framework 'can be compared with myth, whose function is to build a collective identity by masking the inner conflicts and contradictions within a community' (Jobert 1989: 380).

Clearly, in Jobert's analysis the focus has been shifted from epistemic communities and scientific paradigms to the social conception of policy and its institutionalisation. However, what are the main political attributes of social conceptions of policy, and how does institutionalisation proceed? It is to this question that we now turn, considering the literature on discourse structuration (Wagner *et al.* 1991) and frames of reference (Rein and Schön 1991; Schön and Rein 1994). This body of literature shares with the study of economic orthodoxies a macro approach and carries further the analysis of the relationship between social sciences and state structures illuminated by Hall.

Discourse structuration is an approach emphasising the way policy-makers and social scientists interact, using discourses to understand and make sense of secular social and economic transformations. In the long run, these interactions may go through discourse institutionalisation, when the links between social science and societal institutions become more firmly established, for instance by means of ad hoc governmental commissions. Both intellectual rules (i.e. the discourse within intellectual communities), and institutional settings contribute to the creation of specific dispositions and policy-oriented capacities. The attention to discourse is typical of another body of literature which is specifically concerned with how symbolic languages, discursive practices, vocabularies, and intersubjective meaning affect policy decisions. As shown by Yee (1996: 94), not only does language create reality, but intersubjective meaning is the key element in explaining how 'ideas and beliefs prescribe, shape, constrain', and guide courses of action. This area of research, in which interpretative, humanist and post-modern approaches are predominant, is particularly useful for understanding why certain policy ideas and paradigms are considered more persuasive than others by policy-makers. Put differently, this body of literature investigates the 'capacity' of ideas themselves (Yee 1996). By contrast, the epistemic community approach attributes the political power of knowledge to specific actors (i.e. experts with policy-relevant knowledge and advisory power) and the literature on policy paradigms (i.e. Hall and Goldstein) focuses upon political and administrative institutions that govern the access of ideas into the policy process.[6] With the literature on discursive practices, instead, the very power of ideas themselves is explored.

The literature on discursive practices emphasises the crucial role of cognitive variables in shaping political action. Additional tools for the exploration of political cognition are provided by a body of literature which specifies the content and the dynamics of 'frames of reference'. If in Jobert the notion of policy framework is used in a macro political context for denoting empirically the political functions played by policy paradigms, the literature on 'framing' is rooted in micro analyses that aim to explain why and how actors recur to 'frames' for coping with uncertainty. In brief, when faced with problematic policy situations actors tend to rely on 'frames', in which values, social science models, and interests are integrated.[7] Framing is an activity of selection, organisation and interpretation of a complex reality, 'so as to provide guideposts for knowing, analysing, persuading and acting. A frame is a perspective from which an amorphous, ill-defined situation can be made sense of and acted upon' (Rein and Schön 1991: 262). As shown by psychologists working in the related field of prospect theory (Kahneman and Tversky 1979; 1982) preferences depend on the frame used in the formulation of decision problems. In addition, linguists working in the area of categorisation (Lakoff 1987) have shown that different categorisations of an issue (for example, an issue of tax policy can be categorised as a redistributive problem or as a regulatory problem) empower certain actors while disempowering others. The point therefore is not only that facts need to be interpreted in order to be acted upon, but, most crucially, that different frames lead to the selection of alternative courses of actions, instruments, and solutions. Put differently, frames matter in the policy process because they affect decisions. Consequently, the choice of one frame instead of another can trigger competition and conflict: alternative frames can vie for attention and different policy-makers push their favourite frame in the policy process.

The conversion of a problematic situation into policy problems and policy agendas is the result of the intense relationships which characterise the policy discourse. In this analysis, there is room for a dynamic element: in fact, frames shift when a frame-reflective discourse becomes feasible. This happens when in a policy controversy 'participants would reflect on the frame-conflicts implicit in their controversies and explore the potentials for their resolution' (Rein and Schön 1991: 267; Schön and Rein 1994). Schön had analysed in the past how 'generative metaphors' originate learning and ultimately policy change (Schön 1979). With their more recent work, Schön and Rein (1994) show how 'intractable' policy controversies can be treated, provided that the conditions for critical reflection upon policy-makers' own frames are met. The essential point to observe is that, thanks to the concept of frame reflection, Rein and Schön are able to explain policy change without recurring to exogenous variables: policy change results from the interaction among participants, and precisely from the capability to re-consider frames of reference which orient political action.

Agenda setting

The previous discussion has proceeded from knowledge utilisation to political cognition, thus reaching the earlier stages in the policy process. Accordingly, it is to the stage of agenda setting that we now turn. Indeed, the process of agenda setting is not a simple matter of socio-economic inputs generating policy agendas via their transmission into the political system. On the contrary, there is room for arguing that agenda setting is mostly an endogenous process of the political system. Thus, models and concepts such as the 'inside initiative model' (Cobb, Ross and Ross 1976), the 'professional bureaucratic complex' (Beer 1977), and 'bureaucratic demand creation' (Milward 1980) are all images of a policy process in which the agenda is built within the political system, often with the significant contribution of policy experts not easily classifiable as academic, bureaucratic, political or professional actors.

Kingdon's analysis of knowledge in agenda setting based on a version of the garbage-can model (Cohen, March and Olsen 1972), is particularly interesting for the tax issues considered in this study, as will be shown in subsequent chapters. His thesis on the relative independence of three streams – problems, policies and politics – can be stated as follows. To begin with, problem recognition is crucial to agenda setting. Socio-economic events come to be defined as problems only when political actors believe that something should be done to change them. Moreover, problems are continuously structured and restructured by alternative arguments and public deliberation (Majone 1989).[8] Problem definition is therefore a political process in which different actors compete for setting the agenda in terms of their favourite specifications. Clearly, there is a convergence between the literature on frames and the literature on the politics of problem definition (Rochefort and Cobb 1994). In both cases, the stress is on how political actors engage in debate, arguments and competition not only for understanding a puzzling reality, but above all for shaping courses of action (i.e. 'what can be done' once a given problem has been defined in a certain way), and ultimately for influencing public policy.

Independently of problem recognition, political events have their own dynamics: elections, interest group behaviour, and ideological conflict set up specific developments in the political sphere, thus modifying existing agendas, or structuring completely new agendas. Finally, the generation of policy alternatives, i.e. the process of selecting solutions to problems, defines the 'policy stream'. Therefore there are three streams that shape agenda setting: the stream of problems, the 'politics' stream, and the policy solutions stream. Participants are conceptually distinct from these three streams: experts are usually more involved in devising policy alternatives, but they may show up also in the political stream.

It must be stressed that Kingdon's model has nothing to do with a rational, linear view of the policy process, in which actors first identify problems and then elaborate solutions for them. Kingdon is extremely clear on this point: 'Agendas are not first set and then alternatives generated: instead, alternatives must be advocated for a long period before a short-run opportunity presents itself on an agenda' (Kingdon 1984: 215). The crucial theme of knowledge transmission as the key element of the process, rather than the origin of ideas, appears once again in Kingdon's analysis. However, this does not necessarily mean that political scientists should disregard the discourse within social science communities. On the contrary, Kingdon highlights two components of this discourse: the criteria that allow the existence and later the emergence of an idea in the 'primeval soup' (such as softening-up, technical feasibility, value acceptability inside the expert community, and anticipation of future constraints), and the linkage between the ideas eventually selected and policy-making. This linkage is the major function played by policy entrepreneurs (Kingdon 1984: 129), defined as advocates for proposals, who are willing to invest their resources in the hope of any kind of future return. As stated above, problems, policies and politics flow according to independent processes, but on occasion they can be coupled. This happens when a policy entrepreneur can benefit from a short-run opportunity (a policy window) to push the favourite solutions or to focus attention on a certain problem. Policy entrepreneurs perform the function of 'coupling solutions to problems, problems to political forces, and political forces to proposals' (Kingdon 1984: 214). Hence this model of policy change breaks with a long tradition in political science, dedicated to structural variables: by contrast, in Kingdon's model, individuals (i.e. policy entrepreneurs) are placed into the limelight.

Policy change and learning

The different ways in which policies may be constructed, modified, and influenced by knowledge have been considered. However, what is the typical 'mode' of knowledge access to the policy-making process, and how can we model knowledge-induced policy dynamics? The study of policy change and advocacy coalitions (Sabatier 1988; Sabatier and Jenkins-Smith 1993) proceeds from the recognition that the most frequent mode of professional knowledge affecting policy decisions is via coalitions, in which policy experts play a significant role.

Generally, a policy subsystem has one dominant advocacy coalition, challenged by one or more opponents. The 'glue' of an advocacy coalition is a core of shared beliefs, and the line-up of allies and opponents is fairly stable over a period of at least a decade or so. The key variable of the model is therefore the belief system. This is quite different from the epistemic community approach, where the key variable is knowledge. The 'core' of belief systems is mostly normative, and is hence immune to empirical challenges. However, knowledge, in the broad Lindblomian sense of 'well-probed belief, empirical or evaluative', can impinge on belief systems of advocacy coalitions, albeit usually only on the secondary aspects. Sabatier and Jenkins-Smith (1993: 48–56) outline a few conditions conducive to policy-oriented learning across belief systems of different coalitions. These include the level of conflict, the analytical tractability of the issue and the existence of a policy forum 'prestigious enough to force professionals from different coalitions to participate, and dominated by professional norms'.

Overall, the advocacy coalition approach offers a link between policy and politics. Most crucially, it implicitly suggests a model of adversarial democracy. Indeed, policy change is explained as the result of confrontation between different coalitions. This framework may assist the medium- to long-term comparative analysis of policy dynamics. The main set of independent variables explaining the policy change is composed of dramatic shocks external to the policy subsystem: for instance, 'politics' can induce policy change through new trends of electoral behaviour.

The potential of this approach will be assessed below (Chapter 6) by using the empirical analysis of European taxation (and later, in the conclusion). At this point it is sufficient to observe that, when contrasted with the view of the policy process outlined by the garbage-can model (Cohen, March and Olsen 1972), the advocacy coalition approach is less fluid, as advocacy coalitions bring a more stable structure into the process. The crucial causal relations of policy paradigms – i.e. the 'core' elements of paradigms – are quite resistant to change. As a consequence, advocacy coalitions, organised around belief systems, represent, at least in the short term, a stable feature of the policy process. However, as Dudley and Richardson have noted (1996), the advocacy coalition approach undervalues a spatial element, i.e. 'the importance of policy arenas as a dynamic of change'. They draw upon Baumgartner and Jones (1991; 1993), who underline the interaction between the construction of a policy problem (the 'image') and the 'institutional venues', i.e. the institutional structures within which policies are 'made'. Losers in a policy controversy can turn into winners by the selection of a new venue: the study of trunk roads policy in the UK (Dudley and Richardson 1996), of nuclear policy in the United States (Baumgartner and Jones 1991), and the shift of lobbying from national capitals towards Brussels (Mazey and Richardson 1993) seem to confirm the existence of more endogenous elements of change than predicted by Sabatier. Also, the interaction between venues and images shows that the impact of professional knowledge is not independent of the particular kind of image prevailing in a policy area. In particular, when issues 'are portrayed as technical problems rather than as social questions, experts can dominate the decision-making process' (Baumgartner and Jones 1991: 1047).

A key feature of the advocacy coalition approach, and more generally of the whole cognitive perspective on politics, is the emphasis put on time, context, meaning and agency. These elements are usually treated successfully in individual case studies, but are not easily linked to macro perspectives. This raises the problem of micro-macro linkages. The problem, as Ashford has eloquently argued, is that

> a particular policy study is not simply a building block for one or more lawlike generalisations as conceived in normal social science, but is simultaneously a historical narrative, a portrayal of particular motives and intentions at work in a particular setting, an account of prevailing ethical and moral standards at work in political and social life at some moment in history, and an exercise in defining political and social reality for policy-makers and for the public.
>
> (Ashford 1992: 4–5)

The works of Douglas Ashford (1982) and Jeremy Richardson (1982) and more recently, the advocacy coalition framework, with its emphasis on the connections between subsystem dynamics and external macro changes, seem to map the puzzling analytical territory of the micro–macro linkage. However, as the previous quotation shows, the linkage is not a mere question of the number of cases, but rather it seems to highlight different perspectives and, ultimately, different variables. There are no clear rules of commensurability, and hence, in the walk 'from micro to macro' (one might translate 'from policy to politics') analysts are climbing a scale of abstraction (Sartori 1970) in which a few steps are missing and certain steps are of a different nature. Most crucially, the knowledge perspective assigns a different status to the very concept of explanation, certainly more similar to the Weberian *Verstehen* (or, one could argue, to hermeneutics) than to lawlike generalisations. Probably future research on the subject could benefit from the insight provided by the analysis of discourse structuration and of institutionalisation of knowledge. In any case, the direction suggested here is not towards a reconciliation with lawlike models of science: even though it seems possible to investigate macro processes 'taking knowledge seriously', these processes are rooted in unique historical and contextual boundaries. Micro–macro linkages can be found, but not in a narrow positivist framework. If policy-making becomes subjectively defined, the positivist presumption that lawlike behaviour at the macro level can be consistent with lawlike behaviour at the micro level is definitively challenged (Ashford 1992: 342).

KNOWLEDGE AND METAPHORS OF THE POLICY PROCESS

At this point a question introduced at the beginning of the chapter (i.e. what is 'new' in the rediscovery of knowledge?) can be answered to. Indeed, recent research on the cognitive dimension of politics introduces a new perspective in the study of the *policy process*, whilst previous studies, for example on technocracy and the 'power elite', were more interested in the *macro characteristics of political systems*. To be more precise, it is argued here that recent literature on the role of knowledge has the advantage of introducing a new *cleavage* which is useful for sorting out two different approaches to the analysis of the policy process. What is this cleavage about?

The traditional analysis of power accords only an advocacy role to knowledge, or even no role at all. Thus, the main distinction is between models in which knowledge is endogenous to the policy process, and models in which knowledge is nothing but an input to the 'black box' or merely a 'hook' on which interests hang their case. In the models reviewed here, knowledge has different kinds of relevance, from justification to learning. The endogeneity of knowledge in the analysis of public policies brings loose and contextual features into policy studies. This new perspective on the policy process is manifest even at the level of metaphors used by different authors. Most pertinently perhaps, the preference for metaphors rather than 'hard' concepts illustrates the definitive escape from any determinism. The traditional, deterministic approach in political science tends to explain the making of collective decisions as the result of a 'parallelogram of forces' (Macridis 1961: 32). By contrast, scholars emphasising knowledge are keen on using such metaphors of the policy process as 'unending social enquiry' (Lindblom 1990), 'collective puzzlement' (Heclo 1974), 'evolution' (Haas 1992), 'learning' (Heclo 1974; Sabatier and Jenkins-Smith 1993), and 'garbage-can with policy windows' (Kingdon 1984).

Some general tendencies appear to emerge: a new perspective on the policy process, capable of interpreting both stability and change, rather than the mere question of 'do ideas matter?', arises as the key theoretical issue. Other tendencies include a 'post-positivist' thread;[9] the alignment of policy, problems and politics; the increasing internationalisation of epistemic communities (and as a consequence the decreasing importance of the national focus for the study of knowledge diffusion); the changing nature of the political discourse; and finally, the relationships between knowledge, on one side, and institutions and political power, on the other. The general trend is also gently debunking the world of 'number-crunching' contributions of social science; instead, the rhetorical contributions of social sciences (cf. the analysis of economics in McCloskey 1985; 1994), the construction of meanings, and the shaping of shared understandings seem more relevant.

On a more epistemological note, however, scholars dealing with the role of knowledge in public policies give dramatically different answers to the crucial question 'why is a policy paradigm accepted or, alternatively, why does it fail to access the political agenda?' There is a sort of continuum, with Hall (1993) and Kingdon (1984) representing the opposite poles. The former thinks that a paradigm is refused after repeated falsification,[10] the latter underlines the faddish elements of the life-cycle of ideas. The corresponding epistemological references for the two poles of the continuum might be Popper or Kuhn, on one side, and post-modern scholars on the other. March and Olsen criticise Hall's idea that the rejection of policy paradigms is determined by repeated failure, by observing that 'failure is subjective. . . . Change is often driven not by demand but by supply, by the existence of an alternative that attracts attention and support and thereby stimulates a perception of a problem to which it is a possible solution' (March and Olsen 1995: 119).

Furthermore, Hood (1994: 7) argues that 'the further we move from "harder" to "softer" versions of the "primacy of ideas" approach, the harder it will be to distinguish "ideas" from "interests"'. If repeated experimentation is not the key motive of acceptance or refusal, then policy knowledge inevitably blurs with power and interests, Hood argues. However, Goldstein (1993) has successfully shown how the transmission of interests into a specific policy choice can be impossible without road maps provided by shared causal beliefs. And even if we assume (but we should not) that power directs the policy choice, knowledge plays a fundamental justification function: political actors must persuade and convince, because politics is not sheer 'powering' (Heclo 1972; 1974; Majone 1989; Sabatier and Jenkins-Smith 1993: 45).

'IT IS NOT IDEAS WHICH ARE IMPLEMENTED, BUT POLICIES'

The quotation above (Pirie 1988) reminds us that the study of knowledge in political science is ultimately concerned with political choices. Pirie, who has been director of a British think-tank for a long time,[11] remarks that the political impact of knowledge goes beyond sociology of knowledge or philosophy of science: it is not ideas or policy paradigms *per se*, but their effect on policies which is of primary interest to political science. Accordingly, the concern here is the *link* between social science knowledge and public policy-making. However, what are the implications of adopting this particular point of view? Notwithstanding the benefits of considering the endogeneity of knowledge, a cost in terms of research design is evident. Indeed, if the link between the cognitive dimension of the policy process and policy choices becomes the main focus, it follows that empirical analysis cannot proceed simply by measuring the impact of, for example, policy paradigms and ideas on a given policy choice independently from interests and other variables. Of course, when this can be done the research design becomes powerful. However, the transmission of cognitive elements into policy choices involves advocacy coalitions (Sabatier and Jenkins-Smith 1993), the alignment of politics, policy and problems (Kingdon 1984), or the adoption of certain interpretative frames by policy-makers (Schön and Rein 1994). In these circumstances experts participate in political events in conjunction with pressure groups, policy entrepreneurs intervene in the definition and adoption of policy solutions, and cognitive elements and interests are ultimately intertwined. Therefore, assessing the impact of knowledge is not a simple matter of inserting an additional variable into the conventional research design based on more traditional variables. To use the language of econometrics, cognitive variables are not independent from the other explanatory variables: indeed, there is always, in any circumstance, a strong *prima facie* suspicion of multi-collinearity! This is the reason why authors working on cognitive factors of political life prefer metaphors and narratives to more structured research designs: the latter are often inconsistent when explanatory variables exhibit multi-collinearity.[12]

The difficulties in terms of research design are compounded by another problem to which we turn now. Put succinctly, it would be desirable to assess the political role of knowledge by considering the independent impact of specific categories of actors (most pertinently, social scientists) on the policy process. Social scientists should therefore be considered apart from politicians and other more conventional actors. However, this situation, although desirable for fleshing out a strong research design, is often fallacious. Indeed, it seems possible to challenge the view which sees the linking of social science and governmental communities as the most important problematic aspect, and accordingly sees the two sects of actors as two separate communities (Dunn 1980). Unfortunately, this view is misleading, because it does not take into account the large number of positions of policy influence held by social scientists. Many are, of course, in the academic world, but they are also in policy institutes and think tanks, in international organisations (OECD, IMF, etc.), in political cabinets, and may even occupy top elected positions in politics.

For example, as Regonini and Giuliani suggest (1994), Italian policy-making over the past decade has involved an increasing number of professors, who either became ministers or were active in the ministerial cabinets. They helped shape the agenda of political debate, with a particular emphasis on electoral reforms and constitutional engineering. Also, there is an increasing literature on the role of economists in government (Colander and Coats 1989; Pechman 1989): sometimes, as in the Israeli case described by Keren (1993), economists have direct political roles in economic management and in political communication. At other times, as Markoff and Montecinos (1993) underline, they play more symbolic and ceremonial roles. Economists and social scientists are also active in non-bureaucratic advisory services.[13] In Britain during the 1980s, the importance of the transmission of policy ideas via think-tanks has been highlighted (Gaffney 1991; Pirie 1988; Stone 1996). During this period the policy role of the Civil Service in the UK may have changed from policy advice to management, as suggested by Hayward and Klein (1994), thus giving more leverage to specific economic advisers and policy think-tanks. In addition, professionals, often from the main accountancy firms (Power 1993; Ward 1993) rather than universities, have been important in UK policy, and the analysis of European taxation will show how professional bodies have played a role in corporate tax harmonisation (see Chapter 6). Finally, the European Community political system has often been considered a privileged territory for specialised and highly technical policy-making, as witnessed *inter alia* by the neo-functionalist explanation of European integration (O'Neill 1996: 42).[14] H. Wallace (1996: 22) has gone so far as to assert that the debate on the role of epistemic communities 'in some senses is a reprise of the Monnet approach to European integration'.

Therefore, the relative neglect of the role of social scientists in public policy is, perhaps, puzzling. However, Lindquist (1990) suggests two possible explanations. First, a number of studies have systematically overlooked the role of a peculiar breed of social scientists, namely economists in government. The literature just mentioned, on the contrary, illustrates how instrumental economists are in the making of public policies. Second, the role of knowledge in the policy process has been treated within the 'two communities' conceptual framework, in which only two separate communities exist: the academic community and the political one. Consequently, in order to illuminate the rather grey area between the two communities, Lindquist (1990) suggests the notion of a third 'community', in which 'the range of actors and information that needs to be accounted for when discussing the impact of social scientists is necessarily broadened'. The third community is composed of individuals with policy-relevant knowledge who participate in policy-making, even though they are not policy-makers: for example, political consultants, advisers, ideas brokers (Smith 1991), directors of influential policy institutes. Taking into account the relative 'ubiquity' of social scientists – and especially of economists – and the different forms of knowledge, it seems reasonable to claim that actors with policy-relevant knowledge are active in multiple points of the political systems (Table 2.1) and their impact is in all probability greater than predicted by the conventional 'two communities' models of knowledge utilisation.

There is also a certain symmetry between the form of knowledge and the characteristics of decision-making situations (Lindquist 1988): when the decision-making process is very specialised and policy-making rules are institutionalised, as in monetary policy, there is room for knowledge as information. Indeed, in many Western countries the quantity of money – under normal conditions – is set by an econometric equation. In contrast, when a policy is in crisis or under major scrutiny (and also in the rare cases in which a public policy enters a 'virgin' area) decision-making is permeable to new slogans and ideas in

Table 2.1 Different kinds of knowledge, knowledge-oriented actors, arenas

Knowledge *'What'*	*Actors* *'Who'*	*Arenas* *'Where'*
Information data	Academics in universities International data providers Governmental units Think-tanks	Co-operative games Stable decision-making Sophisticated depoliticised arenas
Ideas	Academics in government Think-tanks Ideas brokers Policy advisers Social scientists in policy fora	Uncertainty Crisis management Policy revamping New policy areas
Argument	Experts operating within advocacy coalitions	Zero-sum games Post decision-making (justification) Learning across coalitions

Source: Radaelli, C. M. (1995) 'The role of knowledge in the policy process', *Journal of European Public Policy*, 2(2), June.

good currency. Finally, when controversies and struggles stymie the policy process, knowledge can gain access to the political debate as argument, as shown by the bottom row of Table 2.1.

In analysing the role of knowledge in the policy process, it would be a mistake, however, to search only for the establishment of new paradigms and research programmes, thus overlooking the contribution of single individuals, for example. The cases of Mr Laffer in the USA and, more recently, Professor Tremonti (Italian Minister of Finance in the Berlusconi cabinet, 1994) are two examples of unorthodox individuals (when judged by the policy paradigms prevailing in the domestic economic communities) who, nevertheless, exercised considerable political influence.

The problem of how to identify the impact of knowledge on policymaking might be solved by tackling two of the analytical dimensions identified earlier: the micro–macro dimension, and the individual-community divide. Figure 2.1 shows how different approaches and threads eventually suggest different research foci.

The approaches are placed along two continua, instead of being collocated in rigid matrix cells: for this reason, the advocacy coalition

Figure 2.1 The different fields of the knowledge perspective in a two-dimensional space

Source: Radaelli, C. M. (1995) 'The role of knowledge in the policy process', *Journal of European Public Policy*, 2(2), June.

approach tends to shift from the study of social scientists towards the analysis of social sciences. This happens when this approach considers the development and change of belief systems in policy fora. By the same token, the study of epistemic communities may easily lean towards the macro pole, when knowledge becomes institutionalised. Nothing illustrates the possibility of a bridge between the poles of each dimension better than the concept of policy enlightenment: micro studies gradually permeate the frames of reference employed by policy-makers, thus creating the conditions for macro changes in key-words, causal belief systems, and, eventually, policy choices. This is the reason why policy enlightenment is in the centre of Figure 2.1.

It seems reasonable to suggest that the institutionalisation of ideas is the main factor at work when we move from the micro to macro level. Institutions are important in the cognitive perspective: they provide stability for shared causal beliefs, set up structures of meaning, create networks of actors, and constrain the perception of interests and socio-economic change. As shown by March and Olsen (1995) institutions contribute to democratic governance by developing political identities, political capabilities, political accounts, and political adaptiveness. Action is taken on the basis of a logic of appropriateness which is provided by institutions. As specified by March and Olsen (1995: 32, emphasis added) 'appropriateness has overtones of morality, but it is in this context primarily a *cognitive* concept'.

Moreover, it is precisely at the institutional level that we find the importance of the interpretative approach to policy studies. As Ashford (1992: 347) has argued, policies are subjectively defined within institutional contexts: 'institutionalised activity cannot be imagined without some prior understanding or trust concerning the nature of the activity itself. . . . Institutions provide the contextual or situational foundations for collective action'.

Each approach in Figure 2.1 contains a more or less implicit 'drive' towards the empirical investigation of different impacts of knowledge: a 'knowledge utilisation study' looking for the concrete results of an evaluation study will probably overlook the contribution of knowledge to the structuring of political discourse in the long run. Considered as a whole, Figure 2.1 reveals a much greater impact of knowledge (instrumental, conceptual, and institutional) than single approaches can detect.

At a more theoretical level, the cognitive perspective in political science might appear at first glance as a modelling of the policy process in which knowledge becomes the new independent variable explaining the dependent variable of policy. This is *not* being argued here, for the reasons discussed earlier: put simply, knowledge interacts with other important elements of the policy process. Accordingly, a causal modelling of the policy process with cognitive independent variables presents serious drawbacks. In contrast, the interaction of knowledge with the main elements of the policy process (policy problems, policy styles, and decision rules) is a more promising avenue for research. Contingency models stressing connectedness, rather than causal models, are probably the most useful.

Finally, we turn to the question of what might be learned about the nature of poliarchic policy-making when knowledge becomes one of the main analytical foci. In the cognitive perspective the co-operative nature of politics appears to be emphasised. Thus, Rein and Schön (1991: 282–283) distinguish between the 'political' and 'co-operative' views of policy-making. In both views, conflict and co-operative enquiry exist, but have different meanings. In the 'political mode' democracy resembles a zero-sum game, and the co-operative enquiry turns out to be an appeal to the shared interests of actors in reducing or minimising the costs of the game. In the 'co-operative' mode, instead, participants perceive themselves as enquirers and members of a co-operative social system, rather than interested parties. Further, the epistemic community approach shows the role of experts in the depoliticisation of controversial issues and their capacity to transform political conflict into the search for a 'correct', mutually beneficial solution. Accordingly, authors working in the field of the 'politics of ideas' (Quirk 1990) often support a view of politics which goes beyond self-interest (Mansbridge 1990). The advocacy coalition approach is an important exception in this scenario, however, as the emphasis on the struggle between the dominant coalition and the opponents lends itself towards a model of adversarial democracy, even though the action of policy fora can bridge the gap between the belief systems of different coalitions.

Considering the co-operative 'bias' of the studies reviewed, there might be theoretical scope for a closer match between the cognitive perspective and rational choice theory. From very different points of departure, Dryzek (1992), Quirk (1989), and Scharpf (1990; 1991; 1994a) explore the conditions for positive-sum games and the pursuit of joint benefits. However, the characteristics of games are not given: both Scharpf and Quirk stress the difference between a 'given' matrix of payoffs, and the 'effective' or 'perceived' matrix. In other words, knowledge can change the perceived characteristics of the games, through cognitive and affective processes. Cognitive processes are crucial to the understanding of the policy stake. In any case, every game is a strategic situation in which conflict and interdependence are both present: the journey from power to knowledge is probably a sophisticated route between the Yin and Yang of politics, that is, conflict and co-operation.

3 Policy-making in the European Union

> The European Community fascinates observers and scholars because it is a unique object of study.
>
> (Tsebelis 1994)

> The European Union is not as sui generis as those engaged in European studies are inclined to think. It remains only a rather sophisticated trade area.
>
> (Strange 1994a)

> It is neither a state nor an international organisation.
>
> (Sbragia 1992)

> It is less than a federation, more than a regime.
>
> (Wallace 1983)

> Middle ground between the cooperation of existing nations and the breaking of a new one.
>
> (Scharpf 1988)

> The EU is not, and cannot be, a unitary nation state; it can at best be a multi-level political system.
>
> (Scharpf 1994b)

> Whatever the arguments about the true nature of the EC, it certainly exhibits at least this state-like characteristic [to make authoritative allocations for society] .
>
> (Mazey and Richardson 1995)

EXPLORING POLICY DYNAMICS IN THE EU: WHICH ANALYTICAL PERSPECTIVE?

What are the main characteristics of the European Union (EU)[1] political system? This is the question around which theories of European integration have revolved since the late 1950s. The development of integration theory has proceeded along dramatically different lines: the quotations above give an impressionistic idea of the huge theoretical divergence among different interpretations. The theoretical dispute is hence a long way from arriving at a stable equilibrium point.[2] This fact can be interpreted in different ways: it could be argued that it is a sign of intellectual vitality, or that it reflects the objective difficulties posed by the 'nature of the beast' itself[3] with its genuinely polymorphous characteristics. Following the latter interpretation, Wallace (1983), in his classic work, concluded that elements of different systems are present in the European political system. This also explains the success of syncretic theories of European integration which confront rather than ignore 'paradoxes at the heart of regional integration' (O'Neill 1996: 80).

The main objective of this chapter is not to offer a systematic review of integration theories, but to reflect on existing theories for extracting theoretical underpinnings and hypotheses that can be used in the empirical analysis of the EU direct tax policy process. However, when public policy becomes the main empirical object – as it happens in this book – the theoretical debate presents more signs of discomfort than fruitful stimuli. In fact, when viewed from the public policy analysis perspective, theoretical difficulties are compounded by the dominance of approaches which focus on linear, mono-dimensional dynamics of integration, rather than acknowledging and explaining contrasting dynamics. Even a superficial observer of policy dynamics in the EU notes that certain policy areas have progressed steadily on their path to integration, whereas others are still in their infancy. Yet the traditional 'dominant' approaches, namely neo-functionalism and varieties of inter-governmental approaches as represented by neo-realism *à la* Hoffmann (1966) and more recently, by the 'liberal inter-governmental' approach put forward by Moravcsik (1991; 1993), are not focused upon this fundamental aspect of integration. The situation has improved with the emergence of what has been dubbed 'the syncretic paradigm' (O'Neill 1996) based upon the theory of interdependence (Keohane and Nye 1989), but the tone of the dominant theoretical debate is still essentially centred on issues different from the variability of policy integration in the EU.

What then are the issues that 'monopolise' the debate? For the functionalist approach the process of European integration stems from co-operation in limited sectors of economic policies which then spills over to other sectors. Neo-functionalism has added a political determinant to this explanation, by showing how elites steer spill-over mechanisms.[4] In its recent refinement, neo-functionalism contemplates a threefold logic of spill-over (Tranholm-Mikkelsen 1991). First, the functional logic of integration, which represents the traditional claim of neo-functionalism: tasks assigned to European institutions have an inherently expansive nature. Second, the already mentioned political logic, according to which governmental and non-governmental elites become immersed in a system of *engrenage* conducive to further collaboration amongst states and ultimately integration. Third, the logic of 'cultivated' spill-over, which enables autonomous institutionalised mediators (such as the Commission) to upgrade the common interest by facilitating interest accommodation and providing solutions. This element, which is however ancillary to the main thrust of neo-functionalism, paves the way to a dialogue between neo-functionalism and policy analysis because it acknowledges that integration is characterised by the purposive behaviour of European institutions. Indeed, policy analysts have almost invariably observed that European institutions are much more than passive spectators of states' decisions. However, even sympathetic scholars of neo-functionalism such as Tranholm-Mikkelsen recognise that this approach lacks a clear causal explanation of integration, fails to pin down precisely how spill-overs work, and does not identify 'true dependent variables'.[5]

Realist and neo-realist approaches conceptualise European integration as an outcome produced by sovereign states coping with a world of anarchy (Hoffmann 1966; 1982). The capability of European institutions to act relies ultimately upon the willingness of states to delegate powers. Inter-governmental relations and their dynamics are the single most powerful explanatory variable according to this conceptualisation of European integration. At the cost of crude simplification, it can nevertheless be argued that both inter-governmentalism and neo-functionalism have very little to say on policy dynamics. In essence, policies are independent variables in the functionalist approach (roughly, integration in one economic policy spills over into other policies) and nothing more than outputs in inter-governmentalist approaches, with the typical qualification that policies embedded in 'high politics' dynamics will show a very poor record of integration, whilst 'low politics' issues will exhibit increased integration. The impression is that policies are never in the right place: too important in the one case, because the complex politics of policy-making is ignored, and too marginal in the other.

Arguably, the main cleavage between these dominant approaches appears to be a different view of politics. Indeed, for inter-governmental approaches, which draw upon the time-honoured tradition of realism, politics is structured around the crucial issue of sovereignty and, accordingly, conflict and co-operation within the system of sovereign states are investigated. By contrast, according to neo-functionalists, politics is shaped by deep economic integration, and the same, with important qualifications of course, can be said for syncretic approaches (O'Neill 1996). At the cost of over-simplifying a sophisticated debate once again, it could be said that for inter-governmentalism the focus needs to be put on the political nature of politics, whilst for neo-functionalism it is the economic determinant of politics which is of prime consideration. The 'nature' of politics is then perceived in dramatically different ways.

These two conceptions are extremely interesting for elaborating questions of political theory (i.e. the discussion on the 'nature' of politics) and are relevant for the progress of international relation theory (e.g. they have potential for assessing European integration in the context of the more general study of regional integration and global regime building). The question raised here, however, is different and can be articulated as follows: putting aside the implications for political theory and international relations theory, are grand theories really useful for understanding policy integration? More precisely, how do they perform in the explanation of policy integration? It is to this question that we now turn.

In their comprehensive review of theoretical work on European integration, Caporaso and Keeler (1995) observe that the era of 'grand-theorising' is definitively past, and that it is high time that political scientists dedicated more attention to middle-range models, possibly with the aim of explaining how institutions affect European integration. Notwithstanding this illuminating observation, the impression is that the legacy of grand theories[6] still obfuscates our understanding of European integration. To put it bluntly, the problem with grand theories is that our knowledge of integration is not so advanced as to allow political scientists to engage in grand theory building. The European polity has undergone dramatic changes since the Single European Act,[7] the relationships between institutions are so fluid, and the very character of EU institutions is so experimental and provisional (H. Wallace 1996: 26) that grand theories are intrinsically unable to capture the multi-faceted aspects of European integration, not to mention the details of public policies. The road to theory building advocated here faces the complexity of the European Union in the first instance, with micro analyses of public policies which do not contain heroic assumptions on the pivotal mechanisms of integration, and then seek to penetrate the meso level. Put differently, when the object of analysis is as elusive as the European Union certainly is, there is no benefit in assuming that there is such a thing as *the* explanatory variable of integration (be it member states or spill-over effects).

Indeed, conceptual benefits are copious if strong assumptions are combined with rational-choice models: the latter allow for the introduction of extremely precise analytical tools. Accordingly, the cost of radical hypotheses is compensated by the accuracy of conclusions that can be reached by rational-choice models of politics. The analyses conducted by Tsebelis (on 'nested games' and on the agenda-setting power of the European Parliament) and Putnam's model of two-level games (although not elaborated with the EU case in mind) are illustrations of the potential of rational choice in the study of European integration (Putnam 1988; Tsebelis 1990; 1994). The same cannot be said of dominant theories such as the ones mentioned above. In this case the explanation of European integration is not strengthened by the precision of rational-choice models, and at the same time the analytical perspective is constrained by the Procrustean bedstead of strong assumptions about core actors or core mechanisms. It seems then pointless to pay the cost of rigid assumptions without gaining any conceptual benefit. Why not start with a more flexible approach, then?

It is precisely this question that is at the root of the public policy approach to the study of European integration.[8] It must be stressed that the study of the policy process is not considered here as just a way of qualifying dominant theories. Public policy analysis should not be limited to the provision of knowledge on public policies for the sake of controlling dominant theories of integration. Instead, it is argued here that the application of the policy approach provides invaluable insights on European integration. As a consequence, it can be examined as an alternative to dominant theories.

The main strength of the policy approach is its flexibility: the unit of analysis (i.e. public policy) is analysed without positing that certain categories of actors or certain mechanisms are predestined to prevail. The approach contemplates pluralistic decision-making (as opposed to the hypothesis of a unitary decision-maker), limited information, and partisan mutual adjustment (as opposed to maximisation) as the main criterion of choice. Of course, the flexibility of the public policy approach entails its own costs. Most notably, the difficulty of this approach is elaborating upon the macro characteristics of the European polity (H. Wallace 1996: 5).

The remainder of this chapter is dedicated to a discussion of how the policy approach has coped with this difficulty. In the next section one of the main results of the policy approach is presented, focusing on the European polity as a regulatory state, whereas in the following section institutional agency and preference formation are introduced. Taken together, these insights certainly do not provide a macro framework of European integration. In this respect, the challenge of the policy approach to dominant theories has as yet to be completed. In addition, engaging in grand theorising is not a rewarding exercise for the time being (Caporaso and Keeler 1995). With these important limitations in mind, it will be contended that the results of policy analysis shed light on the meso configuration of the European polity and consequently constitute promising preliminary thinking towards a better theoretical understanding. For example, the regulatory state as a conceptual template for the EU is more than a tool kit for the analysis of policy types. Indeed, as indicated by Caporaso (1996) the concept of a regulatory state – developed by Majone (1991; 1992; 1993a; 1994a; 1994b; 1996) – refers to the macro institutions of the EU. As such, it should be compared to other highly stylised forms of state, such as the Westphalian state or the post-modern state (Caporaso 1996). This interest in the theoretical potential of public policy analysis is of particular importance in the current stage of theoretical development: whilst in the 1960s and 1970s scholars were mainly concerned with creating taxonomies of integration as process and outcome (for instance, categorising the European institutional structure as 'concordance system', 'confederation', or 'emerging federal union'), today, as Caporaso has put it: 'The study of European integration is moving into a *post-ontological state*; scholars are less concerned with how to categorise than how to explain process and outcome, paying less attention to the "nature of the beast"' (Caporaso 1996: 30, emphasis added).

Most importantly, the public policy approach provides useful leverage for originating hypotheses. It is precisely with this aim that the results presented in this chapter will be developed into hypotheses for the analysis of the main object of this research, namely corporate direct taxation in the EU. Therefore the aim of this chapter is not an in-depth discussion of approaches to European integration, but, instead, a clarification of the most useful theoretical underpinnings for the study of the EU policy process.

A REGULATORY STATE?

In European integration scholarship, one of the main drawbacks of dominant theories is that, as already mentioned, they fail to explain the divergent integration patterns of different policies (Majone 1994a: 86). The development of EU policies has proceeded steadily in some areas (e.g. telecommunications and environment) but not in others (e.g. direct taxation and transport policy). Legal resources contemplated in the treaties do not offer much explanatory leverage because certain policy areas were (at least partially) integrated before they were consecrated in the treaties: environmental policy is the obvious and often cited case in point. More precisely, legal provisions are resources available to actors and are important when an actor can and does decide to use them. However, legal resources do not define the policy process: arguing that they do would be a typical conceptual mistake, dubbed by Hjern and Hull (1982) as 'methodological constitutionalism'.

The puzzle of uneven policy development can be explained by taking into account differences in policy types, most crucially the political properties of regulation.[9] The European state[10] is not characterised by the extraction of resources or by the development of the distributive and redistributive public programmes associated with the welfare state. A process of integration reproducing the evolution of the welfare state at the national level is unthinkable in the EU, due to the lack of fully-fledged European public finance, based upon genuine extractive capacities of EU institutions, and due to the limited dimension of the Community budget (no more than 1.5 per cent of the EU GDP). Social and redistributive policy becomes impossible, given these constraints.

By contrast, regulatory policy is not constrained by a limited budget (Majone 1993a). If the production of redistributive policy requires a considerable amount of financial resources, the cost of production of regulation is negligible. The regulator needs only expertise and 'know-how' and bears only a small 'internal' cost, that is the rule-making cost. The more substantial costs of regulations are borne by firms and individuals who have to comply with them. To sum up, the budget constraint is not a serious hurdle for regulatory policy; production costs of regulation are immensely lower than the ones of welfare policies; the regulator needs expertise more than financial resources; finally, the costs of regulatory policy are borne by firms and individuals. Therefore member states are not extremely sensitive to regulatory costs in the decision-making process: these costs do not impinge on public finance directly. Of course, the implementation stage of regulatory policy has implications for public finance and public administration. However, these costs are discovered by states in the medium term, when learning processes illuminate implementation costs that were not politically visible in the decision-making stage. An example of this is Richardson's study on EU water policy-making which illustrates the opacity of the cost structure, particularly in the earlier stages of the policy process (Richardson 1995).

The emergence of the European regulatory state can be understood in terms of demand and supply. To begin with the latter, the Commission is the main actor on the supply side, being interested in expanding its competencies. The resources of expertise of this small but formidable (in terms of competencies) bureaucracy and the intimate knowledge that EU bureaucrats have of the regulated industries (Majone refers in his articles to the notion of *copinage technocratique*) place the Commission in an ideal position for the production of regulation. Turning now to the demand side, why should actors in the EU policy process, most notably states and pressure groups, demand European regulation? For firms, the development of European regulation means that the European business community is able to 'speak with one voice' in the international context, thus challenging the competitive supremacy of Japanese and US companies. Instead of coping with fifteen different regulatory regimes, companies prefer to deal with a single European set of regulations.

But what about national governments? Why should they not oppose European regulation? It is true that regulation, being efficiency-oriented,[11] is fully consistent with the doctrine of economic liberalism that pervades the treaties, but this does not automatically secure consensus on regulatory policy. The strong rationale for EU regulatory policy comes from another source, namely the failure of national regulation. If that is not the case, efficiency can be presided over by domestic regulatory regimes, without the need to set up supra-national regulation. However, domestic regulations tend to fail for various reasons, including imperfect information, transaction costs and other barriers to negotiation and contract (Coase 1960), and finally lack of trust and credibility of domestic regulators (Majone 1994b).

The demand side of EU regulation therefore has something to do with the credibility of national governments *vis-à-vis* the regulated industries and the electorate. Are governments really independent from the regulation, or are they subjugated to the economic power of firms and to the retaliatory power of the vote (i.e. citizens who do not want to be regulated can vote against the incumbent government)? Credibility is the Achilles' heel of national regulatory regimes. Institutions such as the Commission are in a better position. Not only is the Commission less politically and physically 'close' than national governments to companies in various countries, but, most crucially, given its bureaucratic nature, it is not sensitive to electoral cycles and inter-party competition. When regulation is 'politically expensive' for governments and credibility of domestic regimes is low, delegation of regulatory powers to supra-national institutions represents the most viable solution.

Far from being a technical discussion of policy types, the arguments proposed by Majone constitute a theory of the European state. It is then surprising that O'Neill (1996) does not even mention the theoretical leverage of Majone's theory of integration in his 144-page description of European integration theory. A note of caution on the European regulatory state is however needed at this point. The growth of the European regulatory state is not unconstrained, and it should not be interpreted in a historicist fashion. Institutions designed to manage regulation with low political visibility are bound to be put under pressure by policies – such as the single currency – that challenge the political symbols of the nation state (Dyson 1994) and by the increasing political visibility of the 'democratic deficit' issue (W. Wallace 1996: 442). However challenged, the regulatory essence of the European state maintains deep implications for the assessment of the EU taxing powers. Caporaso has summarised this point with the following words:

> It would be theoretically misplaced to judge development of the EU in terms of the growth of its taxing and spending powers. Its weakness in terms of extraction and broad spending powers is not due to an 'early stage of development', nor are these functions likely to be supplied by the dynamics of functional linkages (spillover). The regulatory state is not the Westphalian state, the extractive state, or the social democratic state. Its future contours are not likely to resemble these state forms more than at present.
>
> (Caporaso 1996: 41)

At this point it appears that the very status of direct taxation – the object of this study – in the EU regulatory state is not a trivial issue. Are EU direct tax policies part of an embryonic – but as yet very incomplete – European welfare state, or, following Majone, should we consider them within the conceptual template of the regulatory state? It is this important question which will be elaborated upon in Chapter 6, dedicated to the analysis of the EU direct corporate tax policy process.

POLICY-MAKING IN THE EU: AGENCY AND PREFERENCES

The politics of regulation illustrates a number of important characteristics of policy formation in the EU: the focus on domestic regulatory failures, the opacity of cost structure, and the tendency to emphasise efficiency are all factors contributing to the de-politicisation of policy-making. Policies concerned with fairness tend to bring about social conflict and class considerations, whilst efficiency policies are relatively immune from political confrontation.[12] Accordingly, they can be processed within relatively de-politicised arenas, wherein bureaucratic politics prevails (Peters 1992b).

The contribution of the policy approach is not limited to the politics of regulation, however. A further two major aspects of European integration can be conceptualised by the study of public policy in the EU. They are the agency of institutions and the endogeneity of preferences to the policy process. Both aspects have already been mentioned in Chapter 2, but it is useful to turn to them once again, this time not in general terms but in the context of the EU policy process.

Institutional agency

An important theme in current research on European integration is the above mentioned move towards a post-ontological analysis. The real question does not seem to concern the ultimate 'nature of the beast' (inter-governmental or supra-national) but rather to identify the main mechanisms active within the European political structure. This new analytical focus has drawn attention to the policy-making process, as observed by Caporaso and Keeler:

> Scholars increasingly assume that some institutional structure is in place and examine what goes on inside these structures. Politics and policy-making within institutions have assumed an analytical place alongside the politics of institutional change.
>
> (Caporaso and Keeler 1995: 56)

The recent interest in historical institutionalism (Pierson 1996) can be interpreted as a new emphasis on the EU policy-making process. Integration is no longer explained exclusively in terms of single history-making decisions – such as the Treaty of Rome or the Single European Act[13] – but is analysed over time. It is particularly important to study what happens over time between one historical decision and another, in the 'daily grind' of the policy process (Cram 1997; Wincott 1995a) when significant divergencies between the preferences of member states and the actual functioning of EU institutions and policies emerge (Pierson 1996: 131 calls these divergencies 'gaps'). The analysis of public policies over time provides an excellent point of observation: it is there, away from the limelight of grand bargains, that 'gaps' emerge and, as shown by Pierson, cannot be so easily closed. Whilst authors working within the inter-governmentalist approach stress the efficiency of institutions (i.e. institutions emerge to reduce information asymmetries, monitor compliance and solve other problems of international policy co-ordination), policy scholars tend to emphasise institutional 'slack', purposeful opportunism of agents (Cram 1997; Pollack 1997) and unforeseen consequences. According to policy analysts sensitive to arguments of historical institutionalism, institutions are not mere efficient devices in the hands of member states.

The difference between history-making decisions and the 'daily grind' of the policy process raises the problem of the levels of analysis. Peterson (1995) has argued that alternative approaches to integration can be applied to different levels of integration: for example, the inter-governmentalist approach is more suitable for analysing 'high politics' and history-making decisions, whilst the policy approach explores micro decisions.

Basically, Peterson suggests an 'ecumenical' solution to the theoretical controversy: theories are not commensurable because they explain different levels of integration. Peterson's suggestion makes good sense: after all, is it not true that even at the height of history-making negotiations, that is at the table of an inter-governmental conference, core executives engage in 'high politics' negotiations, whereas bureaucrats and experts weave the fabric of specific policies? Yet where Peterson cuts, seams are needed. The reciprocal interactions between the micro and the macro level should not be neglected. Otherwise the theoretical usefulness of the policy approach would be confined to filling in the details of broad trajectories described by macro approaches.

The most obvious interaction between policies and 'high politics' in the EU is that macro events such as the Single European Act influence the development of policies. Therefore micro dynamics is not comprehensible without consideration of the macro political environment. The analysis of the EU direct corporate tax policy process (Chapter 6) will show how the policy environment had a fundamental, although not exclusive, role in bringing about policy change.

Yet there may also be opposite interactions. Both Cram (1995, 1997) and Wincott (1995b) argue that interactions amongst actors involved in the policy-making process generate mechanisms of adaptation and learning that eventually impact on the historical development of European integration. Wallace makes the point that 'significant institutional changes are improbable unless linked to changes in the level of agreement about policy' (H. Wallace 1996: 26). The historical institutionalist model of integration put forward by Pierson (1996) is also compatible with this public policy argument. Another thread of studies which is consistent with institutional agency is the rational-choice institutionalist theory presented by Garrett and Weingast (1993).

This analytical interest in the reciprocity between the policy process and the macro sphere is interrelated with the 'rediscovery' of European institutions – to use March and Olsen's expression (1989) – suggested by the policy approach and rational choice institutionalism. To begin with, European institutions work in a system that is more fluid than domestic political systems. The EU system of governance is multi-level and multi-dimensional (Hooghe 1996; Marks 1993); the agenda-setting process is extremely unstable (Peters 1994); and the relationships between institutions are not yet settled (Mazey and Richardson 1995). Furthermore, European bureaucracy does not respond to a European executive backed by a governmental coalition, and this has an impact on the principal–agent relationships in that the European Commission enjoys higher degrees of freedom than the ordinary domestic bureaucracy.

This fluid political system is acknowledged by the most sophisticated varieties of inter-governmentalism (Moravcsik 1993), but the problem with these is that they conceive of European institutions as passive structures: European institutions have degrees of freedom within a set of constraints imposed by member states.[14] By contrast, a considerable number of studies have proposed an active characterisation of the Commission (Bulmer 1994; Cram 1993; Majone 1994a; Peters 1992b), the European Court of Justice (Burley and Mattli 1993; Garrett and Weingast 1993; Wincott 1995b), and the European Parliament (Richardson 1995; Tsebelis 1994). Rational-choice scholars such as Garrett and Weingast have stressed the crucial role of European institutions in the interaction between ideas and interests, taking into account how institutions provide shared belief systems and 'constructed focal points'. In their own words:

> By embodying, selecting and publicising particular paths on which all actors are able to co-ordinate, institutions may provide a *constructed focal point*. Such institutions can also mitigate potential breakdowns in cooperation associated with ambiguity by providing the critical information about when an actor has defected and by resolving problems raised by unanticipated circumstances. Acting in this capacity, institutions not only provide individuals with critical

> information about defection but also help construct a shared belief system that defines for the community what actions constitute cooperation and defection.
>
> (Garrett and Weingast 1993: 176, emphasis in original)

Garrett and Weingast's argument is particularly important in that not only does it develop a preliminary theory of the role of ideas[15] but it also explains institutional agency.[16] Their argument can be summarised as follows. First, member states face multiple paths to co-operation. Second, institutions are devices through which ideas are transformed into shared belief systems. Third, within a whole range of possible paths to co-operation only one is selected; this path is discovered by actors thanks to the 'constructed focal points' created by institutions.

The stress on agency has potential, therefore, for exploring the role of knowledge in the EU policy process. There is a symmetry between what has been suggested in Chapter 2, and Garrett and Weingast's suggestion. On the one hand, the study of knowledge leads to the exploration of agency and actor-based models (Richardson 1996). On the other hand, the acknowledgement of EU institutional agency leads to the investigation of the role of ideas in the policy process, thus completing the full circle.

Preference formation

It has already been shown that the difference between the policy approach and other approaches, with reference to institutions, does not lie in the endogeneity *versus* exogeneity of institutions, but rather in the active *versus* passive characterisation of them, as argued by Cram (1995, 1997). Something similar happens in the domain of preference formation. In their most mature versions, inter-governmentalist approaches acknowledge the endogeneity of preferences. According to Moravcsik (1993), the preferences of states are moulded by domestic socio-economic interests; at the same time, governments have relative autonomy from domestic interests when national positions are articulated in the EU.

However, the policy approach underlines something deeper than this notion of endogeneity. Here the key issue concerns the consequences (in terms of preference formation) of actors' participation in the policy process. What are the consequences of the participation in the policy process? The following observation by Sandholtz seems poignant:

> Membership in the EC has become part of the interest calculation for governments and societal groups. In other words, the national interests of EC states do not have independent existence; they are not formed in a vacuum and then brought to Brussels. Those interests are defined and redefined in an international and institutional context that includes the EC. States define their interests in a different way as members of the EC than they would without it.
>
> (Sandholtz 1993: 3)

Similarly, Cram undertakes her analysis of integration theory by arguing that:

> European institutions, operating both as passive structures and as 'purposive actors', may have the capacity to alter the very perceptions which national governments and domestic interests hold of their interests. Thus participation in the 'day to day' policy process may significantly influence the environment in which major 'constitutional' decisions are taken in a number of important respects.
>
> (Cram 1995: 16–17)

It is with the aim of showing preference dynamics that policy studies describe how the Commission promotes networks of support for European policies by encouraging the emergence of Euro-associations, 'public concern' groups, networks of expertise and even drawing the attention of citizens towards the EU.[17] All these activities aim at forging favourable attitudes towards European integration. More importantly still, member states themselves discover and change their preferences in the EU policy process, as argued by Sandholtz in the quotation above.

The final question to be addressed concerns the relation between institutional agency and preference formation, on the one hand, and the conceptualisation of European integration, on the other. By and large, policy analysts are somewhat reluctant about the glib elaboration of macro hypotheses (not to mention fully-fledged models) of European integration. Presumably, this is the reason the policy approach is not considered one of the dominant theories of European integration. For the time being, policy scholars prefer to maintain fluid and 'open' analytical characterisations of European integration. Ultimately, it is the instability of the policy process itself (Mazey and Richardson 1993; Peters 1994; Richardson 1996) that hampers the recognition of a single path to integration. In addition, as argued above, institutions themselves are too 'young' and their relations are too unsettled to permit a definitive assessment on the European polity, particularly when policy studies show an amazing variety of institutional relationships in the EU policy process.

In this scenario, it seems plausible to limit oneself to asserting the unpredictability of the EU policy process, and perhaps recurring to the garbage-can model as the most satisfying analytical approximation (Richardson 1996). However, although the garbage-can model should not be disregarded, a promising research strategy ought to consider the elements of structuration (as opposed to the most volatile elements) of the EU policy process. The emergence of advocacy coalitions, the political role of epistemic communities, and the construction of focal points have potential in this respect. These elements will be taken into consideration in Part II of this study, dedicated to empirical analysis.

CONCLUDING REMARKS

This chapter has discussed the theoretical relevance of a little researched domain, i.e. the analysis of the EU policy process.[18] The main thesis argued in this chapter is that the investigation of the EU policy process does not represent a mere micro complement to the macro mosaic of integration provided by dominant theories. On the contrary, the study of the politics of policy-making provides insights into the development of integration theory, even though grand theorising is not an ambition (and presumably should not be) of the policy approach.

The first insight refers to the role of regulation in the emergence of the European state. The growth of the European regulatory state is explained by the political properties of this policy type. Without the study of policy types (which is a cornerstone of the policy approach) this essential feature of integration theory could not be singled out.

The second insight concerns the political consequences of institutional agency in integration theory. It is not the question *do institutions matter* that is most useful in the debate on integration. The real question is *how institutions are conceptualised* by different approaches: according to dominant theories, they are a passive set of constraints and opportunities, whilst in the policy approach they are assigned agency. This has dramatic consequences. Indeed, dominant approaches appear ultimately to understand the EU policy process as a zero-sum game between member states and EU institutions: for neo-functionalists the game is won by European institutions at the expense of member states' sovereignty, whilst the contrary is true for inter-governmentalists. By contrast, the study of public policies over time (especially in the historical institutionalist's view) shows that *all actors lose degrees of freedom* when institutions undergo a process of consolidation: 'historical institutionalism [as Pierson observes] emphasises how the evolution of rules and policies along with social adaptations creates an increasingly structured polity that restricts the options available to all political actors' (Pierson 1996: 147).

A third element to be stressed is preference formation. Preferences are discovered and changed by actors' participation to the policy process. In this sense, the EU policy process is not different from any other policy process (see Lindblom 1990 for this generalisation). Preferences are endogenous in two respects: from the point of view of the observer, they are part of the research design (and this marks a major difference from economic analyses of integration), and, as far as the observed reality is concerned, they are sensitive to what happens within the EU policy process. This means that the policy process itself produces change in preferences.

In conclusion, it seems that the policy approach has potential both for empirical analysis and for theory building. Incidentally, potential for theory building is enhanced by a number of important results of rational-choice institutionalism. Therefore, contrary to the conventional wisdom (H. Wallace 1996: 25), it has also been argued that the rational choice approach is useful for the understanding of the EU policy process. Indeed, authors working on the long-term dynamics of public policies have already emphasised that there is no need to argue for or against the rational-choice approach: for example, historical institutionalism, at least in Pierson's usage, 'cuts across the usual sharp dichotomy between rational choice and non-rational choice work' (Pierson 1996: 131). Both the analysis of the role of knowledge in the policy process (Chapter 2) and the discussion of EU integration presented in this chapter lead to the conclusion that rational choice models and the policy approach share elements of complementarity that should not be overlooked.

Perhaps the time has not yet come for 'closing' policy models with strong assumptions and generalisations that would unjustifiably neglect the multi-faceted essence of European integration. However, the opposite is not necessarily true: the interpretation of the policy can be less loose than a garbage-can model (Richardson 1996). As Wallace persuasively contends, the 'instability' of EU policy regimes does not mean that 'everything is uncertain'. The record of policy development has accumulated policy authority at the European level, although in unintended or unexpected ways (H. Wallace 1996: 28). The empirical analysis of EU direct corporate taxation will provide a fertile terrain for elaborating upon this point.

4 The politics of tax reform

> Most of the models of tax politics available appear better suited to explaining why the reforms were impossible, than for explaining how and why they did succeed.
>
> (Peters 1991: 271)

> One headline in the Washington Post told the whole story: THE IMPOSSIBLE BECAME THE INEVITABLE and the dream of America's fair share tax plan became a reality.
>
> (Birnbaum and Murray 1987: 285)

> Tax reform is not a station we arrive at, it is a way of travelling.
>
> (Slemrod 1990: 11)

THE DYNAMICS OF TAX POLICY: AN ANALYTICAL PUZZLE

Exploring policy change in tax policy presents a double challenge to comparative public policy. First, an explanation of domestic dynamics of tax reform is called for. The second analytical step consists of the explanation of the international diffusion of tax reform. Considered together, these two steps require *dynamic* models of tax policy as the first step highlights innovation and the second emphasises policy diffusion (or policy transfer, see Dolowitz and Marsh 1996). However, the study of tax policy has traditionally illustrated the *inertial* characteristics of this policy area, not its dynamism (Robinson and Sandford 1983; Rose and Karran 1987). Indeed, Witte examined the long-term dynamics of US federal tax policy only to conclude that radical policy change was most unlikely (Witte 1985: 380). Presumably, until the end of the 1980s the single most renowned theme of the tax policy literature was the quasi-impossibility of tax reform; during the same decade, this thesis had to be overhauled in view of the extraordinary diffusion of tax reform throughout the world. Accordingly, a second generation of policy studies appeared, this time more concerned with the explanation of change than with the thesis of policy inertia.

The main goal of this chapter is to review the literature on tax reform with the aim of highlighting hypotheses for the study of tax policy change in the European Union. Another aim in this chapter is to present the background of cross-national tax policy change in which the Italian and British cases – which will be discussed in Chapter 7 – are situated. In order to draw the correct lessons from this literature, it is useful to pin down the relevant analytical elements as precisely as possible. To begin with, which type of tax policy change is considered by this literature (i.e. limited, even though substantive and therefore not merely symbolic, change or comprehensive tax reform)? And second, how did tax reform develop over time (i.e. can a pattern of policy diffusion be detected)?

The nature of tax reform (comprehensive as opposed to limited) has been the cause of much debate, most notably amongst economists, who have drawn attention to the lack of a coherent approach in the reforms of the 1980s (McLure and Zochow 1987). Most importantly, economists have observed that new structures of taxation of the type suggested by economic theory have not as yet materialised in any country. Economists have been particularly keen on showing how the political system has distorted the initial proposals for tax reform. The US tax reform of 1986 is a case in point. Whilst economists have indicated that the process of US tax policy change was stopped a long way from the frontier of efficient taxation (Minarik 1989), political scientists have commented favourably upon the capability of political institutions to defeat particularistic interests and to bring about tax reform (Mucciaroni 1995). The diffuse tendency to broaden the tax base and to cut the number and the level of tax rates has led political scientists, and on occasion economists who have an interest in the tax policy process (Sandford 1993), to refer to the 1980s as a period of incisive tax reforms throughout the world (Peters 1991). Obviously, political scientists have looked at the impact of tax reform on the political system (e.g. how the process of tax reform has changed the relationships between policy-makers, pressure groups and institutions), whilst economists prefer to use economic theory as a yardstick for assessing tax reform.

It is important to observe that the impressive intellectual development of public economics has generated radical proposals for tax reform. Kaldor (1955) and Meade (1978) in the UK, Bradford in the US (1986), and Lodin (1978) in Sweden have all emphasised the need for a radical shift in tax policy based upon the introduction of new types of taxation. In more recent times, proposals for a flat-rate tax (Hall and Rabushka 1995), which were first put forward at the beginning of the 1980s, have gained good currency in public opinion.[1] Yet world tax reform has not gone so far as to follow economists' suggestions for new tax structures such as the Kaldorian expenditure tax or the flat-rate tax.

What is the main lesson to draw from this state of the debate between economists and political scientists? An important lesson for the study of policy change is that its measurement is deeply embedded in the analytical framework employed by the observer. What for political scientists is radical tax reform, for economists can be a limited revamping of tax policy. Therefore models of policy change based upon an allegedly objective nature of change, such as the one suggested by Hall (1993) and discussed in Chapter 2, show some limitations in this respect. The measurement of policy change is in fact contingent upon conceptual parameters.

A second theme of theoretical interest is related to the fact that tax reform, as we are reminded by Slemrod's quote introducing this chapter, often comes about in a series of decisions. This implies that tax reform should be conceptualised as a process, perhaps characterised by 'waves' of tax policy change across the world. Indeed, the cross-national diffusion of tax reform shows that an earlier wave of reforms dealing with the reduction of personal taxation and a mitigation of taxes on wealth took place at the beginning of the 1980s. Since the second half of the 1980s the process of tax reform has proceeded steadily, but this time with a major focus on closing loopholes, simplification and rationalisation of corporate and income taxation (Peters 1991). This second wave of tax reforms is the most important one, for the breadth of its international diffusion. The process of tax reform has spread throughout the OECD area, with some notable exceptions however (Italy and France). In the 1990s, the process was carried on once more, especially in the area of capital income taxation, as shown by the emergence of new tax regimes in Scandinavian countries (Sorensen 1994). Another impressive example of tax reform in the 1990s is the one taking place in the former communist countries (Tanzi 1993).

Having established that tax reform must be studied as a process, what can be said about its origins? At first glance, the second and most important wave of tax reform appears to have originated in the US, with the Tax Reform Act of 1986, and been swiftly imitated by other countries. However, corporate tax reform occurred in the UK in 1984: therefore the UK, more than the US, pioneered the second wave of corporate tax reform in the 1980s. But the fact remains that US tax reform attracted the attention of scholars, probably because it materialised in a single decision (the Tax Reform Act of 1986), whilst the UK tax reform was more of a continuous process (see Chapter 7).

Be that as it may, the process of diffusion stimulates the question of what factors motivated the adoption of similar reforms in the 1980s. For example, could it be argued that imitation of the US reform was the result of cross-national intellectual currents? Or would it be better to look at more 'hard' economic facts, such as the process of structural adjustment of public finance in the OECD area? Surprisingly, economists have suggested the former hypothesis, with analyses which, unintentionally, bear resemblance to the model of epistemic communities reviewed in Chapter 2. Public finance literature, which one would deem inherently distant from political science's preoccupation with cognitive variables, instead appears to be sensitive to this issue. The mosaic of cross-national tax reform thus becomes an intriguing one.

Having presented the main themes of this chapter, it is useful to proceed in order, first taking stock of the domestic level in order to move to the international process of tax reform. Therefore the next section examines the case of US tax policy innovation, the following one looks at the process of diffusion, and the final section draws some concluding remarks.

HOW CAN THE IMPOSSIBLE BECOME INEVITABLE? THE PARADOX OF TAX REFORM

Three dates mark the development of tax policy in the US. The first Reagan tax reform was in 1981 (the Economic Recovery Tax Act), inspired by general supply-side aims, and hence mainly targeted towards the reduction of the tax burden on corporations. In 1984 the US Treasury, concerned with federal budget deficit hikes, decided to undertake a comprehensive revision of the tax system. Finally, 1986 was the year of the Tax Reform Act, the very time in which, as the *Washington Post* put it, the 'impossible', that is a tax reform oriented towards diffuse interests, became 'inevitable'.

Why should a tax reform be considered 'impossible'? A group of authors have investigated this subject and it is useful to consider them here because their analyses shed light on the stringent constraints that render tax reform one of the most difficult exercises in public policy. Given the concern of this study with EU tax policy, a clarification is needed at this point. The EU polity is completely different from domestic polities. Hence the analysis of tax reform in the US is of limited applicability to the EU case. However, insofar as it shows the political difficulty of tax policy change, the examination of domestic tax policy change provides insights which can be considered when turning to the elaboration of hypotheses for the EU case. It is with this aim in mind that, after a short review of incremental and inertial models of tax policy, we will turn to the case of US tax reform.

Incremental and inertial models of tax policy

What do models of tax policy say about the likelihood of tax reform? Witte, author of a monumental history of the politics of the federal income tax, has contended that US tax policy is ruled by incrementalism (Witte 1985). The incremental rule of tax policy is interrupted by abrupt change caused by dramatic events such as wars. In these extreme conditions, taxes suddenly rise and tax rates become steeper. However, under normal conditions incrementalism produces an accommodation of concentrated interests: no comprehensive tax reform can appear, given the huge political difficulty of allocating concentrated costs.[2] This does not necessarily mean that tax reform revolves around the status quo. Indeed, incremental changes are cumulative. Year after year, tax expenditures and fiscal exemptions can alter the very structure of direct taxation, thus generating an unfair system (Witte 1985). Briefly, in incremental models, changes originated by the political intention to please interests create tax 'monsters': incoherence, an extensive presence of loopholes and ultimately profound unfairness.

Rose and Karran (1987) proposed instead an inertial model[3] in which politicians have no interest in championing tax reform. The point to stress is that inertia does not imply a static model of tax policy. In inertial models, the cumulative effect of inertia brings about the mobilisation of the losers. In more general terms, the long-term impact of inertia is the activation of forces that demand a new tax system. Abrupt policy change – the main point raised by Hood (1994) – is explained by this class of models, without the need to use exogenous shocks such as wars. Hood employs the term 'policy self-destruction': short-term distributive choices[4] revert in the long term to politically untenable configurations and at that point a policy regime 'explodes'. Here inertial and incrementalist models diverge: for the former the process becomes irreversible from a certain point on, whilst for the latter there is always the possibility of reversibility (Hood 1994). Clearly, the US tax reform of 1986, in which a number of tax loopholes were closed and diffuse interests were advantaged, is better explained by the irreversibility thesis. Accordingly, it is to the explanation of this extraordinary case of 'irreversibility'[5] that we now turn.

Solving the puzzle of tax reform: experts, interest groups, and institutions

Political scientists (Conlan, Wrightson and Beam 1990; Mucciaroni 1990; 1991; 1992) and economists directly involved in the formulation of the US Treasury reform plan (McLure 1992; McLure and Zodrow 1987; 1994) provide the best explanation of US tax policy change. The agenda of tax reform was set by the presidential request to the Treasury to elaborate a plan (known amongst the pundits by the name 'Treasury I'), which comprised the following elements:

- reform of the whole income tax structure;
- choice of income (as opposed to consumption) as the tax base;
- revenue neutrality;
- distributive neutrality amongst different individuals;
- investment neutrality (i.e. neutrality in respect of the forms of investment and investment financing);
- shift of the tax burden from individuals to companies;
- swift implementation.

The plan was devised in relative isolation by no more than ten individuals, without leaks that could have prompted the reaction of powerful pressure groups in the initial phase (McLure 1992: 102). In addition, the plan did not raise the issue of redistribution (one of the main characteristics was in fact 'distributional neutrality'). The problem of tax reform was not 'framed' as a class conflict (that would have been the case if the plan had not included distributional neutrality), but rather as a conflict between people who paid their 'fair share' and others who did not. Further, revenue neutrality was an element of discipline in that it restrained Congress from decreasing tax rates without taking into account the necessity to widen the revenue base (McLure 1992: 103). Conlan, Wrightson and Beam observe that in this stage of the policy process the role of economists and of 'professional consensus' was influential:

> This professional consensus was especially important because Treasury's tax experts initially got virtually free rein. Once the President requested the Treasury produce a reform proposal, 'outsiders' had virtually no further input. Consequently, the initial

> Treasury I plan was an astonishingly pure expression of expert views. Although never formally proposed as legislation, it – rather than the existing law – set the standard against which subsequent proposals were measured.
>
> (Conlan, Wrightson and Beam 1990: 243)

Curiously enough, economists had the impression that their political role in the policy process was in the end limited (Aaron 1989; 1990; McLure 1992; McLure and Zodrow 1987; 1994). This has something to do with the fact that the 1986 tax reform did not employ the state-of-the-art tools of public finance, but relied mostly on principles of public economics elaborated in the 1950s and the 1960s, if not even earlier. In any case, the role of economists in this process should not be neglected.

As outlined earlier, the main political determinant of this episode of policy change is policy self-destruction. How did self-destruction come about? To explain this phenomenon, the evolutive dynamics of tax policy have to be taken into account. Not only did the long-term consequences of clientelistic tax policy become politically visible, thus shedding light on the unfairness of the tax system, but the very system of incentives sustaining tax policy changed. As time went on, tax choices of the past turned out to be advantageous to some industries, but not to others. New industries, such as high-tech firms, dealers and other tertiary industries did not reap particularistic benefits from existing tax policy. Most importantly, for a number of firms the advantages of tax expenditures and tax loopholes had to be balanced with the costs of accurate tax planning. Within the business community the structure of incentives was no longer biased in favour of the current tax policy: in the long term a number of economic actors began to realise that they would have been better off with a level playing field (Mucciaroni 1991; Peters 1991). Consequently, influential firms such as IBM, Procter & Gamble, and General Motors challenged the status quo. This 'defection' enabled the champions of tax reform to present it as a genuine public good, and not as a zero-sum game between companies and citizens. These attitudes within the business community facilitated the construction of a bi-partisan alliance for tax reform, convincing reluctant Republicans that tax reform was not a policy 'against corporations'. Parenthetically, this point has potential for the analysis of EU corporate taxation and international taxation in general. The point can be articulated in the following way: do companies prefer a loose international tax order and seek the gains of an incomplete international tax framework (via tax planning and tax avoidance)? Or do they manifest a preference for a level playing field, thus joining actors (such as the Commission of the European Communities) who advocate international tax co-ordination? This question will be addressed in the context of the analysis of the EU policy process (see Chapter 6).

Until this point the politics of US tax reform has been analysed without considering the role of institutions. Of course, experts and corporations are important actors, but what can be said of institutional actors? The question is not confined to tax policy alone, but has wider theoretical implications. In fact, the role of institutions in tax reform has stimulated a critique to Kingdon's model of policy change.[6] Whilst Conlan, Wrightson and Beam (1990) find this model useful for understanding US tax policy change, Mucciaroni holds the opposite view. What is the bone of contention? Essentially, Mucciaroni argues that

> Political institutions are structures with perhaps the greatest impact on policy. Kingdon's garbage-can model views the role of institutions almost exclusively in situational terms. They constitute part of the changing 'political climate', which leaves untheorised the role of their structural characteristics and decision-making processes in the model. They are identified as 'players in the game' and 'participants in the streams'. But institutions also make up the topography, the banks and riverbeds that channel and shape participant behaviour.
>
> (Mucciaroni 1992: 466)

To begin with, according to Mucciaroni, tax reform became feasible because reform plans were coherent with the Treasury institutional remit, that is, to guard the revenue base. According to Mucciaroni, policy change materialises when it represents an acceptable course of action from the point of view of structures. Not surprisingly then, the main reforms of the 1980s – not just the US reform – have been revenue neutral. As will be shown in Chapter 6, concerns about the revenue base have been a long-standing obstacle to corporate tax harmonisation in the EU. Second, Mucciaroni argues that institutional autonomy from pressure groups was essential: otherwise the behaviour of Senator Bradley, who championed tax reform without fear of interest groups' retaliation, remains unexplained. Third, tax reform offered President Reagan a historical opportunity to challenge Congress, thus shifting the balance of power between the two most important institutions of the US in favour of the presidency. To sum up, committed 'institutional' policy entrepreneurs are a fundamental aspect of tax policy change.

Tax reform and the study of policy change: linking the three streams of policy change?

Perhaps the most important point made by Mucciaroni relates to Kingdon's view that the three streams which originate policy change (i.e. politics, policy solutions, and problems) are relatively independent. Policy solutions and politics – Mucciaroni argues – are not independent: as mentioned earlier, tax reform as a 'policy solution' had 'politics' (to use Kingdon's terms) implications for the balance of power between institutions, and its revenue-neutrality feature avoided an ideological battle over the dimension of the federal budget. Another political implication of the tax reform solution is that the latter, by advocating the cause of the public interest, tapped 'into widely shared values and potent symbols' (Mucciaroni 1992: 478).

Problems and politics are also linked: the long-term consequences of particularistic tax policy turned policy problems themselves into 'a catalyst for splitting the solid bloc that had supported loopholes' and mobilised 'a pro-reform business constituency' (Mucciaroni 1992: 479). Finally, is there a link between problems and policy solutions? Kingdon subverts the rational notion that problems are individuated first and then solutions are devised. For him, the Cohen, March and Olsen (1972) notion that solutions search for problems is true instead. However, Mucciaroni (1992: 481) argues that 'solutions do not need to "search" for problems because they are regarded as having intrinsic, rather than instrumental, merit'. The goal of horizontal equity, that is, the goal of fairness in the tax system, made tax reform good in principle, as it were. Moreover, the model of policy self-destruction follows a rather rational pattern in which problems and solutions are linked: the existing policy evolves into a major problem and therefore the solution becomes the repeal of the policy itself (Mucciaroni 1992: 481). At this stage we do not need to elaborate further upon the Kingdon-Mucciaroni controversy: it is in the context of the empirical analysis of EU tax policy that this point will be re-considered and discussed at length.

THE DIFFUSION OF TAX REFORM

Although economists have debated in great detail the question of the extent to which the implementation of the 1986 reform has significantly changed US taxation (Aaron 1990; Kasten, Sammartino and Toder 1994; Slemrod 1990), the fact remains that this reform has been considered a fundamental determinant of the cross-national diffusion of tax policy change. Our interest in the process of diffusion is limited to a specific aspect. Simply put, given the role played by tax policy paradigms in the EU tax policy process (Chapter 6) it is interesting to know whether the process of tax reform has been promoted, sustained or accompanied (obviously the three verbs denote different degrees of importance) by the emergence of a new tax policy discourse in the world. Should the answer be affirmative, the policy debate on EU taxation could be collocated in the broader shift of the tax policy discourse.

In this respect it is interesting to consider the analysis conducted by an economist, John Whalley, on seven national cases of tax reform (i.e. Japan, Canada, Sweden, New Zealand, Australia, Mexico, and the UK). An eighth case, i.e. US tax reform, is treated as an independent variable. The first hypothesis controlled by Whalley stresses economic factors. In this hypothesis, US tax reform of 1986, given the US pivotal position in world trade, triggered economic pressure for tax reform elsewhere, via tax base erosion and relocation of firms and portfolios. The alternative hypothesis, surprising for an economist, is that the diffusion of tax reform was not the direct effect of US reform but, rather, the outcome of 'common intellectual influences'. In assessing the two hypotheses, Whalley notes that certain characteristics of world tax reform follow the US model. Yet policy imitation as a hypothesis does not match the empirical evidence that other countries had already initiated tax policy reforms before the US, the UK being one of these countries. Therefore it would be better to consider the US in the more limited role of catalyst, particularly for small countries with closer links to the American economy, and for corporation tax (Whalley 1990).

However, as far as larger economies and other areas of taxation are concerned, Whalley finds that common intellectual influence is the better explanatory variable. The paradigm of neutrality, rate reduction, horizontal equity, and tax simplification appears to be the determinant of this epochal change in tax policy. Briefly, in the 1980s tax policy discourse shifted from equality and redistribution to neutrality and efficiency. Of course, the declination of this paradigm in different countries has respected the peculiarities of each national case. More importantly still, it should be kept in mind that Whalley examines two alternative hypotheses *coeteris paribus* and consequently has nothing to say on other crucial political factors of tax reforms. Peters (1991) shows how important Conservative governments with populist accents were in the diffusion of tax reform across the world. In a similar vein, Sandford (1993) employs a comparative public policy design for concluding that a committed policy entrepreneur allied with the president (or the prime minister in non-presidential democracies) is the most typical aspect of tax reforms, thus emphasising the role of domestic political actors. Policy diffusion would have been impossible – Sandford contends – without this type of political support. The comparative study of tax reform corroborates one conclusion of the analysis of US policy change, i.e. the pivotal role of committed policy entrepreneurs operating within the institutional framework. Hallerberg and Basinger (1997) add that the ability of governments and policy entrepreneurs to produce tax policy change depends critically on the number of institutional veto players required to approve change.

Another important element underlined by authors who have studied the diffusion of tax reform is the strategy of consensus building. The presence of a comprehensive package for tax reform is a political device which emphasises the public good benefits of radical tax policy change because it highlights the interdependence between the minuses for certain interest groups and the pluses for the ordinary citizen. The (few) costs have been presented as the only way to gain access to the (large) gains.

This observation leads to the problem of constructing the legitimacy of tax policy change. Peters (1991) stresses the contribution of public interest or common cause groups in the construction of legitimacy. This element is absent from the EU scene. There are no citizens' movements advocating European tax reforms, even though some domestic policy fora (the Institute for Fiscal Studies in the UK, for example) and some European organisations (see Chapter 6) could be considered – to a very limited extent, of course – as functional equivalents of public interest groups in that they have wider concerns than pressure groups. The European professional tax bodies are not generally composed of ordinary citizens but of tax experts, professionally active in the academic field or in the business community (or, as is frequently the case, both). Almost invariably they tend to advocate the point of view of the average corporate tax payer. Indeed, the political behaviour of these European tax organisations is modelled around the economic paradigm of efficiency and tax neutrality. EU-wide tax bodies are vehicles which transfer into the European tax policy process the same ideas and paradigms that sustained domestic tax reforms in the 1980s.

CONCLUDING REMARKS

There is a fundamental discontinuity in the shift from policy-making at the domestic level to the making of public policies in the EU.

Accordingly, the study of tax reform at the domestic level does not provide any lesson for the EU. Yet the analysis conducted in this chapter suggests hypotheses. Therefore the main point argued in these conclusions concerns *hypotheses-building, and not lesson-drawing*. The first element of reflection pertains to the presence of institutional policy entrepreneurs. In the EU political structure, the Commission is the best candidate to play this role. Empirical analysis will hence establish if and to what extent the Commission has been a pivotal actor in the EU corporate tax policy process.

The second element to bear in mind is that the political behaviour of firms should be included in empirical analysis. The assumption that firms are in favour of loose international tax co-ordination (because this situation offers more advantages in terms of tax avoidance) should be challenged or in any case empirically controlled with extreme caution. Domestic tax reforms have in fact witnessed the alignment of firms or segments of the business community with the pro-reform coalition. The question then can be raised: are firms in the EU prepared to advocate for a European level playing field? Is the degree of uncertainty in EU taxation high enough to push firms towards the demand for tax policy co-ordination?[7]

There is a third element to consider when investigating tax policy change: consensus-building. The construction of legitimacy is indeed a crucial factor in tax reform. In turn, consensus-building is related to the characteristics of 'package deals' offered by tax reform advocates (i.e. the political properties of policy solutions). This stimulates an empirical assessment of the linkages between policy solutions and political variables within the process of policy change. In more general terms, the Kingdon–Mucciaroni controversy over the independence versus interdependence of streams seems intriguing. Mucciaroni argues that 'by stressing the mutual *inter*dependence of the streams and tracing them out, agenda-setting seems less indeterminate and random and more purposive and strategically based' (Mucciaroni 1992: 474–475, emphasis in original). The Kingdon–Mucciaroni debate, in conclusion, has considerable potential for the investigation of tax policy change in the EU, in which agenda-setting is a fluid and extremely random process (Peters 1994).

Part II

Empirical research

5 Problem definition in EU direct corporate tax policy

> To a large extent, the international institutions of the post-war period have been shaped by economists. . . . Economists can offer another very substantial contribution in the area of capital income. This opportunity results from the historical evolution of tax laws and international capital markets.
>
> (Giovannini 1990)

INTRODUCTION: ALTERNATIVE 'FRAMES' FOR EU TAX POLICY

The problem of European direct corporate tax harmonisation (throughout the book, this term is referred to as policy co-ordination, and its precise meaning is defined on a case-by-case basis) is addressed in different ways by distinct perspectives of analysis. When conceptual lenses vary, European tax harmonisation acquires changing meanings, suggests diverse policy instruments, and, most importantly, implies alternative approaches to European governance of corporate taxes. This chapter considers four approaches (namely, tax neutrality, fiscal implications of monetary union, fiscal federalism, and international tax complexity) with the aim of arguing three analytical points. First, tax policy problems are not incontestable givens, but are the result of an interpretative act (an act of 'framing') which makes problems amenable to human action: this is consistent with the literature on the politics of problem definition and frames reviewed in Chapter 2. Second, problem definition has implications in terms of the structuring of the policy process as suggested by the literature on advocacy coalitions, target populations, knowledge utilisation, and interpretative frames (Sabatier and Jenkins-Smith 1993; Schneider and Ingram 1993; Schön and Rein 1994; Weiss 1979). Third, not every approach has entered the European tax policy process. Therefore this chapter prepares the ground for the presentation of a wider discourse on

European tax harmonisation. A wider discourse will be presented and assessed in Chapter 10.

A preliminary delimitation of the field of analysis is needed at this point: all the approaches considered here have been developed within public economics. Hence they belong to the same family, share common theoretical foundations, and proceed with similar assumptions relating to economic behaviour. Yet their policy conclusions differ markedly. This renders the investigation of the policy solutions advocated by these approaches an intriguing intellectual exercise.

The chapter proceeds along the following lines. Four approaches to European direct taxation are presented in the following four sections. The analysis will necessarily be confined to the most important elements of each approach. Indeed, the main point in this chapter is to show how elusive the cognitive structure of the EU tax policy process is, rather than conducting a review of specialised approaches. Not only are solutions diverse, but the very identification of policy problems is a puzzle. After having discussed the pieces of this puzzle, some concluding remarks will be presented in the final section of this chapter.

FOUR DEFINITIONS OF EUROPEAN TAX PROBLEMS

Even though no systematic attempt to highlight the different analytical perspectives on international tax policy problems has been presented in the literature, it is argued here that pointing out differences rather than similarities is extremely useful for the understanding of this policy domain. Admittedly, the perspectives analysed here reveal contiguities and can be joined by means of bridge propositions. However, stressing diversities has three advantages. To begin with, the choice of underlining differences shows that policy problems can be defined only through conceptual moves (an approach, a model, or a series of causal propositions concerning the economy). In the absence of an interpretative act, a policy problem cannot even be detected. Second, not only is defining policy problems an interpretative act, but problem definition is not univocal: distinct analytical moves do not lead to the same policy conclusions, notwithstanding the analytical contiguity of the approaches considered here. Given these two arguments a third proposition follows: what is presented in this chapter is not a review of the literature, but an exploration of how problem definition brings about identification of chains of phenomena, problems and solutions around which political action evolves.

A cursory view of alternative problem definitions is provided by

Table 5.1. It can be seen that the four approaches do not share the same causal structure, as illustrated by the selection of independent variables, dependent variables, and analytical foci. To be sure, the notion of dependent and independent variables should not be considered strictly; indeed, this notion is employed here only for shedding light on the causal chain which represents the backbone of each approach. Obviously, the most important column is the fifth (labelled 'policy instruments') as it illuminates the consequences of distinct causal models in terms of political action: it is here that the politics of problem definition becomes visible and politically salient.

TAX NEUTRALITY

This approach is extremely important because during the late 1980s it introduced a common set of beliefs and arguments in the European tax policy process. However, the concern for tax neutrality is not limited to European issues; indeed, public economics as a whole has exhibited an amazing paradigm shift, from the goals of redistribution and fairness to allocative efficiency (Quigley and Smolensky 1994 and Chapter 4 of this volume). However, in the field of international taxation the concept of neutrality has peculiar connotations. The policy discourse on international neutrality is based on the notions of capital export neutrality (CEN) and capital import neutrality (CIN). When

Table 5.1 Problem definition: four approaches to EU corporate taxation

Approach	*Dependent variables*	*Independent variables*	*Focus*	*Policy instruments*
Tax neutrality	Tax wedges	Taxes on income from capital	CEN CIN	Removal of cross-border withholding taxes
EMU	Fiscal implications of EMU	Monetary union	Anchor-tax Spatial disparities Second best	Community budget
Fiscal federalism	Tax assignment	Externalities Economies of scale Indivisibilities	Non-centralisation	Side payments
Internal tax complexity (tax globalisation)	Tax regimes	Capital flows (tax base mobility)	Globalisation	Global agreements Institutional reforms

CEN is achieved there is no tax incentive to locate investment in one country rather than another; CIN instead assures that in a given country there is no tax-induced competitive advantage of a domestic company over a foreign company (Devereux and Pearson 1989). CEN and CIN can then be employed as yardsticks for assessing the efficiency of taxes affecting cross-border company activity in the single market. Besides, CEN and CIN can be conceived as intimately linked to the essence of the Single European Act, the thrust of which is to eradicate obstacles to the free movement of workers, capital, and goods. Similarly, CEN and CIN can be seen as an extension of this principle to cross-border tax obstacles. As Devereux and Pearson argue: 'it is possible to make a case that *both* CEN and CIN are required for the aims of the 1992 programme not to be subverted by differences in corporate tax burdens' (1989: 23, emphasis in original). However, a perfectly neutral European tax regime, i.e. a regime with the same tax effective burden on all European businesses, would require 'identical tax systems, rates and bases in each country' (Devereux and Pearson 1989: 24). Economic efficiency would be achieved, but the political cost would be unacceptable. This is why policy-makers – who are particularly aware of the costs of total harmonisation – are compelled to choose between CEN and CIN. Devereux and Pearson (1989: 24), reflecting a view shared by many economists, suggest that 'achieving CEN is more important than achieving CIN'. CEN is achieved by residence-based taxes, whilst CIN requires source-based taxes. The residence principle stipulates that residents' income, whether earned at home or abroad, should be fully taxed by the country of residence.[1] Economists such as Devereux and Pierson (and the OECD) recommend tax systems based on residence taxation rather than territorial taxation.

During the 1980s a model capable of measuring the distance of existing tax systems from the benchmark of neutrality became available. This model, originally developed by King and Fullerton for the analysis of the cost of capital in closed economies (King and Fullerton 1984), was later extended to the analysis of open economies. In a nutshell, the open-economy version of the model allows the measurement of tax wedges, which represent synthetic measures of the tax incentives and disincentives originated by the impact of different tax systems on transnational economic activities. The advantage of this model is that the impact of several taxes (for example, national and local taxes, corporate taxes and income taxes on the individual who receives dividends from companies) is condensed into one synthetic measure of the tax burden on investment.

The policy implications of this model are evident and can be articulated in the following steps. In the place of abstract models of optimal taxation, tax wedges measure concrete tax distortions present in the European market. In turn, distortions can be ascribed to specific taxes, particularly withholding taxes on cross-border company profit, interest, and royalty flow. Finally, the need for European tax harmonisation can be proven on a case-by-case basis because the analysis of tax neutrality sheds light on specific taxes which are the major impediments to the completion of the internal market. Thus the approach has potential for structuring the discourse on European direct tax harmonisation in a pragmatic way: instead of harmonisation for its own sake, the approach advocates the removal of specific cross-border withholding taxes. Mitigation of tax distortions through limited intervention of the Commission, rather than full harmonisation of European tax systems, appears the most straightforward policy consequence of this approach. Accordingly, the tax neutrality approach argues that political action for co-ordinating taxes in the EU should *not* proceed along the track of harmonising tax rates, tax bases or tax systems; on the contrary, the most needed reforms – the approach asserts – consist of the elimination of withholding taxes which present obstacles to cross-border trade (Devereux and Pearson 1995).

FISCAL CONSEQUENCES OF EMU

The independent variable is defined in another way by this approach, as shown by Table 5.1. Whilst the approach of tax neutrality detects its own independent variables by looking at the interwoven mechanisms of different domestic tax regimes, for the economic and monetary union (EMU) approach it is within the EMU policy process that independent variables have to be chosen. Consequently, the approach investigates the repercussions of monetary variables upon fiscal variables. Obviously, it is impossible to sum up the huge debate on EMU. Hence, it seems better to focus upon the following critical themes illuminated by this debate: the identification of anchor-currencies, as opposed to anchor-tax systems; the second-best implications of EMU; the issue of spatial disparities; and the fiscal prerequisites of an optimum currency area.

The 'anchor' theme points out differences between the creation of a single currency and corporate tax harmonisation. It argues that harmonisation makes sense when there is an indisputable centre of gravity – a sort of 'anchorage' of the policy process – around which national systems converge. The anchor can be represented by one European system which possesses greater power and is regarded as somewhat virtuous. In the case of monetary policy it seems sensible to argue that the German system (independence of the central bank, credibility of monetary policy, structural power of the Deutschmark) could be the anchor for harmonisation (Dyson 1994). By contrast, there is no tax-anchor in Europe, which, thanks to its desirable properties and its structural power, can inevitably attract the other tax systems. To make things worse, the alternative choice of harmonising around the mere average of existing tax systems (for example, selecting a European tax rate which is the average of the current fifteen rates) is inefficient as the average of a series of non-optimal units is in itself non-optimal (Tanzi and Bovenberg 1990). In conclusion, if a centre of gravity does not exist, the EU could be better off without tax harmonisation. This leads Cnossen to argue that complete corporate tax harmonisation is neither necessary nor desirable:

> The crucial question with regard to taxation is not, it appears, how the various taxes can be equalised as soon as possible, but, on the contrary, how much tax diversity can be permitted without interfering with the establishment of a common market and further down the road to a monetary union.
>
> (Cnossen 1990: 473)

A second theme linking European taxation and EMU has to do with the second-best implications of the single currency. Briefly, the theory of second-best, when applied to EMU, states that removing monetary barriers in a market in which other barriers are still present (cross-border withholding taxes are a case in point) can decrease the degree of economic welfare (Frenkel, Razin and Sadka 1991). Therefore monetary union must be implemented in conjunction with the removal of tax distortions, otherwise the efficiency of the single market would be put in jeopardy. Here there is a case for constructing a bridge proposition between second-best analysis and tax neutrality as the latter can be seen as the necessary complement to EMU.

The themes of spatial disparities and fiscal prerequisites of currency areas have a long history which dates back to the well-known MacDougall Report (Commission 1977), but they have been rejuvenated by the economic analysis of the monetary provisions enshrined in the Treaty of Maastricht. The 'school' of spatial disparities (Prud'homme 1993) argues that the unification of monetary policy in Europe can exacerbate spatial differences in Europe. Even though these gloomy perspectives are not considered real threats (Santos 1993) there is still concern that (a) the loss of flexibility in economic policy associated with the renunciation of flexible exchange rates, together with (b) the elements of regressivity currently present in the Community budget could aggravate spatial disparities in the EU. Consequently, the Community budget should be restructured in two directions. First, more effective transfers, themselves compatible with a limited increase of the budget, are needed. Second, the problem of regressivity should be solved, possibly by means of a new emphasis on European corporate tax harmonisation and on the so-called European 'green' taxes.

Whilst students of spatial disparities tend to focus upon the redistributive functions of the budget, the theory of optimum currency areas – originally elaborated by Mundell in the 1960s – when applied to the EMU policy process highlights the need to empower the stabilisation function of the Euro-budget. Accordingly, the federal budget ought to absorb asymmetric shocks which, in a single currency scenario, cannot be stabilised by means of a flexible exchange rate. Spatial disparities and optimum currency areas analyses hence advocate tax harmonisation for reasons which are not the same as used by the tax neutrality approach. The key policy instrument within which tax harmonisation has to be considered is the Community budget. Furthermore, the study of spatial differences and currency areas lends weight to the arguments of fiscal federalism in that a federal budget is considered indispensable for coping with these problems (Eichengreen and Frieden 1994).

FISCAL FEDERALISM

The point of arrival of optimum currency areas studies, that is fiscal federalism, can be conceived of as a point of departure for the understanding of European taxation. The strength of fiscal federalism is that it provides a comprehensive analysis of all the Musgravian functions of economic policy, namely allocation, stabilisation, and redistribution. To these a fourth federal function, regulation, has more recently been added (Oates 1994). The classic argument for federal tax assignment is the presence of externalities, economies of scale, and indivisibilities. However, recent research on fiscal federalism in the EU has steadily progressed beyond classic arguments, and has stressed the peculiarities of tax assignment in the EU (Reichenbach 1993).

It should never be forgotten that fiscal federalism is not a theory for centralisation, but a stock of economic and political arguments for non-centralisation. As such, fiscal federalism should be considered as intimately melded with the principle of subsidiarity. This is why recent research on fiscal federalism does not advocate measures such as, for example, the introduction of a federal corporate tax in Europe.

At the same time, specialists on fiscal federalism do not show any hesitation in recommending a more incisive tax harmonisation, articulated along the following lines:

> Economic conditions appear therefore united for recommending the establishment in the medium term of a single corporate tax regime characterised by a harmonised tax base, a minimum statutory rate and a common country-apportionment formula relative to the profits of enterprises operating in more than one Member State.
>
> (Reichenbach 1993: 88)

More importantly still, the approach maintains that the creation of a fiscal federal structure in Europe cannot be achieved without the introduction of compensatory measures (i.e. side payments). Existing federal systems contemplate a flow of equalisation grants. These intergovernmental grants preside over consensus among members and compensate for the absence of state-level flexibility in absorbing asymmetric shocks. By the same token, fiscal federalism in the EU is simply inconceivable without side payments deliberately planned for mitigating the huge political and economic costs (from the point of view of member states) of tax harmonisation. Side payments are a relevant aspect of many EU decisions, as illustrated by the political mechanisms at work in the Single European Act negotiations and in the Social Protocol of Maastricht (Lange 1993; Marks 1992). Simply put, fiscal federal arguments insert the political logic of side payments into the discourse on European tax harmonisation. We will turn to a more in-depth consideration of the political implications of fiscal federal arguments in Chapter 10, when we discuss the perspectives for development of the EU policy process.

INTERNATIONAL TAX COMPLEXITY (TAX GLOBALISATION)

Never has capital been more mobile than in the contemporary global economy. This is not just a consequence of the directive liberalising capital movement in the European Community (1988) but represents a more general trend in the international political economy (Owens 1993; Tanzi 1995). In the previous world of limited capital mobility, the problems of international taxation were more or less effectively governed through the residence principle and the time-honoured network of bi-lateral tax treaties (Arnold and McIntyre 1995; Picciotto 1992). The situation has now changed dramatically. Managing the residence principle when capital becomes fully mobile is extremely difficult: legal, technical and administrative problems, compounded by political constraints, seriously limit the exchange of information among tax administrations (Tanzi 1995). Savers and companies are increasingly sophisticated, but the 'internationalisation' of capital has been accompanied by a limited degree of internationalisation of tax administration (Picciotto 1992). This explains why the residence principle, even though it represents a cornerstone of OECD policy recommendations, is far from being fully implemented by states. Quite the contrary, the trend is towards an increasing application of the alternative source principle.

In addition, for some economists the mere existence of a single tax haven somewhere in the world can trigger a process of unbridled tax competition (Frenkel, Razin and Sadka 1991). In turn, this 'race to the bottom' can bring about a downward pressure on capital and skilled labour taxes. At the end of the process the whole tax burden will be placed on unskilled labour, which can provide a very limited revenue. The bottom line is that the welfare state will be disintegrated by deep economic integration (Sinn 1990).

Intriguingly enough, as far as policy conclusions are concerned this approach does not necessarily recommend harmonisation. Harmonising taxes in Europe is not a solution to the problem of tax base mobility because attractive tax regimes outside the EU can thwart any effort to limit unbridled tax competition through European legislation. Monitoring foreign controlled corporations' income and capital movement – the approach goes on – requires a global multi-lateral initiative under the auspices of an organisation such as the World Trade Organisation. The EU could be, at best, a catalyst of a multilateral initiative, to be developed within appropriate policy fora such as the OECD, in concert with the United States and Japan. In any case, European institutions (in particular the Commission) should look outside Europe (global initiatives) and not inside (tax harmonisation) in their search for ways of governing international tax problems (Owens 1993). Giovannini shares the view that EU tax harmonisation cannot be an effective solution, but prefers to focus on institutional reforms, such as, say, persuading Switzerland to abolish bank secrecy laws, or promoting a co-ordinated international campaign for dismantling laws such as deferral regimes[2] which favour fiscal arbitrage of transnational corporations (Giovannini 1989; Giovannini and Hines 1991).

CONCLUDING REMARKS

This chapter has shed light on the radical uncertainty surrounding the EU corporate tax policy process. The four approaches under examination, although partially compatible, are inherently diverse in their construction of policy problems and policy solutions. For the neutrality approach, the most crucial policy problem of EU corporate tax harmonisation is represented by tax distortions and the solution has to be found in the elimination of cross-border taxes which affect international trade and investment. For the EMU approach, it is the balance between real and monetary convergence that is the guiding principle of EU tax harmonisation. Fiscal federalism 'frames' tax policy problems by looking at the functions of the Community economic policy: when this approach advocates the harmonisation of corporate taxes, it does so for reasons mainly linked to the allocative function of the budget. Finally, the tax globalisation or tax complexity approach does not even address EU solutions as the main concern. Indeed, according to the tax complexity paradigm, the crucial concern is the search for appropriate arenas in which tax co-ordination can be brought about. Consequently, this approach considers the pros and cons of different arenas: the EU arena, bi-lateral inter-governmental arenas, and multi-lateral inter-governmental arenas with the OECD or similar organisations as main policy fora.

The fact that different approaches are available does not necessarily mean that all approaches have been included in the system of interaction between actors involved in EU taxation. The policy discourse on EU corporate tax harmonisation is not so wide as to include all approaches. Indeed, one of the main arguments of this book is that the EU policy process has a thin cognitive component. Only the tax neutrality approach (and that only belatedly) entered the EU policy process. The next chapter will analyse how it all came about. We will then return to the cognitive structure of the EU policy process in Chapter 10, in order to discuss the implications of a wider discourse on EU tax harmonisation.

6 Corporate direct taxation in the European Union

> Countries that have become aware of the damage done by tax competition might be able to agree on the harmonisation of national taxes on capital incomes and corporate profits.
>
> (Scharpf 1996a: 13)

> It is only when the European Union will become politically accountable in a democratic way for those policies that should be conducted at the European level, that it is justified to grant the Union the power to decide the basic issues of taxation. . . . Only in this way will we continue in the glorious tradition of 'No taxation without representation'.
>
> (Vanistendael 1994: 144)

INTRODUCTION: THE PARADOX OF INACTION AND CHANGE

This chapter analyses the EU corporate direct taxation policy process (referred to hereafter as TP, as in 'tax process'). Two questions introduce this area of investigation. First, what does this process consist of, and second, what are the theoretical underpinnings of the analysis? The second question will be dealt with in the section entitled 'Building hypotheses'. It is now important to set out the main characteristic of the TP.

To begin with, the TP has produced few outcomes. The European Commission has been advocating the necessity to harmonise direct corporate tax since the 1960s, but only in 1990 were measures (two directives and a convention) ratified by the Council. In the wake of that event, the Commission set up a Committee of independent experts, dubbed the Ruding Committee after its chairperson, Onno Ruding, in the hope that its proceedings would provide the background necessary for further tax policy integration. Nevertheless, none of the policy recommendations advocated by the Ruding Committee (Commission 1992) have yet been implemented: in November 1994 Madame

Scrivener concluded her mandate as European Commissioner with a *de profundis*, withdrawing a draft directive mitigating international double taxation which had been deemed essential by the Commission. Only recently, in March 1996, did the Commission seek to re-launch the TP, drawing attention to corporate taxes by means of a consultative paper dealing with taxation in general (i.e. value-added tax, excise duties, social security contributions, personal income taxes, and capital income taxation; see Commission 1996).

This course of events traces a very uncertain integration pattern as the European tax policy process is characterised by three stages: a long stalemate from the 1960s to the end of the 1980s; an episode of policy change in 1990; and, after a short phase of enthusiasm, resumed difficulties later on. The puzzle of policy areas in which long periods of stability, and even inaction, alternate with episodes of policy change has attracted the attention of public policy analysts. Most of the research has been conducted at the national level (e.g. Dudley and Richardson 1996; Richardson *et al.* 1992) but the European policy process examined here presents a similar puzzle: how can we explain stability (inaction, in the case of EU direct tax harmonisation) *and* change?

The development of the TP is indeed very demanding: to begin with, how can one explain the 1990 policy change which materialised after a period of inaction? If – as it will be argued below – policy development is interpreted from the perspective of learning, how can one explain that the Commission has gradually learned apparently successful strategies only to be frustrated once again in the most recent period? Was this just an erratic episode? Did it all happen by chance? And can the transfer of direct tax power – one of the milestones of statehood – to the supra-national level be interpreted as a mere random episode?

The chapter is organised in the following way. First, it will turn to the theoretical underpinnings. The analysis of the three bodies of literature conducted in Part I of the book is useful here. In fact, three hypotheses contained in the public policy literatures relating to the politics of tax reform, policy change and European integration will be set out in this section ('Building hypotheses'). Some background information on the main policy problems in European taxation will be provided in the subsequent section; and the TP will be analysed in detail in the section which follows. Within this section the main factors explaining the varying degrees of success of the Commission over time are presented, namely the changing policy environment, the policy frame in which proposals are encased, and the political role of knowledge. Finally, the concluding section assesses the hypotheses and draws implications for the study of knowledge utilisation, policy change, and policy types.

BUILDING HYPOTHESES

Politics of tax reform

The literature on the politics of tax reform has been considered (in Chapter 4) with the aim of building hypotheses, and not with the intention of drawing lessons for the EU. Three elements have been underlined in this respect. The first concerns institutions, from two points of view. Institutional policy entrepreneurs are present in the most studied cases of domestic tax reform. This leads towards the investigation of the Commission as potential policy entrepreneur in the TP. At the same time, tax policy change has to be agreed upon at the Council level by domestic institutions which have a long-standing goal of guarding the revenue base: can tax harmonisation in the EU be compatible with this institutional remit?

The second element refers to the political behaviour of firms. After a long period in which companies had been funnelling tax policies toward complicated tax exemptions, sophisticated tax avoidance, particularistic tax expenditures and, ultimately, a logic of client politics (Wilson 1980), the 1980s witnessed a split within the business community. An increasing number of firms became persuaded that they would be better off on a level playing field, with a simplified and fair tax system. Can one draw analogies with the EU case? Is the TP similar to domestic cases in this respect? In any case, what can be said of the political behaviour of companies in the TP?

The third element is a tremendously important 'ingredient' of tax policy change, namely consensus building. Tax reforms necessitate the construction of a strong, widely supported legitimacy in order to defeat particularistic actors. We observed that domestic tax reform tends to assume the characteristics of package deals in which the costs and benefits, the problems and solutions, and the winners and losers of the reform are connected. Put differently, interdependence of the main issues of tax reform is a typical feature of this policy area. It could be argued then that the construction of the 'tax policy change package' is a crucial determinant of policy dynamics. This is equivalent to saying that the construction of policy problems and policy solutions is decisive. There are good reasons for exploring the politics of problem definition because, as Chapter 5 demonstrated, the policy discourse on EU taxation is extremely elusive. How did problem definition emerge in the TP and with what effects on agenda-setting?

As mentioned in Chapter 4, Peters (1991) stresses the role of public interest or common cause groups in the construction of legitimacy. This raises the following question. Can Europe-wide professional organisations (and policy fora such as the Institute for Fiscal Studies) bring into the EU tax policy process diffuse interests, thus 'widening' the TP?

Policy change and the role of knowledge

The study of tax reform has triggered a debate on the degree of uncertainty in tax policy change. Whilst Kingdon argues that the three streams of policy change (policy, politics, and problems) proceed with relative autonomy, Mucciaroni has considered the case of US tax reform for contending that Kingdon overlooks institutions and constraints. Most pertinently, Mucciaroni (1992: 466) argues that 'Kingdon's garbage can model views the role of institutions almost exclusively in situational terms' and that the three streams are interdependent. Accordingly, the analyst should investigate linkages among politics, policy, and solutions. Briefly, Kingdon's model allows for radical uncertainty, whilst Mucciaroni suggests a relatively more structured model.

Apart from the Kingdon–Mucciaroni controversy, the debate on policy change, reviewed in Chapter 2, has highlighted the crucial role of knowledge in explaining policy dynamics. Arguably, it seems important to understand how the political discourse on European taxation is constructed by framing. The latter, as already mentioned in Chapter 2, is defined as

> a way of selecting, organising, interpreting, and making sense of a complex reality so as to provide guideposts for knowing, analysing, persuading, and acting. A frame is a perspective from which an amorphous, ill-defined problematic situation can be made sense of and acted upon.
>
> (Rein and Schön 1991: 263)

Framing is an essential component of the cognitive dimension of public policy. But how is knowledge transmitted into the policy process? According to Sabatier (1988), knowledge is usually transmitted into the policy process via advocacy coalitions. Change is normally facilitated by professional policy fora that promote policy learning across adversarial coalitions. However, policy learning across coalitions is not a common occurrence: therefore Sabatier and Jenkins-Smith (1993) point out that environmental variables are more frequent in the generation of policy dynamics. A question then arises: does EU tax policy change conform to Sabatier's model in that policy change is mainly produced by environmental dynamics, or are there more endogenous elements of policy change?

European integration

In scholarly debate on European integration the relevance of public policy analysis has increased during the course of the last decade or so. This literature generally points out the relevance of bureaucratic politics (Peters 1992b) and the learning processes leading the Commission to achieve its goals *vis à vis* member states. Majone in particular has shown in a number of influential articles how a European regulatory state has grown, whereas a European welfare state (with the competence to tax and spend) is still underdeveloped. Hence policy types make a difference in the policy process:[1] regulatory policy, for example, is processed in arenas of power which differ from the arenas where distributive policy is made (Pollack 1994). This introduces a challenging question relating to the nature of European taxation. What policy type (e.g. regulatory or redistributive) better suits European tax harmonisation? Can one explain direct tax harmonisation as a component of an emerging fully fledged welfare state, or, as is argued below, should it be explained within the framework of regulatory policies?

In any case, the European public policy literature is very cautious in predicting a universal growth of regulatory policies at the European level. Policy development at the EU level has been uneven. Cost considerations are of central importance in gaining acceptance of regulatory measures. When costs fall on companies or individuals rather than on national governments there are less objections at the Council level (Cram 1993: 142). Tax harmonisation proposals, on the contrary, typically imply costs for domestic revenues.

Three hypotheses

The examination of the literature brings us to the formulation of three hypotheses. The politics of tax reform literature and, most notably, the literature on the political role of knowledge suggest that policy change has more to do with learning, consensus building and policy frameworks than with mere power mechanics and with particularistic pressure group behaviour. This leads to the first hypothesis:

1 Coeteris paribus, the feasibility of tax policy change is crucially influenced by the frame selected by policy initiators. Tax policy reforms that are not feasible when encased in a frame become acceptable in another frame.

The literature on policy change and learning stimulates an assessment of Kingdon's model in contrast with other models concerned with the role of linkages in the policy process (Mucciaroni) and environmental factors (Sabatier). For simplicity's sake the hypothesis is set out by two distinct statements:

2(a) Policy change is better explained in terms of the links between policy, politics, and problems rather than in assuming independence between the streams.

2(b) Significant modifications external to the policy sub-system (briefly, perturbations of the policy environment) are likely to change the policy core attributes.

Consequently, knowledge, which is crucial in defining the policy stream in which solutions emerge, should be seen in connection with other elements of the policy process. Finally, the literature on European integration and policy types suggests the third hypothesis:

3 Direct tax harmonisation measures in Europe can be explained as regulatory policies, rather than as examples of an emerging European welfare state.

If corroborated by empirical evidence, this hypothesis means that the emergence of the Commission's competence in direct corporate taxation should not be confused with the traditional function of taxation at the domestic level, that is to provide revenue in order to sustain welfare expenditure.

'PROCESSING' INTERNATIONAL TAXATION: INTER-GOVERNMENTALISM VERSUS SUPRA-NATIONALISM

In Chapter 5 different approaches to EU tax harmonisation were presented. Here it is sufficient to recall that different political strategies are available for processing international tax issues. States have a choice between inter-governmental strategy and the use of EU institutions. It is to these two fundamentally diverse strategies that we now turn our attention.

Inter-governmentalism has been the typical way of tackling these problems: from the 1920s, under the aegis of the League of the Nations, up until the 1950s and 1960s, this time at the OECD level, a 'treaty network' – that is a network of bi-lateral tax treaties – was gradually built up, with the aim of mitigating the double taxation of income (Picciotto 1992, Chapters 1 and 2).

However, the treaty network is not complete and presents asymmetries. This means that voluntary inter-governmental co-operation has not solved European tax problems. This does not necessarily imply that the alternative of tax harmonisation remains the only feasible solution. The OECD, for example, has argued that co-ordination (within a framework of dialogue and collaboration provided by the OECD itself) is more desirable and more feasible than formal harmonisation of tax systems (Owens 1993).

The point is not trivial as some member states (for instance, the UK) have always insisted on the distinction between a facilitatory role *versus* a mandatory function of the Commission. 'Facilitation' implies that the Commission facilitates voluntary co-operation between the states, especially in the negotiation of multi-lateral agreements which therefore remain inter-governmental.

A second way of dealing with international aspects of direct taxation, at least in the European Union, is via supra-national institutions. Here the choice is mainly between selecting a strategy to remove specific tax obstacles (for instance, cross-border withholding taxes), as suggested by the tax neutrality approach (see Chapter 5), or aiming towards a more comprehensive harmonisation of European fiscal structures.

To be more precise, it is necessary to take into account the three main features of the fiscal structure: the system chosen for the taxation of profits, the rates, and the fiscal base (for instance, the ways in which income and profits are defined for fiscal reasons). Systems differ according to the presence (in which case there is an imputation system) or absence (in which case the system is dubbed classic) of an integration between the fiscal treatment of corporate profits and the fiscal treatment for the shareholder of dividends paid out of those profits (Cnossen 1993; Messere 1993a).

A third system – i.e. the so-called split-rate – has been chosen by countries where there is no link between corporation tax and income tax, but nevertheless distributed profits are treated differently from non-distributed ones (Messere 1993a: 345).

EXPLAINING THE POLICY PROCESS

The search for a supra-national solution

Legal resources for harmonising corporate taxes are scarce in the treaties: whilst in indirect taxation Articles 95–99 of the Treaty of Rome constitute a relatively sound legal frame, in direct taxation only Article 100 (a general, catch-all regulation for the establishment and the functioning of the internal market) and Article 220 can be employed. In particular, Article 220 has a definitively inter-governmental nature, for it stipulates that 'Member states shall, so far as is necessary, enter into negotiations with each other with a view to securing for the benefit of their nationals: . . . the abolition of double taxation within the Community'. Unanimity at the Council level is required, and the Treaty of Maastricht has not modified the voting system, even though some have highly recommended the introduction of majority voting as soon as possible (Vanistendael 1992).

Given this situation, it is not difficult to explain the long stalemate. However, the real *explicandum* is the policy change of 1990 and, in particular, why it happened so late. It is difficult to interpret the 1990 tax decisions considering exclusively the role of member states in a policy process characterised by unanimity voting. By contrast, consideration of the political role of knowledge seems more promising.

In any case, it is necessary to investigate the policy process itself, pointing out at least a few facts (cf. Easson 1992). As anticipated, the presence of the Commission's solutions to European corporate tax problems is a long-standing feature of the TP. The Neumark Report of 1962 (which suggested a split-rate system for every member state) and the Segrè Report on capital markets (1966) are the earlier (unsuccessful) examples of supra-national strategies. In 1967 the Commission launched a comprehensive programme, advocating a general tax on profits (with the same tax base and the same structure of rates in all member states) for the long run, alongside a complete VAT and excise harmonisation. In 1969, the Commission presented two draft directives – finally approved in 1990 – for the abolition of double taxation of dividends between parent and subsidiary companies and for the treatment of mergers and acquisitions, in an attempt to implement at least some parts of the 1967 programme (European Taxation 1969). Van den Tempel, in his independent study prepared for the Commission (1970), even though aware of the huge difficulties of harmonisation, did not resist the temptation to specify a final fiscal system for the Community as a whole. This time the 'classic' system had to be selected, owing to its simplicity.

The behaviour of the Commission in the tax field was influenced by broader developments in European integration. Around 1970, the expectation of achieving concrete results was high. The policy environment was characterised by the own resources principle (April 1970, see Easson 1980: 3–6) – that broke the fiscal taboo which stipulated that only member states (at the central and local levels) were entitled to extract resources – and, most importantly, by the Werner Report (1970) on economic and monetary convergence. The Werner Report was followed by two resolutions of the Council (22 March 1971 and 21 March 1972). The 1972 resolution was extremely encouraging as it maintained that fiscal and capital market proposals elaborated by the Commission would have priority in further Council decisions. In this political discourse on European integration, it appeared reasonable and feasible to propose tax measures as necessary complements to economic and monetary union. However, this attempt was doomed to fail.

Contrary to expectations, the 1970s was a gloomy period for direct tax harmonisation. The policy environment soon became less rosy than expected. On the one hand, macroeconomic difficulties implied that member states were less prone to concede revenue losses for the sake of mere harmonisation. On the other hand, the entrance into the Community of problematic countries such as the UK (in terms of its general attitude towards harmonisation) rendered the direct tax harmonisation dialogue ineffective at the Council level. Real progress was inevitably stymied. Moreover, the 1970s were in general a period of tax concessions to taxpayers (capital allowances, stock relief, and tax expenditures) and this resulted in a greater differentiation of the tax base, thus making the road to harmonisation more difficult.

However, in 1975 a new Commission programme[2] indicated the intention to proceed along the road to harmonisation, and in the same year a new draft directive[3] outlined a final fiscal system, namely an imputation one, thus jettisoning the previous choice of a 'classic' system. The idea at that time was that an imputation system might have proved more politically viable at the Council level because the majority of national systems in the Community appeared to be headed in that direction. Once again, the aspiration of the Commission turned out to be wishful thinking. The 1975 proposed directive included the provision of a common tax rate structure, with a range between 45 per cent and 55 per cent. The 1975 package remained the official strategic view of the Commission until the late 1980s, when it was eventually withdrawn.

What are the main elements of this frame, which constantly appeared in the Commission's documents from 1967 to the late 1980s? Commission *fonctionnaires* claimed on many occasions that their intention was by no means to centralise, but, on the contrary, to encourage all indispensable moves for the completion of the internal market (Burgio 1990; Easson 1980: 118–120). Yet it seems possible to address another interpretation. To begin with, there is the question of the necessity of a single European tax system. The 'preferred' system has varied over the years, but the idea of a uniform corporate tax system did not disappear until 1990. The convergence of the Council towards a single system turned out to be impossible given the voting requirement of unanimity, especially in periods such as the 1970s, when the economic difficulties of the European economies structurally hampered the tax concessions necessary to reach co-ordination.

Second, the choice of solutions had priority over the analysis of problems. It could be asked: if a common fiscal structure is the solution, what is the problem? Looking at the experience of federal countries, it does not appear immediately evident that a single market requires the degree of uniformity suggested by the Commission (Bird 1987). In this period the Commission was criticised by member states for supporting a framework in which eventual harmonisation-standardisation would be necessary, desirable, and feasible – almost a natural progression.

Third, within this frame even incremental proposals (the 1969 draft directives, for instance) were damaged by the image of centralisation surrounding the proposals of the Commission. At the Council level there was strong opposition to the idea of granting the Commission even the mere general entitlement to regulate direct corporate taxation. Every specific tax concession would have been interpreted by member states as the beginning of a centralisation process. Even limited directives, when contained within a frame of centralisation and confrontational decision style (in the sense used by Scharpf 1989), are therefore doomed to fail.

The policy change

In 1990 three measures were ratified by the Council: a directive on the common system of taxation applicable to mergers, divisions, transfers of assets and exchanges of shares between companies of different member states (the so-called mergers directive, 90/434/EEC); a directive against the double taxation of profits distributed between parent companies and subsidiaries of different member states (the so-called parent–subsidiary directive 90/435/EEC); and a convention aiming for the elimination of double taxation in connection with the adjustment of profits of associated enterprises (also known as the arbitration convention on transfer pricing 90/436/EEC). Parenthetically, the adoption of a convention rather than a directive (as the Commission would have preferred) prevents the European Court of Justice from gaining authority in the field of transfer pricing.

The 1990 tax policy change is directed towards the rules governing the tax aspects of transnational operations. In particular, the three measures eliminate a series of tax obstacles and disadvantages to the operation of the single market. However, this emerging European corporate tax regime does not affect the rules set out in national legislation which govern domestic operations. As a consequence, the magnitude of its importance should not be exaggerated.[4] Furthermore, the three measures are restricted to certain companies.[5] The removal of tax obstacles to the cross-border distribution of profits is restricted to companies linked by parent–subsidiary relations in which the parent company has a minimum holding of 25 per cent in the capital of a company of another member state. Most importantly, the package presented by the Commission in order to create tax conditions within the Community similar to those existing in an internal market included further corporate direct tax proposals which are still pending (e.g. the compensation of losses proposed directive) or have been withdrawn (e.g. the proposed interest and royalty directive). In order to establish a level playing field, the European regime presumably also requires the adoption of directives on company law (the long-awaited European company statute) and on the taxation of savings (e.g. a common European withholding tax) which have not as yet materialised.

Notwithstanding these limitations, the business community reacted with extremely positive comments to the 1990 policy change and multinational companies seem to have much appreciated (and supported with their lobbying) the initiatives of the Commission. The economic efficiency of national norms governing transnational operations has also benefited from the introduction of European corporate tax measures (Fantozzi and Manganelli 1993: 33). One commentator even went to the extent of considering the 1990 tax directives 'a cornerstone on the way to the completion of the internal market' (Thommes 1990: 464). Indeed, the parent–subsidiary directive covers a tax regime which had previously been regulated by a messy jungle of norms: fifty-seven different bi-lateral tax treaties between twelve states, with a lack of nine bi-lateral treaties between seven member states. It should be emphasised that the parent–subsidiary directive stipulates that certain sections of the directive are valid 'until the date of effective entry into force of a common system of company taxation'. This provision represents the most far-reaching concession of tax power to a supra-national level that could be imagined. Indeed, whilst the Treaties of Rome and Maastricht do not even mention a direct tax competence of the Commission, the directive promises nothing less than a common system, even though a date is not specified.

The mergers directive is also important because it disposes of some tax obstacles to the creation of competitive European companies. Admittedly, the implementation stage of the mergers directive has shown problems, as some operations considered by the directive are not specifically provided for under national laws, but in any case its substantive content has been considered positive – even though limited – by tax specialists. As far as the transfer pricing convention is concerned, it reached the implementation stage recently, after ratification by all member states, and at the beginning of 1996 no company had yet made use of it (CFE 1996: 61).[6] However, the structure of the convention has been appreciated by commentators, and Hufbauer (1992) has recommended that similar provisions would be used by the United States.

Whatever the assessment of the 1990 measures may be, it is in any case necessary to explain how they materialised in the TP. How can one explain this policy change, in which, oddly enough, the same solutions originally put forward in 1969 were accepted (with modifications, of course) twenty-one years later? Three factors were at work in this event: the policy environment, the re-definition of the policy problems, and the new arguments and evidence (in the sense used by Majone 1989) provided by an emerging epistemic community. It is to these aspects that we now turn.

The policy environment

Environment dynamics can modify the set of opportunities and resources available to actors. The second half of the 1980s was more favourable for tax directives in terms of the macroeconomic conditions. Also, during the 1980s the *de facto* integration of firms and markets increased dramatically: hence tax impediments tended to be increasingly important for corporations and employers' organisations. In the perception of the business community the advantages of a

European market without fiscal barriers have become preferred to tax planning and tax avoidance. Hypothetically, an unharmonised European tax system attributes pay-offs and competitive advantages to a company able to exploit the possibilities of tax planning and tax avoidance. However, with a process which resembles that at the national level (see the section 'Building hypotheses' above), the definition of corporate interests in Europe has shifted towards a relative rejection of the advantages of tax avoidance. Consequently, in this period UNICE and other employers' organisations supported with increasing conviction the Commission and its proposals for a level playing field for taxation.

Most crucially, the set of political resources (as opposed to legal resources) available to European tax harmonisation changed during the second half of the 1980s. The emphasis here is on the political consequences of the Single European Act. The White Paper on the internal market dedicated no more than two paragraphs (Numbers 150 and 151) to direct taxation, announcing a Commission White Paper (which was delayed until 1990). However, the political relevance of the White Paper for tax harmonisation does not rely on specific tax aspects, but, rather, on the commitment to remove barriers to the free movement of individuals, goods, and capital. This implicitly stresses the negative impact of tax distortions: in a market where n-1 variables are harmonised via the Single European Act, the remaining variable (in our case, taxation) becomes increasingly important and politically visible to policy makers and corporations.

Finally, the broader process relating to economic and monetary integration has gradually created favourable dispositions of policy actors towards supra-national solutions at the ECOFIN (the Council of Economic and Finance Ministers) level. During the second half of the 1980s – and crucially around 1990 – there was 'greater capacity of the European Commission, post the Single European Act, to infuse Council bargaining with a more supra-national style' (Dyson 1994: 129) and an 'increasing concentration of a sense of mutual responsibility and accommodation within ECOFIN. . . . A greater sense of collective identity emerged' (Dyson 1994; 195). Thus ECOFIN, which is the Council of Ministers in which tax measures are discussed, presented some favourable conditions for tax harmonisation, given this supra-national policy style.

The re-definition of problems

In this changing environment the Commission modified its strategy in 1989. In that year the new Commissioner, Madame Scrivener, did not hesitate to withdraw the old tax harmonisation proposals, stressing subsidiarity, and, at the same time, pressing upon ECOFIN a series of specific proposals which had to be considered as a coherent package designed to reduce double taxation in the Community (Commission 1990; Scrivener 1990a; 1990b). Scrivener explained in an important speech at the Confédération Fiscale Européenne (Scrivener 1990a) – and the Commission pointed out the same themes in official documents (Commission 1990: 2) – that the new frame, based upon a rigorous application of the subsidiarity principle, did not even include harmonisation, but only problems which, upon closer examination, required the intervention of the Commission. For every other item, market forces would operate efficiently. Easson observes that European taxation is not exactly the field where one expects a discourse in terms of subsidiarity. The latter 'scarcely seems necessary. To date, the problem has not been restricting the Community to doing only what is really necessary, but rather getting the member states to agree to take necessary action within 20 years' (Easson 1992: 626).

Subsidiarity was therefore more a rhetorical component of the frame than a substantial one. Yet it turned out to be an influential symbolic resource because it contributed to shaping a frame usable for real bargaining between the Council and the Commission. Framing of the policy problems in terms of harmonisation correlated with a decision style based upon confrontation, whereas a tax discourse in terms of subsidiarity, neutrality and mutual recognition aided negotiation. The changing definition of policy problems at the end of the 1980s forged (or at least sustained the emergence of) a decision style based on bargaining (Scharpf 1989). The proof is that after two decades ECOFIN accepted the Commission's agenda: the package of two directives and one convention became a real stake for negotiation. Needless to say, an agreement on the agenda does not imply a wholly consensual definition of the alternatives (Kingdon 1984): the short decision process, which in a few months led to approval, was characterised by difficulties, by compromises accepted on the verge of interrupting ECOFIN meetings, and by bi-lateral negotiations between the Commissioner and member states. In this game there were revenue losses to be allocated and finance ministers had to be compensated by the concession of some degrees of freedom in implementation, but at the end of the day the measures succeeded in passing through the Council.

The economic discourse on European taxation

As anticipated, the third explanatory factor of the 1990 policy change is the transmission of knowledge into the TP. Knowledge, following the discussion in Chapter 2 above, can be defined as well-probed belief, both lay and professional (Lindblom 1990). Accordingly, knowledge utilisation is a process involving both academic experts and individuals with policy relevant knowledge, such as auditors, lawyers, consultants, and think-tanks. Rather than relations between the academic community and the political community, what really matters is the grey area of the 'third community' (Lindquist 1990), populated by actors with policy knowledge who participate in the policy-making process even though they are not policy-makers. The metaphor of the third community is pertinent to the European corporate tax arena, in which knowledge is transmitted into the policy process by advisers, practitioners, professional bodies, tax institutes and tax lawyers, and not just by academics working in 'ivory towers', far away from the policy process.

Experts have always been present in the arena of direct European tax policy. However, it is important to distinguish between an emerging epistemic community, characterised by shared causal beliefs, shared notions of validity, and a common policy enterprise (P. Haas 1992: 3) and other actors (e.g. tax practitioners) who certainly belong to the policy community of European taxation, but who do not produce or necessarily use the analytical models of the epistemic community. The epistemic community of European taxation emerged in the second half of the 1980s, when a limited number of economists began to investigate specific tax impediments, tax wedges, and measurable distortions which send the European economies away from neutrality. The main element of their analysis is the calculation of effective tax rates. The latter 'condenses' a number of different taxes into a synthetic measure of the cost of capital. For a firm willing to invest, it is the aggregate impact of taxes on the cost of capital, and not single taxes, that makes a difference to whether to invest or not, how to finance the investment, and where the investment is made (at home or abroad, for example).

The key word in the policy conclusions of this school of thought is 'neutrality' and consequently these experts favour the 'tax neutrality approach' reviewed in Chapter 5. It is interesting to note that economists working within the tax neutrality approach have been aware of the political potential of their calculations since the outset (Bradford and Stuart 1986; Fullerton 1986). Fullerton himself addresses the issue of communicating to policy-makers, arguing that

> The numbers are extremely useful in coming to a summary judgement about tax reform, but any decision about tax reform should be based not on whether it increases or decreases the cost of capital as measured in one of these models, but on whether it's a good reform.
> (Fullerton 1986: 291)

Fullerton employs the vague, slippery notion of 'good reform' for arguing that effective tax rates involve only efficiency considerations and do not cover the fundamental question of fairness. Consequently, effective tax rates do not qualify as the ultimate argument for a 'good tax reform'. Whatever a good reform may be, according to Fullerton it should be based more on broader considerations (such as equity, fairness, political priorities and ultimately – Fullerton argues – good judgement) than on effective tax rates. It seems useful to elaborate upon this point. If the economic discourse is not fully concluded within itself, in the sense that it does not lead to an ultimate assessment of fiscal reforms, then politics is the complementary variable which takes the economic discourse to a conclusion. 'Numbers' are essential resources for political actors. In other words, the calculation of tax wedges is by no means a calculation of the objective solution to distortions and tax impediments. On the contrary, there are good reasons for treating the quantitative aspects of economics within the analysis of rhetoric and language (McCloskey 1985; 1994). The more economic arguments have literary forms – as shown by the famous analysis of the master tropes by McCloskey (1985: 83–86) – the more they have potential for persuading and for re-structuring policy problems and frames. In the case of effective tax rates, their political potential in the TP was enhanced by the 'narrative' linking tax neutrality, the single market and subsidiarity.

Not only does the King-Fullerton model permit the calculation of tax wedges, but, as a consequence, it measures the degree of 'non-neutrality' in international markets, hence providing a hierarchy of taxes in terms of the distortions which they produce. In this conceptual framework, the discourse on European taxation no longer has a standardisation bias; on the contrary, it shifts towards such concepts as CEN and CIN (see Chapter 5). Another element of this construction of the policy discourse is the distinctive meaning of harmonisation. Instead of standardisation, harmonisation denotes a tax environment in which neutrality is the primary goal of European corporate tax policies. Every tax difference between member states is acceptable, provided that it does not affect neutrality in a negative way. Indeed, 'as every musician knows, harmony is a different, more subtle and more agreeable concept than unison – and please spare us the approximate unison!' (Chown 1994: 4). This discourse combines tax diversity and limited European initiatives to remove tax obstacles. The main thesis is that there is a strong case for tax diversity. Therefore, 'the need for tax coordination must be proven because the presumption is that the social benefits of tax diversity outweigh the social costs of inadequate coordination' (Cnossen 1990: 477). Similarly, looking at the integration of personal and corporate taxes (i.e. the issue of a common system for the taxation of profits, Bird concluded that

> There thus seems very little case for *requiring* all member states to adhere to a particular corporate-personal tax structure. . . . The benefits to be obtained from integration are primarily a domestic, not an international, issue and there seems no overriding reason why countries cannot to a large extent be left to do what they want in this area.
>
> (Bird 1987: 242–243, emphasis in original)

Tax wedges, neutralities, and limited co-ordination are the underpinnings of the frame put forward by the embryonic epistemic community in the last decade or so. However, who are these policy experts and where do they operate? The network is composed of just a handful of names spread throughout Europe. The emerging epistemic community has been gradually shaped by common research interests and participation in the initiatives promoted by influential policy fora, such as the Institute of Fiscal Studies (in the UK) and the OECD (cf. OECD 1991 and Picciotto 1992). In this network there are still significant policy divergencies, even though there has been a relative consolidation of the preferred 'correct policy' (Majone 1993b). The individuals considered here do not have consolidated consultation rights, and overall it is preferable to define them as an embryonic epistemic community.[7]

The formation of a common view of the 'correct policy' favourable to the interest of the ordinary tax payer (usually, but not exclusively, a corporate tax payer) has been spawned by professional bodies and by policy fora. In the UK the Institutes of Chartered Accountants (one for England and Wales, one for Scotland and another for Ireland), the Law Society, and the Institute of Taxation are active on European taxation issues, even with comments upon the draft directives of the Commission, that is on the very initial stage of the TP. The Institute for Fiscal Studies (IFS) is English-based but, owing to the breadth of its research, is recognised as an influential institute at the European level. The IFS was instrumental in disseminating the paradigm of international tax neutrality across Europe (Devereux and Pearson 1989).[8] At the European level professional bodies include the Confédération Fiscale Européenne (CFE) and the Fédération des Experts Comptable Européens (FEE). The International Bureau of Fiscal Documentation, based in Amsterdam, is not a professional organisation in the same sense as CFE and FEE. Rather, it is more a professional and scholarly centre. At the world-wide level an important body is the International Fiscal Association, which on occasion issues resolutions on European taxation (IFA 1994).

These organisations have brought broad interests into the TP, and performed a function of knowledge dissemination. Also, they have provided a mechanism of linkage between academics and companies, especially in the case of research projects oriented towards information needs of the business community. The ethos of professional bodies and the research mission of institutes (such as IFS or IBFD) are well developed. It is then impossible to find in their resolutions a substantive content which does not represent a wide-spread concern in the business community[9] and which does not fit in with the bulk of shared beliefs and norms of the community of lawyers and/or public economists. To a limited extent, the TP now contains a functional equivalent of tax 'common cause' groups (Peters 1991). The main distinction is that at the European level there are not social movements, but professional bodies, research institutes, and policy fora.

Having described these actors, the main point argued here is that around the end of the 1980s there was an alignment between the new frame of the Commission and the policy arguments advocated by the embryonic epistemic community. Any causal hypothesis does not appear sound in this respect, with causal 'arrows' from social science to the policy-making process, or *vice versa*. The Commission did not mobilise experts prior to the 1990 decisions; rather, a kind of mobilisation occurred later, with the Ruding Committee. However, the following aspects were at work:

- at the end of the 1980s there was an impressive clustering of economic studies on tax neutrality and tax harmonisation (Cnossen 1990; Devereux and Pearson 1989; Gammie and Robinson 1989; Kopits 1992; OECD 1991). Needless to say, if a book is published in a certain year, the operative links among researchers and clients, especially in the case of a book promoted by international organisations or policy fora, are established earlier;

- the majority of these studies were financed, discussed or produced by policy fora, such as the Institute for Fiscal Studies, the OECD (Fiscal Affairs Division), and the International Monetary Fund. Therefore the process of knowledge dissemination was aided by a wider concern with international taxation, as shown by the involvement of OECD (Owens 1993) and IMF (Kopits 1992);
- finally, on occasion knowledge is not transmitted immediately into the policy process. Knowledge utilisation takes time, and the analyst ought to look at the conceptual use (e.g. the change in the interpretative frames), rather than at the instrumental one. Knowledge enlightens gradually (Weiss 1979; 1986). The fact that nowadays policy-makers talk about European tax co-ordination using the vocabulary of tax wedges, capital export neutrality, and tax diversity is the best evidence of the enlightenment process. In this view, the latter is more important than any instrumental impact on the 1990 decision-making.

The mobilisation of experts

The historical, even though limited, success of 1990 created momentum, and the Commission aimed at new goals. On the one hand, the package against double taxation was completed with two drafts, on interest and international royalty flows (withdrawn in 1994), and losses. On the other hand, the Commission promoted a Committee of independent experts (the Ruding Committee, set up in 1991), with a mandate to formulate a strategy for the long term.

Who were the members of the Ruding Committee and what kind of mandate did they receive? And what were the effects (if any) of their decisions? To begin with, the recruitment: instead of selecting only the traditional heavy-weight professors, the selection stage (activated soon after the 1990 directives) privileged a group of influential members of the European business community, and people operating in the area between international civil service, policy fora, universities, and the professions. The Committee was chaired by Onno Ruding (former Dutch finance minister and president of the Christian federation of Dutch employers). The members were four business executives (Donald de Buitléir, Ireland; Jean-Luis Descours, France; Lorenzo Gascon, Spain; Carlo Gatto, Italy), one international civil servant (Ken Messere, former head of the OECD fiscal affairs division), one tax lawyer working both in the academic and in the professional fields (Professor Albert Rädler, Germany) and one tax lawyer mainly working in the academic field (Professor Frans Vanistendael,

Belgium). At the outset Bill Robinson, at that time director of the Institute for Fiscal Studies, joined the Committee, but he resigned following his appointment as special adviser to the Chancellor of the Exchequer. It was at that point that Ken Messere was asked to join the group of 'wise men'.

The Committee operated in 1991–1992 more or less as a laboratory: the dire straits of mediating between social science and economic power had to be tackled directly inside the Committee. Instead of involving a group of academics and then mediating the various cleavages surrounding knowledge utilisation (i.e. cleavages between academic knowledge and professional knowledge, between experts and bureaucratic politics, between economic and political feasibility), all of these cleavages were deliberately mixed in the Committee at work. The link between the group and the Commission was provided by a secretariat. The latter was partly staffed by ad hoc appointments (Michael Daly, the secretary), partly by *fonctionnaiers* of the Commission. Experts belonging to the emerging epistemic community were only partially involved in the Ruding Committee directly as members. Rather, their contribution came through the secretary (Daly is indeed a typical member of the epistemic community) and through the analyses commissioned by the secretariat itself on behalf of the Committee.

The mandate to the Committee, formalised by Madame Scrivener, consisted of three questions related to a search for usable knowledge:

> Do differences in taxation among member states cause major distortions in the internal market, particularly with respect to investment decisions and competition? In so far as such distortions arise, are they likely to be eliminated simply through the interplay of market forces and tax competition between member states, or is action at the Community level required? What specific measures are required at the Community level to remove or mitigate these distortions?
>
> (Commission 1992: 11)

In addressing its answers, the final Report of the Committee (Commission 1992) presents both an accurate analysis of European tax distortions, and a survey of European companies. Taken together, the calculations and the survey – based upon a questionnaire prepared by the Institute for Fiscal Studies – point out the need for measures at the Community level: the Ruding Report excludes the fact that the sheer market drive or the negotiation-competition amongst member states will provide a substantial mitigation of tax impediments.

Looking at the proposals, the Report offers political ammunition for the Commission, urging the approval of the Commission's direct corporate tax package. For the long-term perspective, the Report avoids the mistake of suggesting a 'final fiscal system' (imputation, classical, or other), even though there is a clear preference for a single, uniform European tax system. This might have caused some embarrassment to the Commission in its attempt to show how pragmatic and piecemeal the new approach was. Most crucially perhaps, the Ruding Report proposes a compulsory range of tax rates and a long list of detailed measures that have given cause for the accusation of centralisation and lack of a 'real basis for some of the recommendations' (Arthur Andersen 1993: 54–55).

More generally, the debate on the Ruding Report,[10] the unsympathetic reaction of ECOFIN (November 1992), and the fact that none of the recommendations have been implemented give the impression that something must have not functioned properly in the Ruding Committee as a laboratory for knowledge utilisation. But what, and why? Obviously, the change in macroeconomic and political environment played a role. The ratification of the Treaty on the European Union raised political difficulties compounded by macroeconomic troubles and tight budgetary policies. These events did not provide a favourable environment for the TP. However, it is useful to investigate whether elements endogenous to the TP also played a role. To begin with, it can be claimed that knowledge creeps slowly into the decision process, and that time is required before a new frame can enter the minds of decision-makers. According to this optimistic view, there is no cause for concern that the Committee did not have any short-term impact. The Report has spawned a huge debate on European corporate taxation. Perhaps the most important result of this debate is that experts and policy-makers are more aware of the political and economic relevance of this policy domain. Thanks to this debate, there is now a common frame for analysing these tax issues, not only in Brussels, but also at the level of national policy-makers.

However, the fact remains that no progress has been made in the TP since 1990. The relative failure of the Committee can be explained in terms of a missing link between academic knowledge and the business community's priorities. It is important to observe that nine out of ten chapters of the Report were prepared by members of the emerging epistemic community, whilst the group of 'wise men' – even though they commented upon every chapter – only discussed the chapter concerning policy conclusions and recommendations in depth. The nine chapters of analysis are not fully compatible with the policy recommendations chapter. The 'wise men' did not have a budget for commandeering resources which might have produced knowledge to fill information gaps. Consequently, the Ruding Committee members had to rely on their own personal experience and on the background material provided by the secretariat and by the consultants of the secretariat.

Most crucially, the relative failure of the Committee might have something to do with the fact that the search for solutions has been given priority over the search for conditions and for methods to devise solutions. The difference between the former and the latter has been extensively analysed by policy scholars such as Wildavsky and Lindblom in their discussion of the meaning of planning. In a situation of limited rationality and turbulent environment, an effective plan is not mere goal definition enriched by a checklist of actions to undertake in a given order; rather, it is the building of conditions for reacting to changing events and for learning from experience (Lindblom 1975). The high potential in terms of internal mediation of the conflicts has not been fully exploited by the Committee: this is probably the reason why the Committee provided a list of recommendations, instead of a mechanism useful for two purposes: devising different solutions in a changing macroeconomic environment, and creating the conditions for political compromise and agreement between the Commission and the Council.

It is not a surprise that, as soon as the macroeconomic scenario assumed by the single currency project enshrined in the Maastricht Treaty began to change and the road towards monetary union became quite bumpy, the political feasibility of many proposals of the Report declined almost to zero. The Committee seems to have failed in that it has not investigated the specific information requested by the TP. An influential policy analyst once expressed this problem in the following effective words: 'What is needed is information that will facilitate negotiation of a compromise rather than information that can be cranked into a decision rule' (Cronbach *et al.* 1980: 116).

ASSESSING HYPOTHESES

How can the empirical analysis be employed in order to assess the initial hypotheses? The first hypothesis required an appropriate frame to be selected by policy-makers to facilitate consensus building and, in the case under examination, ultimately tax policy change. In the political discourse on European taxation language, concepts, calculations, ideas in good currency, and policy proposals flowed into frames that entailed specific perceptions of the European tax policy problems. Consensus building around European directives became a feasible strategy when a frame of subsidiarity, tax wedges, international tax neutrality (i.e. the paradigm of capital export neutrality and capital import neutrality), and a specific attack on tax obstacles entered the TP via the new initiatives of the Commission and the conceptual elements provided by the emerging epistemic community. Furthermore, the construction of legitimacy was supported by the behaviour of the business community, on the one hand, and by policy fora and European professional bodies, on the other. Thus a 'supra-national' advocacy coalition – composed of the Commission, corporate actors, and an embryonic epistemic community – promoted the transmission of new shared beliefs and public policy paradigms into the TP. On occasion (in 1990, to be precise) the 'supra-national' coalition achieved success over the 'inter-governmental' coalition, centred on member states (ministers and domestic public administrations).

Knowledge played an important rôle in this process as experts contributed to the elaboration of policy frames. However, knowledge does not only have an 'expert' component (i.e. the participation of experts in the process) but also a strategic one, concerning knowledge an actor has of other actors' behaviour. The strategic component relating to learning processes (for instance, during the years the Commission has learned that head-on approaches to harmonisation would create a stalemate) is crucial in the explanation of the new approach chosen by the Commission in its relationship with member states. Obviously, the concept of knowledge ought to include interactive knowledge or political learning, distinguished from policy learning (see May 1992).

Another aspect of the frame can be extracted from recent research in European integration. Scharpf observes that

> The European Union is not, and cannot be, a unitary nation state; it can best be a multi-level political system in which national and subnational units retain their legitimacy and political viability. . . . The legitimacy of European rule-making must rest on, and is limited by, functional justifications.
>
> (Scharpf 1994b: 227)

As Scharpf shows, in a multi-level political system the only way to achieve outcomes is to devise forms of co-ordination which do not weaken the authority of nation states, but, on the contrary, accept and strengthen it. The new frame of the Commission is oriented towards the construction of the conditions for games in which the removal of tax impediments is perceived as unrestrictive of national tax policy autonomy. These games create 'saddle-point solutions', which are minimally adequate from a technical point of view; at the same time they represent the maximum sacrifice of political autonomy that can be voluntarily reached (Scharpf 1994b: 232). Arguably, the 1990 measures were saddle-points in that they represented the minimum tax requirements for the functioning of the internal market, and they were the most generous concessions achievable in a multi-level system with unanimity at the Council level. In that event, policy solutions were filtered by structures, just as Mucciaroni (1992) claimed in his critique of the indeterminacy of the garbage-can model. The acceptability of tax measures to national tax structures (i.e. national ministers and administrations concerned with guarding revenue) was a crucial element of the TP.

The second hypothesis – related to the theory of policy change – consisted of two statements: one concerning the connectedness (as opposed to interdependence) of policy, politics and problems, and the other concerning the policy environment as the element most likely to produce policy change. The former statement is probably the most difficult to assess because evidence leads to two opposite directions. On the one hand, there are clear indications of the independence of the streams. Until the end of the 1980s, policy solutions and problems represented two independent streams. The connection between a new frame for policy problems and policy solutions developed by the emerging epistemic community was a window of opportunity in which independent streams converged. Curiously enough, when the Commission deliberately tried to mobilise experts and to link policy solutions and problems (with the Ruding Committee), progress was stymied once again. Arguably, the Ruding Committee is probably an example of strategic failure in planning to meld two streams. Even when learning and new frames are available, the Commission may pursue its goals with poor results.

On the other hand, there is empirical evidence of linkages between the three streams. The stream of problems has links with the politics stream, the latter being defined as the political arena where member states interact (typically at ECOFIN level). Indeed, during the stalemate of the European process (from the 1960s to the end of the 1980s) a particular formulation of the problem contributed to the emergence of a confrontational decision style in the politics stream. In this period the syndrome of the joint decision trap was at work (Scharpf 1988). By contrast, when policy problems were re-structured around 1990 by the 'narrative' of neutrality and subsidiarity, political actors appeared to be involved in a different decision style, one which was more bargaining-oriented.

All things considered, it is very difficult to give a clear-cut response to the question of interdependence *versus* independence. Obviously, further research is needed. However, a general point can be made. When thinking of further research on the role of knowledge in the policy process, the theoretical perspective ought to avoid the sirens of traditional causal models; rather, it might prove interesting to look at developments in contingency theory for inspiration (E. Ostrom 1986) and at knowledge-induced changes between the given and the effective matrix of the games that 'real actors could play' (Scharpf 1991). The policy stake has not been a constant in ECOFIN meetings: for member states the pay-offs of tax directives changed when the stake was articulated within a frame of subsidiarity and limited initiative of the Commission. In sum, contingency models based on connectedness seem more attractive than causal models.

The second statement of the 'policy change hypothesis' draws upon Sabatier and Jenkins-Smith (1993), who argue that substantial policy dynamics is usually triggered by modifications in the policy environment, which can alter the resources available to competing advocacy coalitions. In at least two cases (the Werner Report in the 1970s and the vicissitudes of Economic and Monetary Union in the 1990s) the TP has been influenced dramatically by its macroeconomic environment. To some extent Dyson generalises this proposition, arguing that economic policy co-ordination in the European Union (defined by Dyson as budgetary policy, short-term and medium-term economic policies) remains an underdeveloped area which is more a by-product of monetary policy co-ordination than 'a dynamic factor in its own right' (Dyson 1994: 202).

European taxation should then be investigated taking into account the macro characteristics of economic and monetary integration. However, the preceding analysis shows the existence of more endogenous elements of policy change. The modifications of the policy environment in the second half of the 1980s altered the political resources of the 'supra-national coalition', but it was only when a new frame became available that substantial policy change materialised. This is consistent with the revision of the advocacy coalition framework suggested by Sabatier and Jenkins-Smith themselves. The revision states that exogenous perturbations must be interpreted and exploited by the heretofore minority coalition (Jenkins-Smith and Sabatier 1994: 194). Returning to European taxation, the opportunities created by the Single European Act led to policy change because the 'supra-national' coalition was able and willing to exploit them.

The third hypothesis on policy types, which considered direct tax harmonisation as regulatory policy-making, can be tackled by arguing that the main rationale for European direct tax measures is not redistributive. By no means are they linked to the emergence of a supra-national welfare state which on the one hand levies taxes and, on the other hand, relies on public spending in order to mitigate and to change income redistribution. Taxation, like social policy and foreign policy, is a bulwark of national sovereignty, and each tax system is rooted in specific political and socio-economic traditions: a uniform European tax system is not and will not be on the agenda of feasible policies.

Indeed, the policy choices analysed in this chapter can be seen as an example of regulatory policy in that they are instruments for treating allocative problems and they are justified in efficiency terms. A redistributive policy, by contrast, is not aimed at restoring efficiency when market failures occur, but uses political power to modify the results of the market forces, without efficiency-improving aspects. To sum up, the mitigation of double taxation is an acceptable and feasible European regulatory policy for the following reasons:

- the intervention against double taxation is compatible with the liberal economic constitution of the Union (Majone 1993a: 156);
- there is a strong rationale for the policy in terms of economic efficiency and national regulatory failure. Domestic taxes create areas of double taxation and, according to the Ruding Report, voluntary co-operation between states cannot solve this inefficiency. This is precisely the state of affairs that Majone considers a rationale for supra-national regulation;
- there is no redistributive aim, and no connection with the goals of a hypothetical European welfare state, based upon European taxing and spending policies.

However, a crucial characteristic of tax harmonisation should not be overlooked. The mitigation of double taxation is a game in which revenue losses have to be allocated because at least one member state has to renounce some revenue. This explains the slow progress in this area and the current situation of uncertainty over European tax co-ordination, especially when the policy environment indicates that even the broader project on Economic and Monetary Union seems far from being implemented smoothly.

7 Europeanisation and policy change

Italy and the UK

> When I received Giovannini's paper, I recognised that the telecopy was sent by the 'Ministero del Tesoro'. This reminded me of a conversation I once had with an official from the German Ministry of Finance on European tax harmonisation. He was of the opinion that his Italian colleagues were very creative in developing new ideas on the harmonisation of taxes and norms and that his French colleagues were excellent in formulating the laws establishing these norms. But he was very concerned that the Germans might be the only ones to respectfully and thoroughly execute what has been thought, formulated and established elsewhere.
>
> (Kitterer 1990: 18)

> Several times in the last few months, the press has accused us [the Institute for Fiscal Studies] of knowing more about the tax and benefit system than the Inland Revenue or DHSS do. It is, of course, an absurd assertion. We do not know more about the tax system than the Revenue. . . . The distinctive ability that we do have is one for tax analysis. We know more about the effects of taxation; we have acquired the techniques, the models and the experience to see tax problems as part of a complete tax system, and in turn to see that fiscal system within an economic, social and political context. . . . In the meantime, the press claim is, if taken literally, literally true. We do know more about the tax and benefit system taken together than either the Inland Revenue or the DHSS individually.
>
> (Kay 1986)

INTRODUCTION: CONCEPTUALISING POLICY CHANGE

In this chapter the process of corporate tax Europeanisation is examined through its repercussions at the national level. Accordingly, attention is shifted from the EU policy process to two domestic tax policy processes. The main *empirical* point raised in this chapter is whether the process of Europeanisation has affected domestic corporate tax policy in the two countries analysed here (Italy and the UK). The main *theoretical* points are instead: (a) what type of policy change has occurred as a result of Europeanisation of tax policy? and (b) in what way can the impact of Europeanisation on domestic policy be analysed?

The second point highlights the particular perspective chosen for the analysis presented here. Much European integration literature to date has placed emphasis on the explanation of European public policy, which therefore has a dependent variable status. By contrast, this chapter follows a typical 'second image reversed perspective' (Gourevitch 1978) in that it takes European public policy as the independent variable and explores how it reverberates on domestic policy.

Neo-functionalism and inter-governmentalism – the major approaches to the study of European integration, reviewed in Part I of this book – offer alternative accounts of Europeanisation. For neo-functionalism, European integration tends to weaken the state and strengthens both European institutions (i.e. the European Commission and the European Court of Justice) and networks of societal actors. For inter-governmentalism, instead, the state is strengthened by the process of European integration. Both the historical account provided by Milward (1992) and the liberal inter-governmentalist perspective advocated by Moravcsik (1991; 1994) argue that European integration has increased the political power of states.

Other authors have begun to explore the *continuum* between these two poles. Scharpf (1996b) has shed light on the antinomies of European integration by arguing that negative integration (i.e. the removal of barriers and distortions in the single market) has severely constrained national policy choices. For example, the creation of a single European market for capital has restrained domestic choices in tax and monetary policy (Sinn 1990). At the same time – Scharpf's argument follows – positive integration (i.e. European policies intervening in the socio-economic environment and the regulatory regime within which markets function) is stymied or at least limited by inter-governmental policy-making in the Council. The result is a 'competency gap' (Scharpf 1996b: 15): national governments have less problem-solving capability, but European solutions require an amount of inter-governmental agreement that is often unavailable.

The consequences of the competency gap will not be elaborated here; rather, it is the process linking European integration and domestic policy choices that is further qualified. As already mentioned, Scharpf has contended that negative integration has constrained national policy. How can the relationship between integration and domestic policy change be investigated empirically, and how does policy change come about? Two insights provided by public policy analysis are useful here, the former relating to the political role of knowledge and the latter to the concept of policy change. To begin with, Risse-Kappen (1996b), an author blending international relations and public policy analysis, has produced preliminary evidence relating to the impact of ideas with 'prescriptive status' (in particular, the idea of collective European identity) on domestic politics. This suggests that the relationship between Europeanisation and domestic policy change can be studied within the same theoretical framework (based upon the cognitive dimension of politics) used for Part I of this study. Rather than limiting the research design to analysing how EU directives have constrained national tax policy, it can be argued that a crucial mechanism of Europeanisation operates indirectly, moving from the Europeanisation of policy paradigms to new frames of reference in which domestic decisions are taken. To sum up, Europeanisation occurs when domestic policy changes in response to an ample array of factors emanating from the EU: European law, initiatives of EU institutions, resources made available by European programmes, but also concepts, ideas and other cognitive factors developed within the EU policy process. Briefly, Europeanisation of public policy manifests itself directly, e.g. through the implementation of EU law which constrains the degree of freedom of national policy, or indirectly, when national policy-makers conceive of a domestic issue within a European frame of reference and decide to change their domestic policy to bring it into line with a particular European paradigm even though no specific compulsion (from a directive) exists.

If the first insight pertains to the cognitive dimension of politics, the second deals with the *type of policy change* produced by Europeanisation, either directly or indirectly. As outlined in Chapter 2, P. Hall (1993) has argued that policy change can involve, in order of increasing importance, a variation of levels (with instruments and goals unchanged), a shift to new policy instruments (but without varying policy goals), or the adoption of wholesale change in policy (i.e. a 'third-order' policy change involving the adoption of a new paradigm). Measuring policy change is a difficult task, compounded by the fact that certain aspects of policy change[1] are subjectively defined. Notwithstanding these difficulties, Hall's suggestion that there are different types of policy change is still a valuable input to empirical analysis: altering the level of tax rates is not the same policy change as switching from tax cuts to tax expenditures or, in the case of more dramatic change, re-defining the policy goals of corporate taxation.

The remainder of the chapter tackles the questions of the type of policy change, and how national policy change induced by Europeanisation comes about, through the adoption of a comparative public policy design. The following section prepares the ground for analysis of the two cases (Italy and the UK), which are examined respectively in the two subsequent sections. The final section presents the implications of this study for research on Europeanisation.

BACKGROUND: THE BEAUTY AND THE BEAST?

Before analysing the development of tax policies (with particular emphasis on corporate tax policy) in Italy and the UK it is necessary to illustrate the main differences between the two cases. A conventional (but deceptive) argument can be outlined as follows. To begin with, the performance of Italian tax policy in the 1980s and 1990s has been, comparatively speaking, extremely poor, for many reasons: most notably, the amazingly high levels of tax evasion and the degree of tax complexity. The UK tax system is more coherent. Second, Italy is a laggard when compared to the UK because the process of tax reform, and particularly the reduction of tax rates, has not occurred. By contrast, the UK has been one of the leaders in tax reform, particularly in corporate taxation (Peters 1991).

Third, given the instability of Italian governments and the miserable state of Italian public administration, Italian tax policies have had no long-term perspective. These problems are compounded by a dramatic increase in Italian public deficit and debt. Macro-political variables – the argument goes on – work against the development of a rational tax policy in Italy. The Westminster model and the Whitehall model (i.e. the British administrative model, with its excellent civil service) put the UK in a more favourable position. Since 1979, one political party has held office in the UK, presenting yet another favourable pre-condition for rationalising the tax system. Italy and the UK seem as dissimilar as the proverbial 'beauty' and the 'beast'.

Finally, elites' political attitudes toward the EU differ markedly in the two countries: Italian policy-makers are deemed to be Euro-enthusiasts,[2] whilst UK Conservative Government representatives have developed a rather sceptical attitude towards 'Europe'.[3] Arguably, national attitudes should generate two different responses to the heated issue of direct tax harmonisation: hostility in the UK and acceptance in Italy. 'Beauty' prefers her splendid isolation, and the 'beast' wishes to purify his sins by joining European virtuosity.

What does the empirical evidence show? In Italy taxes were the object of a comprehensive reform in 1971–1974 which *inter alia* introduced a modern European tax, the value-added tax (VAT). The revenue-gathering performance of the new Italian tax system has been good over the past twenty-five years: revenue (i.e. direct taxes, indirect taxes, and social security contributions from employers and employees) has risen sharply, from less than 30 per cent of GDP at the beginning of the 1970s to 45 per cent of GDP in 1994, far above the UK percentage (OECD 1996a). Had the Italian tax system been genuinely backward, it could not have performed so well. Supplementary data confirm doubts on the conventional wisdom. At the end of the 1970s, the British personal income tax had eleven bands, and nine of them were characterised by rates ranging from 40 to 83 per cent; currently, there are only two rates (Leape 1993: 279). In Italy the tax rate schedule was revised three times in the 1980s: tax brackets were reduced from 32 to 6 per cent, and the top rate was decreased from 72 to 50 per cent (Guerra 1993). Clearly, the two systems converged in the same policy direction.

Turning now to the question of unnecessary complexity and lack of rationality in a tax system which is also plagued by tax avoidance and massive tax evasion, the reader could exercise him- or herself in guessing the source (Italian or British) of the following quotes:

> The different nature of these . . . changes underscored the absence of a coherent tax reform strategy.

> We believe something more fundamental is wrong with our tax legislation than the rate at which it is being produced. The style in which it is written has been likened to a puzzle – and one which does not have a picture on the box! It is impenetrable: you cannot see even the broad outline of the picture until you have solved the puzzle.

> In some key aspects, the . . . tax system has become more similar to those of most industrialised countries . . . some significant results have been occasionally attained.

Further, which newspaper does the following quote come from, the *Financial Times* or *Corriere della Sera*? ‘Government officials suspect recent growth in the avoidance of VAT by businesses is a key factor behind an over-shoot in government borrowing’. Well, this quote is from the *Financial Times* (15 April 1996). As far as the previous quotes are concerned, the first and the second refer to the UK tax system (respectively, they are from Leape 1993: 288 and from Tax Law Review Committee 1995: vii), whilst the third is from an Italian source (Guerra 1993: 328).

Moreover, the relevance of macro-political variables seems questionable, or, rather, the consequences of macro-political phenomena can be different from the ones postulated by the conventional wisdom. Could it not be argued that the disintegration of political parties in Italy has given more political clout to intellectual elites eager to champion policy reforms? Dyson and Featherstone (1996) indicate that in monetary policy an elite from the Bank of Italy and the Treasury was able to use EU monetary commitments for disciplining the Italian *partitocrazia*. Regonini and Giuliani (1994) argue in a similar vein, by pointing out that a policy community of intellectual elites seized the agenda of political reforms in the 1980s. It is not surprising then to observe that most Italian ministers of finance were formerly leading figures in the academic debate: Reviglio and Visentini in the 1980s, Gallo, Tremonti, Fantozzi and Visco in the 1990s – all were and still are distinguished *Professori*. Not to mention the plethora of advisers from top universities and, on occasion, from the Bank of Italy who operate in the ministerial *cabinet* (in the French sense). The real question – to be tackled empirically – can be articulated as follows: can the mobilisation of intellectual elites in Italy be considered a functional equivalent of the excellent British civil service? Put differently, do Italian experts in top political positions provide policy-relevant knowledge and leadership that in other political systems are provided by public administration and party leaders?

Elites and mass political attitudes towards the EU are certainly not the same in the two countries, but what is their real impact on tax policies? If the Italian public administration is unable to articulate coherent policy positions in the EU policy process, especially in the various working groups set up by the Commission and the Council, then generic Euro-enthusiast views do not make much difference. If, in addition, public deficit constrains the degree of freedom of tax policy, it can be hypothesised that Italian negotiators at the EU level should not be too keen on suppressing taxes on cross-border trade and investment. In conclusion, these preliminary observations raise more questions than answers. Thus it is useful to scratch the surface and turn our attention to the evolution of tax policy.

ITALY: HOW THE NEGLECT OF EUROPEANISATION IN TAX DESIGN BECAME A PROBLEM

An mentioned above, Italian tax policy was restructured by a comprehensive reform which took place in 1971–1974. The reform was the point of arrival of an intense political and intellectual debate – dating back to the *Commissione* Cosciani, set up in 1962 – which aimed at 'freeing' the country from a system, bequeathed from the nineteenth century, characterised by four drawbacks (Ceriani, Frasca and Monacelli 1992; Cosciani 1950): the old tax system was considered regressive, biased towards indirect taxes, centred around a very narrow tax base, and 'anti-productive' (i.e. it discouraged economic growth). Tax reform assigned more prominence to progressive direct taxes, introduced a modern indirect tax (i.e. VAT), and increased the revenue-gathering performance. Not surprisingly then, for many years the reform was considered a 'sacred cow': very few scholars were prepared to criticise the policy design underpinning it.[4] Nevertheless, problems soared, but they were ascribed to exogenous factors such as the slow implementation, the economic turbulence of the 1970s, the numerous alterations to the original design brought about by the political system over the 1970s and the 1980s, and the difficult situation of public finance in general.

With hindsight, however, the limits of the tax reform seem evident and have more to do with structural drawbacks than with exogenous factors. Four structural limits require attention: (a) the pivotal role given to progressive personal taxation; (b) the neglect of administrative reform, which caused a gradual impoverishment (particularly in terms of human capital and organisational skills) of tax administration;[5] (c) the intellectual foundations of the reform (rooted in the paradigm of redistribution); and (d) the lack of consideration for the international dimension of tax policies. The first three drawbacks, in turn, are related to an underestimation of international aspects of taxation. Therefore it is argued here that *the reform failed because it did not fit in with the process of economic integration with Europe*.

To be precise, the introduction of VAT represented an important element of Europeanisation of the Italian tax system. However, crucial implications of the international context of taxation were overlooked. In order to show this, it is useful to discuss the other three structural limits of tax reform, beginning with the pivotal role assigned to a unique personal progressive tax. The latter resulted in perverse effects because the tax base was not broadened at the same time. Small firms (throughout the country 60,000 firms qualify as non-incorporated), the self-employed, and agricultural rent were granted favourable tax regimes. Poor assessment criteria and an ineffective tax administration jointly determined an extremely limited contribution from these categories to revenue gathering (Guerra 1993). Accordingly, steeply rising marginal tax rates hit a rather narrow tax base, which consisted mainly of employees' labour income. An economist, Pedone (1980), described the Italian tax system with the words *evasori e tartassati* (more or less equivalent to 'evaders and harassed'): an unbearable burden on a relatively narrow group of tax payers.

What is more, in an open economy a progressive tax on all sources of residents' income (with the notable exception of interest income) produced at home or abroad (this is the so-called world-wide principle) triggers perverse effects if tax administration is not able to gather information on residents' income which originates abroad. Tremonti, the 'odd man out' in the Italian debate, given his long-standing total critique of the reform, has argued – in a book written with his aide Vitaletti – that, with the creation of the European market, negative integration would have caused immense problems to domestic politics and policy. In fact:

> Parliaments will no longer choose how to tax wealth, but the latter will choose where to be taxed, thus casting its vote. The broadening of non-conventional types of vote will therefore include not only voting with one's feet, but also voting with one's bank account.
> (Tremonti and Vitaletti 1991: 58, my translation)

Europeans above a certain income threshold – the prediction goes on – will vote in countries in which they do not pay taxes and will pay taxes in countries in which they, being non-residents, have no right to vote. This is tantamount to saying that taxation and representation will be separated. Given this scenario, the Italian tax system has been in the most unfortunate position. On the one hand, an excess of regulation and high statutory rates have pushed savings and wealth abroad. On the other, the regulation of financial instruments created abroad has been rather poor. Therefore, wealth could flow abroad easily, and then come back to Italy under the shelter of foreign financial instruments, for example a foreign investment fund (Tremonti and Vitaletti 1991: 60).

The principle of world-wide taxation was chosen for corporate taxation too, thus reversing the previous choice of territorial taxation. Italy then decided to tax foreign income of Italian companies, in line with the choice of capital export countries, even though it might have looked at the experience of Latin American countries instead. Latin American countries import capital and accordingly tend to favour territorial taxation. In any case, the choice of world-wide taxation is efficient provided that two conditions are fulfilled. First, tax administration must be able to manage the world-wide principle. Second, a pro-active international fiscal policy must be capable of negotiating effective deals and exchange of information with foreign countries. Of course, the two conditions were not fulfilled and hence Italian tax policy choices turned out to be foolishly ambitious.

The corporate tax regime (broadly defined to include the corporation income tax, the proportional *in rem* tax ILOR essentially levied on companies, and the mechanism of imputation which links the distribution of dividends to the income tax) includes a whole series of distortions. The choice between an incorporated or non-incorporated company is affected by tax considerations and therefore taxes are not neutral; taxes introduce a bias towards debt financing; tax distortions discriminate among sectors and geographical areas; and, last but not least, investment at home is penalised (Ceriani, Frasca and Monacelli 1992; Giannini 1994). Neither resident companies nor foreign companies are encouraged to invest in Italy. For multinationals that have in any case decided to run a business in the *Penisola*, Italy is just a place wherein costs can be concentrated, given the high statutory tax rates. In this case again, the tax design failure stems from the neglect of the 'open' dimension of tax policy.

Interest income was the notable exception to the principle of taxing all sources of personal income through the progressive income tax. Interest income of individuals and individual firms is in fact taxed through a final withholding tax. The problem is that withholding taxes vary according to the asset considered: Guerra (1993) notes that more than ten different rate regimes existed at the beginning of the 1990s. Furthermore, certain financial products were not taxed at all. In more general terms, the whole design of capital income taxation did not correspond to any economic rationale. Visco has however observed a political rationale (1995: 51) as the discrimination between different types of capital income has opened many opportunities for 'political trading' (this is the term used by Visco), e.g. assuring low taxation of certain financial products while taxing others more consistently. Negative consequences in terms of non-neutrality (certain financial instruments being privileged by the tax system, thus distorting the market for savings) and tax avoidance were compounded by the existence of an open economy. The growth of negative integration, as witnessed by the European capital market liberalised by the 1988 directive on capital liberalisation, and the proliferation of financial innovation, have exacerbated the inefficiencies of Italian tax policy.

The whole design of tax reform was more appropriate for a country based on a traditional economy (agriculture and mass industrial production) than for an open economy characterised by financial innovation and deep economic integration with Europe. This inherent failure of tax design has been intensified by the absence of administrative reform. Cosciani, one of the founding fathers of the reform, was particularly aware of this, so much so that he resigned from the committee for tax reform when he realised that tax administration would be neglected. The oblivion of tax administration is a typical product of Italian political culture, in which public administration, instead of being perceived as the core actor of any policy reform, is considered secondary to the political system in producing policy change (Dente 1995). Parenthetically, this also explains why the public discussion on the Italian tax system has been rather abstract: experts and politicians have always preferred the debate about how to change tax design rather than engaging in the exercise of reforming tax administration, thus forgetting that without a decent administration all tax reforms are doomed to fail. The Italian tax policy discourse has been characterised almost exclusively by the focus on tax design (Lupi 1996). Efficiency of tax administration, arguably even more than tax design, is the resource that enables a state to cope with the internationalisation of tax policy (Tanzi 1995). A policy discourse centred on tax design was therefore inadequate.

Finally, the intellectual foundations of the reform reflected a redistributive paradigm (i.e. taxes as an instrument for promoting redistribution of wealth and ultimately fairness and equality) that would prove inadequate when the alternative paradigm of neutrality (i.e. taxes as an instrument aimed at the efficient allocation of resources) emerged in the 1980s. The conflict between the liberalism of Einaudi and the redistributive social doctrine advocated by Vanoni epitomised the range of choices available. Italy opted for the latter, only to realise that other countries were moving further away from the redistributive paradigm, as Bernardi acknowledged at the end of the 1980s:

> Theoretical gusts and winds from other countries, on occasion combined with factual evidence, suggest limiting equitable and extra-fiscal goals and giving more room to the goals of neutrality, simplicity, and efficiency. The original structure of the reform, and not just its implementation, is criticised and radical critiques are accompanied by radical proposals for innovation.
>
> (Bernardi 1989: 26–27, my translation)

The Italian tax reform was not designed to preside over neutrality. Distortions and 'political trading' got out of hand, to the point that an MP of the left, Visco, who also held a position as professor of economics and in 1996 became Minister of Finance in the Prodi Government, proposed to constitutionalise tax neutrality (Visco 1986;

see Ceriani and Giannini 1994 on the need to assess the Italian tax system in terms of neutrality). As time went by, the underlying paradigm of Italian taxation, i.e. redistribution, became an element of divergence from countries which took the lead in tax reform and embraced the paradigm of neutrality.

The Italian corporate tax policy process

How is corporate tax policy made? The analysis of the main characteristics of Italian tax system leads to the conclusion that the European dimension of direct taxation has been neglected. Corporate tax policy is not made within a frame of reference wherein European issues play a major role. At this point a question can be raised: is there such a thing as an international direct corporate tax policy in Italy? The question is not trivial, if, following Dunn (1981), a policy is defined by the presence of a collective problem relevant to a set of actors. Actors develop a series of interactions centred around the collective problem and in so doing create decisions, styles of interaction, and policy-oriented interests. Decisions with an international tax component, whether explicit or implicit, are taken daily in Italy, but the salience of this policy area is extremely low. During the interviews conducted for this research, the question 'Why did your organisation play no part in this international corporate direct tax problem?' was almost invariably answered either with 'Alas, there is not a widespread perception of how important these things are', or with the argument that 'In this country there is no policy relating to this area'.

This is not to say that the policy terrain in which actors interact is completely barren. Indeed, the mere transposition of EU corporate tax directives has prodded MPs, bureaucrats, and interest groups into considering international tax issues. However, this terrain does not present tracks, standard operative procedures, and decision styles. In a way, international tax policy resembles a hypothetical disc in which a limited number of scattered files exist, even if the disc itself has not been formatted and labelled. In order to describe how international corporate direct tax policy is made, it is necessary to turn our attention to the actors involved in it: the Ministry of Finance, experts, pressure groups, and Parliament.

The Italian public administration is professionally weak, and the Ministry of Finance, responsible for tax policies, is no exception. However, the common adage that tax administration 'does not work', although definitively correct (Lupi 1996), needs three important qualifications. The first qualification is concerned with two macro characteristics which impinge on tax policy-making. To begin with, Italian public finance has been in dire straits over the last two decades or so, and pressure towards structural re-adjustment has become a paramount concern of the governments since 1992, the year in which the *partitocrazia* lost its hold on public finance. This means that tax policy has been subordinated to the need for catching up with increasingly more ambitious public finance targets. Getting as much revenue as possible in the shortest period of time has been the main macroeconomic constraint on tax policy. Unfortunately, the development of international direct tax policy, particularly in the EU, requires that a degree of revenue concession has to be done in order to eliminate international double taxation. Indeed, EU directives are explicitly targeted towards the removal of taxes that affect the cross-border activity of firms in the single market. The Italian tax system is in the worst possible macroeconomic situation as far as revenue losses are concerned.

Another macro constraint deals with governmental instability. Electoral reforms have been no remedy for this typical feature of the Italian political system. The short life of governments implies that ministers will not invest their resources in championing a long-term design of rationalisation and administrative reform. Nevertheless, Professor Tremonti, Minister of Finance in the Berlusconi government (1994), tried to do so, only to have his fingers badly burned. In fact he was able to present his rationalisation design (publicly, the *Libro Bianco*) only at a time in which the Berlusconi government was already floundering. At the press conference in which his comprehensive White Paper was discussed (December 1994), he had no choice other than to ask the press to call him *Professore* and not *Ministro*! Macro variables are therefore important environmental constraints, although they do not explain the variability between Italy and the UK, as will be shown below.

The second qualification concerns, broadly speaking, the cognitive structure of tax policy. Not only do most people working in the tax administration have a legal background and hence are unfamiliar with economic paradigms, such as tax neutrality, but the most talented civil servants have left public administration in the last two decades or so, following the classic pattern of *pantouflage*. Promising and talented young civil servants have been caught between the Scylla of the strict seniority rules and lack of discretion for promotion in the medium to high career levels, and the Charybdis of total political discretion for top positions (Lupi 1996). Discretion in top appointments has been used more for appointing powerful trades unionists and for spoil-system purposes rather than for rewarding productivity and performance. Senior bureaucrats of the *Ufficio Legislativo*, which has crucial drafting competencies, have joined private organisations such as Assonime (see below) or public holdings, thus contributing to the gradual impoverishment of human resources available within tax administration. The result is that only the most legalistic, rule-oriented and less-prepared bureaucrats have remained in the huge and chaotic towers of *Viale Europa*.[6] The basic problem with this bureaucracy is that it is not prepared to take decisions and hence prefers the proliferation of tax laws to the use of administrative discretion. In addition, the Ministry of Finance does not have a task force able to analyse the substantial (as opposed to formal) content of tax proposals, for example testing a proposal by means of a specific data-base containing microeconomic information. The economic impact of new proposals is therefore assessed naively. Without information specifically organised for the purpose of governing tax policy, how can the Ministry tackle issues such as, say, the impact of tax havens on the fiscal behaviour of Italian multinationals, the benefits and costs of tax base harmonisation in Europe, or the economic implications of different strategies for negotiating bi-lateral tax treaties with foreign tax administrations?

This consideration leads to the third qualification. Given that taxation is a highly technical policy, where does policy-oriented knowledge come from? At first glance, it seems that Italian tax policy draws heavily on a plethora of committees, set up by the Ministry, composed of experts from the academic world and from the business community. However, they do not present a full functional equivalent of a civil service endowed with informative resources specifically created for the management of tax policy. Indeed this plethora of committees has no budget or, on occasion, a very limited budget. Most of the time experts participate in ministerial advisory committees *gratis et amore dei* (i.e. voluntarily). Why do they do this? Simply put, for public ethos or for other less noble reasons, such as to increase their reputation,[7] to improve their portfolio of contacts within the public administration, or to participate in the agenda-setting stage of public policies (Visco 1991: 268). Be that as it may, the bottom line is that advisory committees are intrinsically unable to produce original knowledge and policy-oriented information. Not only is there no budget for producing original research, but most advisory bodies are frequently dissolved or re-shuffled, thus hampering the development of long-term reflection.

However, there is another, more influential, source of advice, situated in the ministerial *cabinet*. The members of this body are recruited by the minister from outside tax administration, and at least one person inside the *cabinet* is in charge of international direct tax policy. This non-bureaucratic advisory body is responsible directly and exclusively to the minister. Members of the *cabinet* come from universities or from the Bank of Italy. In the latter case, the distinction between interests and disinterested advice is blurred, given that the Bank of Italy can have some vested interest in certain policy areas: a proposed EU directive on the taxation of savings could be a case in point. The *cabinet* has partly compensated for the poor resources available within the public administration, but the flip side of the coin is that it has contributed to a verticalisation of tax policy-making, isolating the top ministerial level from the bureaucratic structure. This process of verticalisation has been exacerbated by the fact that, during the recent political season, four Ministers (i.e. Gallo, Tremonti, Fantozzi and Visco) were also academics. Consequently, instead of playing a purely political function, they have been involved directly in the elaboration of tax proposals, using their expertise for drafting tax bills, dealing with EU dossiers, and sorting out administrative problems.

Turning now to the role of experts in the policy process, it has already been mentioned that it is not easy to maintain the distinction between knowledge and interests. Typical tax experts in Italy are not only professors of tax law: they are also successful tax lawyers with their own *studio tributario*. This has something to do with the fact that tax lawyers enjoy a more prominent position than economists in Italian tax policies, reflecting the more general lack of economic culture. Two aspects blur the distinction between expertise and interests. First, corporate tax policy is so important for companies doing business in Italy (without efficient tax planning it is very difficult to survive in the Italian tax jungle) that tax considerations affect crucial managerial decisions. As a consequence, an eminent tax lawyer is placed at the core of many managerial choices. This leads to the second aspect: a top tax consultant is almost a *de facto* partner of the company which receives tax advice.

The distinction between knowledge and interests remains blurred even if we turn to organisations, rather than individuals. In fact the main organisation engaged in corporate tax policy, i.e. Assonime, is a body formally representing the interests of companies on the stock exchange, but at the same time the most eminent figures of Italian tax policy have worked for Assonime. The Ministry of Finance itself has relied on Assonime for many tricky tax law problems (Assonime produces explanatory documents (*circolari*) that often represent the main source of interpretation in certain areas of tax policy) and the Bank of Italy is itself a member of this organisation. Accordingly,

Assonime is a hybrid, part interest group and part organisation with a high technical profile. Apart from Assonime, a handful of think-tanks have gained a good reputation in corporate tax policy analysis, but they have certainly not as yet challenged the pivotal role of Assonime.

Of course, 'real' pressure groups are not absent: the Confederation of Italian Industry (Confindustria), the Italian Bankers' Association (ABI) and single companies (e.g. IMI, IRI, ENI and FIAT) have engaged in lobbying. Moreover, the recent political season, characterised by the collapse of important political parties, has given some members of the Italian business community direct access to political roles. The point to stress is that neither pressure groups nor experts have been particularly active in promoting an international direct corporate tax policy. True, lobbying from companies doing business abroad has not been absent in the negotiation of bi-lateral tax treaties, but this is an episodic involvement in tax policies. The more crucial problem is that EU direct tax harmonisation has not yet become a centre of gravity for bureaucrats, experts, and pressure groups. Accordingly, *there is no such thing as a policy network of international corporate tax policy*.

Even if they wanted to play a more incisive role in policy formation, pressure groups and professional bodies would still have to face a bureaucracy which does not want and cannot manage effective consultation (Lupi 1996). Italian tax bureaucrats are not conceptually prepared to negotiate and use discretion (they are also extremely conscious of the fact that taking a decision today could trigger a suspicion of corruption tomorrow) and, in any case, the time schedule of tax policy is always tight, often so tight that no sensible consultation exercise can be undertaken. Consequently, tax lobbies shift their attention to amendments to be approved at the parliamentary stage and professional bodies organise meetings in which people try to make sense of laws which have been conceived badly, written in obscure language, and often designed without avoiding contradictions. The result is that pressure groups and experts give a limited input to tax policy formation at the earlier stage, where their competence would be useful, although pressure groups are very active in the chaotic process which leads to the formulation of the Finance Bill. The problem is that their intervention in this stage of the tax policy process is often confined to micro-sectional requests.

Parliament is another actor which plays a role short of its full potential.[8] EU direct tax policy was 'discovered' by Parliament somewhat belatedly, when transposing EU directives. Double tax treaties can be politically incendiary in the US Congress (as will be shown in Chapter 8) or in the Danish Folketing,[9] but they make no impact on Italian MPs. Tax treaties are not mere administrative devices for coping with international double taxation. A tax treaty policy directed towards, say, North Africa rather than the Baltic area, affects the balance of economic power between different industries and creates a 'wedge' of fiscal advantages between public holdings (interested in oil from Algeria) and private firms willing to invest elsewhere. Ultimately, tax treaty policy is part of foreign and trade policies. However, neither political parties nor Parliament have played any significant role in this policy area, even though tax treaties are formally ratified by Parliament.

There was no monitoring and no serious attempt on the part of Parliament to influence the position of the Italian government on EU draft directives, notwithstanding the considerable expertise in tax policy accumulated by the *Commissione Finanze* (i.e. the standing committee on tax policies) in the 1970s and 1980s. Members of the *Commissione* had no great opportunity to influence the implementation of EU directives either. In this case, they put the blame on the legislative device[10] compelling MPs to discuss dozens of EU laws in a very short period of time each year. Nowadays the disintegration of the old political system has produced a *Commissione Finanze* (both in the lower and the upper chamber) which does not possess similar expertise.

The EU dimension of Italian corporate tax policy

Given these characteristics of Italian international direct tax policy, it is not surprising that the salience of the EU dimension is low. Even the appointment of an Italian, Professor Mario Monti, as commissioner in charge of tax policy and single market issues (1995) did not stimulate much attention on EU direct tax policy. Monti himself was not even running for that position, as he would have preferred the monetary policy portfolio. The delay of the Italian government in choosing the two Italian nominees for the Commission[11] took Monti out of the running in the competition for the monetary portfolio.

The previous evidence shows a list of conditions contributing to the lack of Europeanisation of Italian direct tax policy. Macro-political constraints – such as public finance and governmental instability – played their role, but the previous analysis has put emphasis on two other conditions: the nature of tax design and the poor cognitive resources available for the development of tax policy in an economy integrating with Europe. What happens to a 'non-Europeanised' tax system when it faces the impact of an emerging EU tax regime? We now turn our attention to the impact of the 1990 EU directives, and to the Italian position on EU direct tax policy since 1990.

The 1990 EU directives

The bulk of EU direct corporate tax policy – examined in detail in Chapter 6 – consists of two directives approved in 1990 (respectively, on the tax treatment of dividends distributed between parent and subsidiary firms operating in two different member states, and on the tax regime of mergers and acquisitions involving companies from two different member states), and one convention (again, approved in 1990) on international transfer pricing tax disputes. Has anything changed in Italy since the approval of these EU laws? Leaving apart some notable exceptions (Giannini 1994), the debate has been dominated by tax lawyers. This – together with the above-mentioned absence of parliamentary scrutiny of EU corporate tax policy – has narrowed the discussion as a number of policy issues can only be fully grasped within the conceptual frameworks of economics and political science. Even so, tax lawyers were instrumental in raising a fundamental question. EU tax directives cannot be fully implemented if an adequate legal 'infrastructure' is not already in place (Di Tanno 1993). Some of the concepts used by EU corporate tax directives are not defined by Italian law. More generally, in order to be effective, tax measures require that taxed entities (e.g. stocks, income, profit, merger, and so on) are disciplined in civil law. In this sense tax law represents secondary legislation. The debate on EU tax directives has thus raised a number of points related to the Europeanisation of Italian law.

A second question raised by the implementation of EU directives concerns the relationship between the parent–subsidiary directive (90/435/EEC) and recent bi-lateral tax treaties with EU member states signed by the Italian government (Escalar 1995). More precisely, this question has triggered a technical discussion on the hierarchical relationship between EU law and international public law (Casertano 1995a; 1995b). The uncertainty of the Ministry of Finance in tackling this issue has produced something more relevant than a technical debate, so much so that in 1994 certain member states retaliated against the Italian government. They decided to suspend payments of tax credits to Italy until the Italian government clarified the relationship between EU law and bi-lateral tax treaties. The problem was partly settled by a Ministerial interpretative regulation (*circolare minis-*

teriale, No. 151/e, 10 August 1994). Technicalities apart (Mayr 1995), the point to stress here is that this tax controversy has shown that Italian tax treaty policy is not developed in synergy with EU policy.

It would be a mistake to assess the impact of EU Italian membership in narrow terms, that is looking solely at the implementation of directives and at the Italian position on draft directives. The EU directive on mergers and acquisitions is a case in point. Not only has the implementation of this directive consolidated the principle that tax policy should be neutral to mergers (i.e. taxes should not create any advantage or disadvantage when two companies merge), but this conceptualisation of neutrality 'spilled over' to other contiguous tax policy areas, in which recent Italian norms have been developed using the EU norm on mergers as a yardstick (Marino 1993b; Mayr 1995; Varazi 1995). This is the case of the fiscal treatment of companies willing to transfer their residence abroad. This example is important but should not be over-emphasised as it covers a minor area of corporate taxation. Italy is still a long way from re-designing its corporate tax regime in terms of neutrality.

Italy and EU policy since 1990

As shown in Chapter 6, EU policy since 1990 has been characterised by the Ruding Committee. The Committee, composed of experts and representatives of the business community, was set up by the Commission for devising a feasible strategy on EU corporate tax co-ordination. However, none of the proposals put forward by the Committee has been approved by the Council of Economic Ministers (ECOFIN). EU corporate tax policy, notwithstanding the publication of the Ruding Committee Report (Commission 1992), has not made progress, to the point that one important directive on the tax treatment of interest and royalties was withdrawn in November 1994.

Even though Italy participated in the Ruding Committee directly (through two executives from FIAT, the largest Italian private company) there was no in-depth consideration of the Committee and its proposals. The Italian representatives in the Ruding Committee (which, however, was a committee of *independent* experts) were not surrounded by a lively policy debate on corporate tax co-ordination at home. Nor were they involved in meetings at the Ministry of Finance, which might have produced a co-ordinated Italian position. The Ministry itself was in a very unstable position as far as political leadership was concerned. Four different ministers alternated over the months in which the Ruding Committee operated: Formica until

September 1992, Goria until February 1993, then Reviglio for one month only, and finally Prime Minister Amato, with an *ad interim* portfolio for tax policy.

Evidence of this lack of interest at the political and administrative level is provided by the monographic issue of *EC Tax Review* dedicated to the assessment of the Committee in different countries. Whilst a British article therein (Elliott 1993) quotes a number of British articles, criticisms and opinions (thus reflecting an on-going policy debate), the corresponding Italian article (Fantozzi and Manganelli 1993) does not contain any reference to it! The lack of attention to the Ruding Committee was a recurring theme in the interviews conducted for this study.

This does not necessarily mean that Italy was permanently absent from the EU tax policy process. Indeed, there is empirical evidence of a limited but not trivial Italian participation. In order to understand this, it is useful to bear in mind the above-mentioned process of verticalisation within the Italian tax administration. As shown earlier, ministers such as Gallo and Tremonti took a personal interest in EU tax development, thus intensifying contacts between Italian ministers and the Commissioner (at that time, Madame Scrivener). One of the main consequences of this direct involvement of ministers in the EU policy process was the capability of articulating Italian interests with coherence. The draft directive on interest and royalties is a case in point. Italy would have been damaged by this proposal, both in terms of revenue and for technical implementation issues. Accordingly, the Italians were able to raise concerns over the draft in a discreet manner, leading prominent member states towards a negative assessment of the Commission's proposal, which was subsequently withdrawn. The point to emphasise here is not whether Italy really torpedoed the Commission's proposal or, more likely, catalysed concerns which were already present in other member states. The political implication is that Italy was capable of articulating a national interest in the EU policy process. Although re-actively (as opposed to pro-actively), *Italy defended its national position in the policy formation stage*. This observation is not trivial, given that according to other, more comprehensive surveys of Italian membership in the EU (Giuliani 1992; 1996), the articulation of Italian interests at this stage of the policy process is the exception rather than the rule.

THE UK: HOW EUROPEANISATION BROUGHT ABOUT POLICY CHANGE

Corporate taxation has been the object of political debate in the UK. Since the establishment of the Royal Commission on the Taxation of Profits and Income (1951), the Conservative and Labour parties have advocated different regimes for the taxation of profits. The bone of contention was whether shareholders should benefit from a tax credit on the profits they receive (this credit is given because of the corporation tax paid on profits by the company), or not. Conservatives preferred the former option, Labour the latter. However, the existence of a politicised tax issue should not be interpreted as empirical evidence of political parties as pivotal actors in the UK tax policy process. As Robinson and Sandford (1983) have shown, the debate between the two major political parties has been eminently ideological. The elaboration of tax strategies within political parties – Robinson and Sandford observed at the beginning of the 1980s – was extremely poor. Prominent figures such as Lord Kaldor used their party as a political vehicle for their tax ideas, rather than *vice versa*. Our research, even though limited to corporate tax policy, confirms this point: neither the interviews nor the literature examined assigns to political parties a significant role in the elaboration of corporate tax policies.

More recently, ideas for tax reforms have come from think-tanks and policy institutes rather than from political parties.[12] Nor can it be argued that political parties have been efficient 'devices' for transmitting mass preferences on tax policies into political choices. The conclusion of the study conducted by Robinson and Sandford, concerned with a sample of taxes, could not be clearer and it is worth quoting at length:

> We do not find much evidence of political rationality in terms of the selection of goals most likely to appeal to the mass electorate. . . . Our study also reveals that the parties showed only limited capacity for rational consideration of their chosen objectives. They did not examine them in sufficient detail, nor did they fully explore the consequences of their chosen actions. . . . If objectives are insufficiently considered and clarified by the party proposing the tax, the policies are more open to influence from the bureaucracy and from affected interest groups.
>
> (Robinson and Sandford 1983: 221)

In addition, British governments since the Second World War have not undertaken a comprehensive attempt to assess alternatives for bold tax reform, with the remarkable exception of the above-mentioned Royal Commission. In Canada, the Carter Commission produced a blueprint for tax reform. In the USA, the Treasury has been the main actor in the analysis of new tax strategies. In the EU, the Ruding Committee produced a series of detailed recommendations, even if they have not as yet been implemented; the plethora of Italian committees flanking the Ministry of Finance attests how the Italian government endeavours to produce usable knowledge (with poor results, indeed). In the UK, the most notable blueprint for tax reform, i.e. the Meade report (1978), was produced outside the government, under the auspices of the Institute for Fiscal Studies. A Select Committee was indeed set up by the Conservative Government in 1971, but with a very limited mandate to prepare the ground for the reform of profit taxation. In 1973 the UK switched from a classic system of profit taxation (this system taxes dividends both at the corporate level and through the personal income tax) to an imputation system[13] and since then the UK has maintained an imputation system. Interestingly, the Committee considered European issues an important element of tax design: 'Finally, your Committee thinks that it is likely that harmonisation within the EEC would be in the first place facilitated by the adoption of imputation here' (HC 622, 1970/1, quoted in Robinson and Sandford 1983: 164).

Another issue discussed by the Select Committee was the link between UK taxation and the flow of foreign investment. The idea at that time was to design corporate taxation in a way that could improve the balance of payments. Even though domestic politics was the primary concern in the ideological confrontation between the two main political parties (Robinson and Sandford 1983), it can be argued that *at least a limited concern with international tax issues was present in the tax design of the 1970s*. This highlights an important difference from the Italian tax design, in which a similar concern was limited to indirect taxes (VAT especially), but did not extend to direct corporate taxation.

Turning now to the exceptionally long era of Conservative rule (from 1979 to 1997), arguably the most striking feature is the propensity for a corporate tax design consistent with the scenario of capital movement liberalisation (as early as 23 October 1979 the Chancellor of the Exchequer, Geoffrey Howe, declared in the House of Commons that the government wanted to lift any restriction on international capital movement), on the one side, and the unwillingness to put European tax co-ordination onto the agenda, on the other. Of course, this apparent paradox is explained by the intra-party tensions on European integration which have beleaguered the Conservative Party.

The main episode of corporate tax reform in the 1980s is represented by the innovation contained in the 1984 budget. In that year the Chancellor, Nigel Lawson, reduced statutory corporate tax rates from 52 per cent to 35 per cent and broadened the revenue base with the abolition of stock relief and capital allowances. In his memoirs, Lawson (1992) stresses that his tax design was considerably different from the supply-side design chosen in the United States in 1981. According to Lawson, tax rate reduction is not a sufficient condition for promoting economic growth, as it originates inflation. Tax rate reduction makes economic sense – Lawson argues – only in conjunction with the removal of loopholes and other tax benefits that create distortions. The debate on the 1984 budget includes different opinions (Chown 1984; Gammie 1984; Leape 1993; Odling-Smee and Lawton 1990).

Whatever the final assessment of the 1984 tax reform may be, it is evident that the UK embraced the new policy paradigm of a more neutral, efficient and transparent tax system much sooner than Italy. Indeed, the UK took the lead in corporate tax reform, in a sense anticipating the most celebrated US tax reform of 1986 (Peters 1991; Sandford 1993). Timing was also of importance: at the beginning of the 1970s, when Italy embraced tax reform, the neglect of the European dimension of corporate taxes still appeared an excusable failure. By contrast, timing was more favourable to the UK, which entered the process of tax reform in the 1980s. This does not necessarily mean that the UK tax system lacks drawbacks. Indeed, one of the main conclusions of this chapter is that British tax policies are not fully able to exploit the 'intelligence of democracy' (Lindblom 1965) in full. It is to this question that we now turn.

The UK corporate tax policy process

At first glance, the UK tax policy process appears an expression of pure rationality when compared to the Italian one. Tax measures are introduced in Parliament during the budget session and are encased in the macroeconomic design of the Finance Bill, whilst in Italy taxes are set in the Finance Bill but then they are continuously modified throughout the year in an attempt to catch up with the latest hike of public deficit, or, if that is not the case, with the failure of preceding taxes in terms of revenue-gathering performance. Since 1993, the macroeconomic coherence of UK tax policy has been enhanced by the discussion of taxes and expenditure in the same budget session. Both taxes and expenditures are introduced by the Chancellor in November, on 'budget day'. As for tax treaties, the House of Commons does not witness any 'hot' debate, but at the same time parliamentary discussion is less apathetic than in Italy. The typical parliamentary debate sees an Opposition MP questioning the government on elements of the tax treaty under discussion when these elements diverge from the OECD model tax convention. The government is therefore compelled to explain why the OECD provision on a certain issue was not adhered to.

Yet the comments on British tax policy are replete with negative remarks: legislation is growing relentlessly and becoming an impenetrable Byzantine structure; tax policies do not react to important socio-economic changes; and the 'purdah' of budget secrecy stifles genuine debate (Gammie 1990; Kay 1986; Special Committee of Tax Law Consultative Bodies 1993; Tax Law Review Committee 1995). This paradoxical state of affairs can be explained by the main characteristics of the tax policy process (Gammie 1990). To begin with, the agenda-setting stage of the policy process is the exclusive competence of the Inland Revenue, in concert with the Treasury. This is the stage in which the context of tax policy is shaped. Of course, neither the Chancellor nor the Inland Revenue examines broad tax strategy without weighing the possible reactions of companies and financial markets. However, if the government decides to review, for example, the taxation of distributed profits, this decision will be taken without consulting the parliament or the business community. In the rare cases in which a consultative paper is produced, there is no institutional body (such as an independent committee) with a mandate to report on the reactions to the paper or to conduct a critical assessment.

Consultation begins when the broad context has already been outlined. Affected parties are consulted in the second stage of the policy process, concerning the definition of alternatives.[14] Accordingly, consultation does not revolve around the question 'What should we do?' but around the different question 'How can we do what we have already decided to do?' (Gammie 1990). In the consultative process, parties have to face an already structured (yet often unveiled) agenda, with scarce time resources (a secret agenda-setting stage implies that there is no time for public discussion), and low transparency (the Inland Revenue does not stress any specific tax measure during consultation; specific tax decisions become public only on budget day). Furthermore, consultation is a voluntary (as opposed to compulsory) exercise (a number of tax issues are not the object of consultation) and operates 'one way' (i.e. from parties to government, and not *vice versa*).

Neither the Treasury nor the Inland Revenue releases information about the tendencies emerging from the process of consultation. Interviews conducted for this study suggest that these characteristics are slowly evolving towards a more open consultative process. One interviewee, commenting upon the increasingly open attitude of the Inland Revenue, exclaimed: 'This is *perestroika*!'. However, a lack of transparency remains.

To sum up, the corporate tax policy process is politically efficient: each year the government has its hands firmly on the agenda and arrives at budget day on time, with tax policy measures fleshed out in the Finance Bill. However, the process appears to be structurally unable to benefit from the mutual interaction of multiple actors who bring to the decision-making process diverse interests, alternative solutions, and different goals.

The problem of a poor cognitive component of policy formation is compounded by the lead taken by a bureaucratic-led department, i.e. the Inland Revenue, in the design of tax policies. In the field of international corporate taxation, for example, the Inland Revenue (not the Treasury) negotiates bi-lateral treaties, liaises with the OECD, monitors EU developments, analyses the relationship between domestic tax laws and EU laws, and prepares documents for the implementation of EU directives. This implies that British tax policies tend to be biased towards purely administrative concerns, thus hampering bold tax reforms, as macroeconomic 'vision' tends to be overlooked (Kay 1986). Put differently, the Inland Revenue has an organisational bias against tax reform. Never has the Inland Revenue produced important macroeconomic documents for tax policy design (such as Treasury I in the USA). Nor has it had a group of economists comparable to the prestigious US Office of Tax Analysis. In a way, the problem of creating an information infrastructure for governing tax policy is almost the same – *mutatis mutandis* – in the Inland Revenue as it is in the *Ministero delle Finanze*!

The Inland Revenue presents structural limits in the production of knowledge for tax reform and the political characteristics of policy formation do not permit the benefit of mutual interaction to be exploited. Where, then, do ideas come from? Of course, the Chancellor is in a pivotal position for fostering broad new ideas for tax policy, as will be shown below. Employers' associations (e.g. the CBI and British Bankers' Association) have a tax board or a tax committee, but these bodies are scarcely endowed with resources for tax analysis. At best, they have a secretariat. The production of usable information in corporate taxation is extremely expensive: academic analysis has to be supplemented with an intimate knowledge of issues such as tax implementation, transfer pricing policies of corporations, and the practice of tax planning within multinational groups. This explains why employers' associations are unable to behave pro-actively. Almost invariably, their lobbying is re-active and constrained by the above-mentioned characteristics of consultation. Interest representation does not bring issues, projects, or ideas onto the agenda of corporate tax policy.

Nor do Conservative think-tanks provide usable knowledge. Institutes such as the Institute of Economic Affairs genuinely have a remarkable track record in taxation, but they have not been terribly incisive in corporate taxation. Multinational accountancy firms are in a better position: not only do they have an accurate knowledge of how taxes impact on the whole of corporate activities (in the UK and abroad), but they participate in the policy process as 'technical' actors. 'We do not have any axe to grind' is a recurring assertion in the interviews conducted with tax partners of accountancy firms in the UK and Brussels. The flip side of the coin is that, by limiting their participation to the technical aspects of tax policy, these firms do not raise broad issues of tax reform. Nor are they allowed to do so, as they do not have a mandate to represent firms: multinational accountancy firms have clients, not members.

Another important technical input to the policy process comes from professional associations, such as the Institutes of Chartered Accountants, the Law Society, and the Institute of Taxation. These bodies, although mainly interested in the legal aspects of tax policy, play two important functions. First, they represent independent authoritative bodies. According to Majone (1993b), the existence of bodies capable of developing a notion of 'correct' policy provides an important focus for public deliberation and policy development. Second, these institutes are linked to European confederations. Accordingly, professional associations are very useful in transmitting the themes and the 'flavour' of European debate into the UK process. Moreover, the European activity of these bodies is not episodic. The Institute of Chartered Accountants has commented directly (that is, apart from the comments provided by the European confederation to which the institute belongs) on the activity of the Ruding Committee and on draft directives presented by the Commission.

The most outstanding actor in the production of policy-oriented knowledge is the Institute for Fiscal Studies (IFS). Set up in 1965, the Institute has articulated its activity in a series of long-term projects. The IFS contributes to the cognitive structure of tax policy in many ways, including the IFS model of the UK corporation tax (Devereux 1986). This model, based upon microeconomic data, captures the impact of corporate tax policy on a disaggregated basis and therefore represents an accurate instrument for the analysis of public policy. Moreover, tax policy is monitored throughout the year and the IFS green budgets assess policy options each year, just before the Finance Bill. Tax policy is investigated by the IFS within the more general framework of public finance: hence the choice of *fiscal* rather than *tax* in the Institute's name. Emphasis should be put on the title 'Institute for Fiscal Studies' in another respect: the denomination contains *for* rather than *of*. In fact the goal of the Institute is to provide tax analysis that can be used for tackling policy issues, and not mere academic problems. In doing so, the Institute has always striven to interact with policy-makers and companies. Accordingly, a number of IFS projects are conducted by teams composed of analysts (mainly economists) and members of the business community.

Presumably, the attempt to amalgamate economic analysis with 'real world' problems and interests is the most important role played by the IFS in the policy process. A second role, partly connected to the first, concerns the contribution of the IFS and the UK-based professional associations to the long-term change of arguments, concepts and paradigms used in British tax policy. This is consistent with the literature of knowledge utilisation which posits the social sciences impact on public policies only in the long term, through the modification of conceptual paradigms used by policy-makers (Weiss 1986 and Chapter 2 of this volume). The IFS studies 'real world' problems, but rarely with the purpose of suggesting to policy-makers what they have to do in the short term. Instead of playing a normative role, the IFS is engaged in a formative role. The major concerns of the IFS are in fact illustrated by the following long-term themes, emphasised year after year via conferences, research projects, and publications: the use of economic analysis for assessing tax proposals, the reliance on the paradigm of tax neutrality as a benchmark for tax policy, the approach to EU tax co-ordination, and the impact of European tax harmonisation on British tax policy. It is precisely to the EU dimension of tax policy that we now turn.

The EU dimension of UK corporate tax policy

In this section the Europeanisation of UK corporate tax policy is examined. First, the reaction to the 1990 directives and to the Ruding

Committee is analysed, with the aim of describing the 'immediate' impact of EU policy on domestic policy. Second, a more 'mediate', but more crucial, effect of Europeanisation is taken into account.

The 'direct' impact

National attitudes seem able to provide a fair picture of the UK reaction to the emergence of EU corporate tax policy. The stereotype of British Euro-scepticism is the most obvious candidate for sustaining the analysis. However, we have already seen that the stereotype of Italian Euro-enthusiasm confines the analysis to an extremely narrow, and ultimately inadequate, corner. Is that true for the UK case too? Euro-scepticism seems to perform rather well, at least at first glance. Williams (1991) observes that the typical Euro-scepticism diverted the attention of the Inland Revenue from the negotiations going on in Brussels, so much so that the Inland Revenue would have been taken aback by the approval of the 1990 directives. By the same token, Elliott (1993: 45) claims that some British officers reacted to the publication of the Ruding Committee with the following exclamation: 'It is as if the lunatics had taken over the asylum.' *The Economist* played the same tune, by arguing that the Commission, with the Ruding Report, had concurred in a ridiculous mistake, trying to freeze the healthy forces of tax competition in Europe: 'If it moves, harmonise it!' (*The Economist*, 21 March 1992).

However, Williams himself notes that the technical content of the 1990 directives contains evidence of typical Inland Revenue concerns. How could it happen, then, if the Inland Revenue had neglected the development of this policy? In addition, the implementation of the 1990 directives has triggered four processes. First, consultation on the implementation has been open, compared to the average for consultative processes: for example, a consultative document was produced promptly by the Inland Revenue (December 1991). Second, the debate on EU corporate tax law has raised the issue of language. The business community has suggested implementing the directives in the same language and the same concepts contained in the directives themselves. An implementation oriented to the English language and concepts would implicitly have taken on board a form of interpretation and a legislative history which, being rooted in British law, could have performed badly.

Third, the emergence of EU corporate tax law has activated a debate on the necessity to shift UK tax law towards a purposive approach, as opposed to an objective approach. According to the purposive approach, EU tax law has to be implemented in a broad sense, looking at the main goals of the directives. For example, given that the so-called parent–subsidiary directive disposes of taxes on cross-border payments of dividends, thus ensuring fiscal neutrality, the purposive approach states that the whole UK legislation on dividends should be re-considered with this conception of neutrality in mind. The purposive approach is a long way from being whole-heartedly accepted in the British legal system, but the point to stress is the role of EU policies in feeding this debate. Fourth, companies such as Hoechst and Pirelli started challenging the British system of taxing cross-border dividend payments in courts. Their main argument is that certain aspects of the system are incompatible with the developing principles of EU law (Gammie and Brannan 1995). This last point can be generalised by arguing that recent European Court of Justice (ECJ) tax jurisprudence on the taxation of individuals in the EU – based upon the doctrine of non-discrimination – could encourage member states to change their tax provisions unilaterally in order to bring them into line with non-discrimination. In the aftermath of recent ECJ cases, the debate in the UK 'has already produced a shopping list of provisions vulnerable to challenge [from the ECJ on discriminatory grounds]' (Nias 1995: 31).

As far as the Ruding Committee is concerned, if one scratches below the surface of Euro-attitudes a different picture emerges. In comparison to the Italian case, the flow of information between London and the experts working on the Ruding Committee was substantial. In addition, the debate on the Ruding Report has been more lively than in Italy (Chown 1994; Elliott 1993; Gammie 1992), mainly thanks to the IFS. Finally, the IFS itself was directly involved in the work of the Ruding Committee with the preparation of a questionnaire which forms an important part of the Ruding Report – not to mention that economists associated with the IFS were consultants to the Committee.

The 'indirect' impact

The transmission of ideas does not follow linear paths, especially in the case of ideas that flow across the borders, from a supra-national arena to a domestic political system. Ideas generated abroad are filtered by national agendas which already contain priorities, by institutions and policy-makers already concerned with specific policy stakes, constraints, and opportunities. This is the main rationale for an investigation of the indirect impact of Europeanisation on UK corporate tax policy. Another rationale for this type of investigation chimes with the so-called bottom-up design in implementation research (Sabatier 1986). A bottom-up approach to the study of Europeanisation investigates the dynamics of corporate tax policies in one country and considers whether European issues have played a significant role in the dynamics of domestic corporate tax policy.

Two changes were originated by the indirect Europeanisation of British corporate tax policy. The first concerns a change of instruments, whilst the second pertains to a change in the market for policy ideas. The change of instruments has to do with a long-standing problem caused by a 'by-product' of the imputation system chosen by the UK in 1973. When a company distributes profits, it is required to pay an Advance Corporation Tax (ACT) which is literally an advance payment of mainstream corporation tax. At the end of the year, the amount paid in ACT is written off against mainstream corporation tax. If profits are earned abroad, for example through a subsidiary, there would still be the payment of ACT when they are paid out to shareholders, but there would be no mainstream corporation tax. In fact, if profits are made by, say, an Italian subsidiary, the latter would pay corporation tax in Italy but the UK parent would have no tax liability because of the double taxation relief acknowledged by the UK–Italy tax treaty. To cut a long story short, this system causes prejudice against companies which make profits abroad: if there is not enough mainstream corporation tax, ACT paid at the moment of profit distribution will never be recovered.[15]

Dissatisfaction with this state of affairs, lobbying, and proposals for alleviating the ACT prejudice circulated for almost twenty years, but without any outcome. After all, from the revenue point of view the ACT prejudice was just a 'natural' feature of the imputation system, whether desirable (for the Inland Revenue) or not (for companies doing business abroad). It was only in March 1993 that the Chancellor announced the intention to tackle the problem. The most important content of the technical solution implemented in the budget for 1994 was the possibility for companies to designate dividends from abroad as foreign investment dividends (FIDs). FIDs still pay ACT, but this payment can be recovered at the end of the year, even though corporate taxes on these profits were paid abroad.

The question then becomes: how did this policy change come about? Interestingly, the Inland Revenue (1993), in its consultative document on the surplus ACT problem, considers the EU initiatives against the double taxation of profits a crucial catalyst. The 1990 directives and the proceedings of the Ruding Committee emphasised the incongruity of the UK corporate tax policy when measured against the yardstick of international tax neutrality. In turn, European issues were put onto the agenda by the IFS and the UK professional associations. These knowledge-based actors promoted a policy discussion on the implication of EU taxation for the UK tax system. It can be argued, then, that the insertion of European issues into the domestic debate was able to break the stalemate, fostering policy change.

The same conclusion can be drawn if the origin of technical solutions is taken into account. Where did the FIDs idea come from? It is always very difficult to track the origins of policy ideas: Kingdon (1984: 148) quotes Ecclesiastes to argue that 'there is nothing new under the sun'. Nevertheless, the FIDs solution quite clearly represents an elaboration of an idea put forward by Malcolm Gammie, an international tax lawyer involved in many IFS projects (Gammie 1991a). The transmission of this solution into the policy process was facilitated by two other aspects. First, the Chancellor who implemented the solution, Mr Lamont, was personally keen on championing this rather technical policy reform. Second, the former IFS director, Bill Robinson, happened to be sitting on the Ruding Committee in the early stage (1991) and later (1991–1992) became special economic adviser to the Chancellor. It is not inconceivable to posit that Robinson was willing to sell some 'IFS ideas' to the Chancellor!

This does not imply that experts in governmental positions 'make' policies *ad libitum*: if so, the Italian tax system would be the paradise of legal precision, and not the inextricable maze we know. This story simply shows the number of circumstances that jointly produce policy change. The presence of economic interests and lobbying is important, but not decisive. A change had been demanded for years by the business community, but with no result. Change materialised when Europeanisation modified the salience of the ACT prejudice. More precisely, the prejudice became hard to sustain in the context of the Single Market. The role of the IFS and British professional bodies in promoting a *European* debate on corporate taxation facilitated a new 'construction' of the ACT prejudice. The re-definition of the surplus ACT problem as a European problem was indeed crucial. As shown by the literature on the politics of problem definition (Rochefort and Cobb 1994; Chapter 2 of this volume), different constructions of policy problems influence the choice of instrument and ultimately the adoption of solutions. Another condition for policy change was represented by the role of individuals (i.e. the Chancellor and Bill Robinson) who acted as purposeful entrepreneurs and catalysed policy change. As shown by Kingdon (1984) change is more often the result of individual entrepreneurship rather than the outcome of structural circumstances. However, a *sui generis* structural characteristic mattered: in the 1970s, British policy-makers had designed a tax system that was more sensitive to the internationalisation of tax policy than the Italian one.

As already mentioned, the second change stimulated by the European dimension of tax policy concerns the market for ideas. The Europeanisation of the debate on taxation and the increasing importance of the paradigm of tax neutrality has led the IFS to promote a project team with the mandate to explore new structures of corporate taxation. In a seminal article, Gammie (1991b) outlined that the existence of an embryonic but crucial EU tax regime had to be completed with an overhaul of corporate taxation at home, based upon a rigorous application of the tax neutrality paradigm.

The main result of the project undertaken by the IFS (see IFS 1994) is the elaboration of a policy proposal which introduces a new type of corporation tax, labelled Allowance for Corporate Equity (ACE). The latter is meant to be neutral towards the forms of investment financing (e.g. debt, new shares and retained profits) and towards the international location of investment (i.e. foreign or domestic investment). According to ACE proponents, this is precisely the type of corporation tax that could be suitable for adoption in a country willing to exploit the benefits of the single European market. The IFS has hinted that ACE could become, if adopted by the Commission, a proposal for harmonisation that could be accepted by member states without the need for harmonising the tax base in fifteen different countries.[16]

CONCLUSIONS

The research design chosen for this article led to the conclusion that Europeanisation of Italian corporate tax policy is still limited to (a) the constraints which negative integration put on the Italian tax design (e.g. the implementation of the 1988 directive on capital movement) and (b) the implementation of the 1990 directives that remove tax obstacles to the single market – yet another example of negative integration. There is also preliminary evidence showing that EU norms and principles are taken into account in tax policy formation, but Italy remains a long way from revamping its tax policy instruments in terms of European paradigms. Therefore the case for indirect Europeanisation of Italian corporate tax policy cannot be made.

Parenthetically, Europeanisation of corporate tax policy is not explained by the 'vernacular' wisdom on Euro-attitudes. Italians found it difficult to articulate their interests in the EU tax policy process, but succeeded in 'saying no' to a Commission proposal. By the same token, the alleged Euro-scepticism of the UK has not impeded the growth of a European dimension of corporate tax policy at home.

As for the British case, the change of policy instruments is the most important empirical evidence of indirect Europeanisation. However, following P. Hall's classification, Europeanisation did not cause any 'third-order' change (i.e. an overall change of goals): radical proposals for tax reform, such as the already mentioned ACE, are now circulating in policy fora, within and outside academic circles, but they have not as yet been translated into political action.

A push towards a 'third-order' change could come about in the future, thanks to the increasing importance of tax neutrality as a benchmark for tax policy. Neutrality is the frame of reference underpinning proposals (such as ACE) for a comprehensive re-formulation of corporate tax policy. For the time being, the articulation of the tax policy discourse in terms of neutrality has not produced a complete change of goals. To be more precise, the policy discourse on taxation has already shifted from redistribution to the goals of economic efficiency and neutrality, as witnessed by the broadening of the revenue base and the reduction of tax rates, with Italy being a laggard in this process. Nevertheless, no country in the world has gone so far as to carry the implication of tax neutrality to the extreme. Looking around the world, a radical revision of tax structures (affecting also the taxation of portfolio income and personal taxation) could manifest in the US – where the 'flat-rate' tax was discussed during the 1996 presidential campaign – and there is evidence that Scandinavian countries are taking the implications of globalisation seriously, but neither the UK nor Italy seem on the verge of a dramatic shift in the foreseeable future.[17]

The predominance of tax neutrality in the tax policy discourse is not a result of Europeanisation alone, but has more to do with an epochal shift of public finance theory and practice, from redistribution to efficiency (Quigley and Smolensky 1994). However, the presence of an embryonic EU tax regime based upon a rigorous application of the principles of tax neutrality has provided a focal point to the British tax policy discourse. The UK thus provides evidence of a 'second-order' policy change induced by Europeanisation. International inefficiencies caused by the ACT regime have been tackled and partly remedied. Macro administrative variables, although important, are not decisive in answering the question 'Why did policy change of the second order occur in the UK but not in Italy?' As far as Whitehall is concerned, the development of tax reform is not facilitated by the characteristics of the consultation process and the role of the Inland Revenue therein. Turning to macro-political variables, the conclusion of this chapter is consistent with the literature on veto players which assigns a higher *potential* for policy change to the British political system (Hallerberg and Basinger 1997; Tsebelis 1995). But in order to understand the *process* of change, the insights provided by the investigation of the cognitive structure of public policies are fruitful. The Europeanisation of the corporate tax policy discourse in the UK has altered the frame of reference in which decisions are taken. Knowledge-oriented actors such as the IFS and British professional bodies have contributed to the Europeanisation of the cognitive dimension of corporate tax policy by arguing persistently that the 'correct' British tax policy is the one in line with European membership of the UK. This empirical result illustrates that research on Europeanisation should explore – alongside the direct impact of directives – if and to what extent domestic policy is influenced by European paradigms. This corresponds to a shift in theoretical focus from a 'top-down' to a 'bottom-up' or 'indirect' approach to Europeanisation.

8 International tax complexity

> Strictly speaking, there is no such thing as an international tax system.
> (Bird 1988)

TAX COMPLEXITY AND INSTITUTIONALISATION

There are two reasons for looking at the wider international context in which European taxation is situated. First, as shown in Chapter 5, the construction of EU policy problems acquires distinctive political implications when problems are 'framed' in the conceptual paradigm of tax complexity. It is therefore useful to examine the globalisation of taxation with the aim of drawing implications for the institutionalisation of principles, rules, and organisations dealing with the international tax order. Indeed, it is within the global process of tax policy institutionalisation that EU tax policy is made. The second reason, which is partly connected to the first, is that the EU tax policy regime is only one of the sources of internationalisation of domestic tax policy. For EU countries, the main challenges to tax sovereignty derive more from the globalisation of capital, tax havens and international tax entropy than from EU directives.

International tax complexity is such a broad theme that only a cursory view of the main issues is presented here.[1] Nevertheless a basic question is raised: is there evidence of increasing consensus, stability, certainty and ultimately institutionalisation in the international tax arena? Alternatively, does evidence point to an increased degree of disorder and hence complexity remains unmanaged? This question is important as it situates the embryonic EU corporate tax regime examined in Chapter 6 into the wider global tax arena. Indeed *if* it could be concluded that the international tax arena is undergoing a process of institutionalisation and convergence of rules, then the drive towards EU tax co-ordination could be strengthened and eased. By contrast, in a world of fundamental tax entropy the few elements of direct tax co-ordination achieved in the EU could be seriously challenged.

Whatever option may prevail, the scenario of global taxation offers insights for assessing EU tax policy as a matter of 'external affairs' of the EU, whilst in the previous chapters the EU direct tax regime was examined as an issue pertaining to the single market, that is to 'internal affairs'. Within this new 'external affairs' perspective, what the EU does (or does not do) in the international tax arena is more important than what it does internally. On this point it should be observed that the EU is not as yet a major player in international tax policy. This argument will be stressed in Chapter 9, but at this stage an implication is that the analysis of international tax policy institutionalisation must be diverted towards players different from the EU. The politics of international tax globalisation revolves around powerful states and the OECD, and it is precisely to the interaction between domestic taxation of international income and international consensus presided over by the OECD that this chapter is dedicated. In doing so, we confine our attention to perhaps the most powerful player in the arena of tax complexity, namely the United States. The next section starts with some general issues; the following one examines how American institutions have confronted international tax issues in the 1990s; the subsequent section discusses the implications of US tax policy for the international tax system, and the final one presents some concluding thoughts.

DOMESTIC INSTITUTIONS: BETWEEN PRIVATE PRESSURE AND PUBLIC INTERESTS

It is impossible to analyse the relationship between domestic institutions and corporations in tax policy without a general view concerning the political impact of pressure groups and particularistic interests on public policy. What does the recent debate say on this question? Are institutions captured by powerful economic interests or is there a ray of hope for contemporary democracy?

Recent research on public policies contends that the political power of pressure groups has been successfully curbed in many policy areas and that the role of private interests in contemporary political systems may have been over-emphasised by previous literature (Majone 1993b: 3). Research based on recent dynamics of public policies argues that theories and models such as extreme 'pressure group' versions of pluralism,[2] neo-corporatism (Schmitter 1974), the syndrome of regulatory capture (Stigler 1971) and the ordinary characterisation of the period from the 1970s to the mid-1980s as the era of 'political resurgence of business' (Vogel 1989) spawned a pessimistic view of the policy process that no longer corresponds to reality.

Political scientists have now contended that in a number of important circumstances American institutions have been able to initiate and implement policies which have allocated concentrated costs (paid by companies) and distributed diffuse benefits (Mucciaroni 1995; 1996). Tax reform (Conlan, Wrightson and Beam 1990; Mucciaroni 1990; Peters 1991) is a case in point. As explained in Chapter 4, within the domain of tax policy, institutions are less permeable to particularistic pressure than they were at the beginning of the 1980s: the contrast between the pessimistic tone of Witte's book, published in the mid-1980s (Witte 1985) and the more optimistic observations made by Conlan, Wrightson and Beam (1990) is illustrative of this debate. Yet a question arises: does this trend in domestic tax policy hold true for domestic taxation of *international* income as well? Indeed, it could be argued that even if diffuse interests are more protected than in the past, their survival in an arena of globalisation and liberalisation can still be questioned. This statement is not confined to tax policy *per se*, but considers tax policy in the wake of trade liberalisation. The latter – the argument goes on – is ultimately meant to be detrimental to national health, safety, and environmental protection. More importantly, it has been argued that the liberalisation of capital movement has triggered a process which will first damage national tax systems and consequently undermine the very essence of the welfare state.[3] However, David Vogel (1995) has argued that the globalisation of trade is not necessarily incompatible with health, safety, and environmental regulations that protect diffuse interests. Vogel makes the important point that business has to take into account the public interest even in the era of international trade. However, this literature does not say anything which could lead to a similar optimistic conclusion as far as international tax policy is concerned.[4]

To sum up, this literature contends that political institutions are not predestined to be captured by powerful corporate actors. The relationship between interest group activity and institutions has hence to be assessed on a case by case basis and there is enough empirical evidence for arguing that, at least under specific circumstances, institutions can be relatively autonomous from particularistic pressure. Building upon these propositions, this chapter argues the following points. The first is that there is empirical evidence of institutional autonomy in the case of US international tax policy. However, the political determinants of autonomy must be explained in order to make sense of the empirical evidence. The second point is that institutional autonomy in domestic taxation of international income cannot be assessed solely in terms of its domestic implications. An examination of its consequences for the international tax order is needed. Can rational and efficient behaviour at the domestic level produce irrational, inefficient and perverse effects in the global tax order?

The third point draws upon the new institutionalist literature (March and Olsen 1989; Powell and DiMaggio 1991) for discussing the problematic creation of order in the international tax system. Indeed, international tax policy can be described as a policy in search of institutionalisation. The main problem is that the demand for institutions is not as yet matched by an adequate supply. In this context more autonomous domestic institutions can paradoxically hamper the institutionalisation of rules and 'ways of doing things' in the international tax system.

DOMESTIC TAXATION OF INTERNATIONAL INCOME: THE US CASE

The political drive

In this section some recent trends in US international tax policy are examined. The main argument put forward here is that American institutions (the Executive, the Congress, a few states, and the Internal Revenue Service) have become increasingly autonomous from transnational-national corporations' political pressures.[5] However, before considering the empirical evidence pointing to institutional autonomy it is necessary to detect the set of independent variables that explain this reassertion of the state. The argument put forward here is that these explanatory variables are political in nature.

True, recent advances in technology should not be overlooked as they provide public administration with new instruments for assessing the revenue of citizens and companies and for exchanging information in magnetic format (OECD 1994). However, technology can work in the opposite direction as well, by providing new ways of evading or avoiding taxes. Briefly, technology represents an important pre-condition for a more incisive tax policy, but it does not seem sensible to adhere to a sort of technological determinism.

Turning now to political variables, the first aspect to take into account is the politics of the federal budget. As is known, the conflict between President Clinton and the Republicans over the balanced budget reached a climax at the beginning of March 1995, when the

Republicans failed (by a single vote) to win a two-thirds majority in the Senate for introducing a constitutional amendment to balance the federal budget by the year 2002. Interestingly, Senator Dole went out of his way to persuade two Democrat Senators from North Dakota who are known to be supportive of the balanced budget. The fact is revealing because one of the two Senators, Byron Dorgan, is the most convinced advocate of a tough approach to the taxation of foreign transnational corporations operating in the USA. In the negotiations Senator Dole was unable to persuade Senator Dorgan that the constitutional amendment could have been achieved without tapping the social security trust fund.[6]

There are now signs that Republicans will not insist on the balanced budget issue for a while (Hager 1996). Moreover, it can be argued (see Schultze 1995) that in any case the balanced budget Republican plan would not be effective in reducing public expenditure (but see Buchanan 1995 for a different opinion). However, the federal deficit remains a hot political issue and governing with huge deficits is now less popular than during the Reagan years. If expenditure were to decrease, then tax policy would be immensely eased: less spending implies less pressure on the revenue. But if public spending is not due to be significantly cut (even the draconian Republican plan might be unrealistic in its claim to limit public expenditure; see Schultze 1995) and if the federal deficit cannot be expanded easily, then revenue has to remain (at least) stable.

Political determination to balance the budget is not the only drive towards an increasing rigidity in public finances. With the conclusion of the GATT Uruguay Round and the launch of NAFTA, less revenue can be obtained through tariffs. In a world of trade treaties and liberalisation of commerce, governments cannot count on tariff revenue. Faced with this problem, a government can decide to raise tax rates or to levy new taxes. In a country in which presidents make such electoral promises as 'Read my lips – No more taxes' this strategy would be politically incendiary and ultimately suicidal. Indeed, both the Republican 'Contract with America' and the generous (for families) tax proposals put forward in December 1994 by President Clinton and by the Democratic Leader of the House, Richard Gephardt, indicate that tax-cut fever is still high in the United States.[7]

Transfer pricing policy

How can the revenue be expanded (or maintained at the current overall level even if tariff revenue is lost) without putting the popularity of the incumbent in jeopardy? And how can revenue expansion become a campaign issue able to bring votes to candidates competing for the presidency? There is a politically sensible answer to these apparent conundrums, provided that an attractive target (or scapegoat) is presented to the electorate. Riding a persistent wave of hostility against foreign-owned transnational corporations operating in the United States,[8] President Clinton did not show any hesitation in solving the tricky problem of making revenue increase electorally attractive by attacking these companies. Hence, during his electoral campaign of 1992 he promised to raise US$ 45 billion over four years from international business. Foreign companies found themselves in the doldrums, charged by the President of the United States with abuses of transfer pricing rules. In particular, foreign-owned transnational companies were accused of abusing the arm's-length method.

The essence of the method is clear and can be articulated as follows:[9] for tax purposes, related enterprises within a transnational company are treated as if they were separate businesses. Consequently, transnational companies must account for transactions (of goods and services) between their subsidiaries at transfer prices which ideally would be the same as those charged to unrelated companies. The aim of the arm's-length and other accounting methods is to allocate taxable income within different jurisdictions and to avoid international double taxation. The resort to criteria for assessing transfer pricing is fundamental in tax controversies between companies and tax officers. In fact, transnational corporations can manipulate transfer prices for tax purposes.[10] The arm's-length method provides criteria for tackling tax disputes when the revenue authorities of a given country reassess the income of an enterprise belonging to a transnational group.

The arm's-length method is extremely difficult to employ when sophisticated transactions occur: sometimes it is impossible to refer a cross-border transaction within a transnational group to a similar transaction between unrelated companies because the product which has been exchanged is unique. If there is not a market for a particular product it is impossible to establish the market value of a transaction. Moreover, the proliferation of transactions involving 'intangibles' and unique products makes the arm's-length method less realistic. Finally, by postulating that enterprises within a transnational group are separate entities, the method goes against the rationale of a transnational company. Indeed, a transnational company is established for the very purpose of dealing with a unitary business. Not surprisingly, then, the arm's-length method has been severely criticised (Bird 1988). Critics such as Bird attack the idea of treating the components of a transnational company (i.e. the parent and the subsidiaries) as separate entities. Accordingly, they raise criticisms over the arm's-length method, which is a manifestation of the separate entities approach to transnational companies.

However, the point is not that this principle has manifested serious drawbacks. All methods for allocating the income of a unitary business (i.e. the transnational business) between separate tax jurisdictions are based on conventions and are ultimately artificial and arbitrary, even though the degree of arbitrariness varies. The point to observe rather is the crucial connection between the arm's-length method and the international tax order. Within the international tax system, the arm's-length accounting method has a pivotal position as it is the typical rule upon which double tax treaties are signed. The OECD, which is the most influential policy forum for international tax issues, has contributed to a gradual institutionalisation of this method. In fact the club of OECD countries has chosen the arm's-length as 'the' method for regulating transfer pricing problems across nations. Accordingly, the OECD official documents and, most notably, the prestigious OECD model tax convention (OECD 1992) have affirmed the priority of this method. The method also has an important political implication: the reference to market transactions, which is the core of the arm's-length method, provides a 'natural' criterion for the allocation of taxable income between one jurisdiction and another. This 'natural' criterion, as noted by Picciotto (1993: 404) has the effect of de-politicising and technicising the process of inter-jurisdictional allocation. The harsh criticisms that surround the arm's-length method in the USA have had the opposite effect of revealing the political nature, and the consequent potential for conflict, of international allocation of taxable income.

The institutionalisation of the arm's-length method has proceeded through an extensive network of bi-lateral treaties which, albeit incomplete and subject to abuse (Picciotto 1992), is the most consolidated structure of the international tax order. The process of institutionalisation, however, has another, more subtle, component, concerning the ultimate meaning of transfer pricing regulation. The legislation on transfer pricing has been interpreted by revenue administrations throughout the world as a defensive resource against price manipulation by transnational companies. This has to do with asymmetry of information between the revenue and the company. The latter has full knowledge of its own international operations, whilst the former, in a world in which international exchange of information is far from efficient (Tanzi 1995), has to play 'defence', reacting to the most evident episodes of tax avoidance.

The United States, probably due to a comparatively more effective administration[11] and to a long-felt concern with international tax avoidance (Gordon 1981), is in the unique position to use transfer pricing legislation not just for 'defensive' goals, but also aggressively, as it were, with the aim of retrieving more money from transnational companies. This is precisely what has occurred. American states with endemic budgetary problems (California is a case in point) have found that transnational companies are an attractive target: by questioning the transfer pricing practices, additional revenue can become available. At the same time, the relationship between the government and the electorate can proceed smoothly: there is no need to raise taxes. All that is needed is a blame game consisting of accusing foreign transnational companies of exploiting the huge US market without paying their 'fair share'.

The US has not been the only country in the world to re-structure the meaning of transfer pricing policy from the 'defensive' to 'offensive'. Canada, Australia, Japan and the UK have tightened their policies. A study on a sample of 210 transnational corporations conducted by Ernst and Young in 1995 found that 49 per cent of the sample were being investigated and 83 per cent had been investigated in a transfer pricing dispute at some time. Roger White from KPMG Peat Marwick in London has defended his clients along the following line: 'Among my corporate clients there is a desire not to avoid tax by transfer pricing but just to get it right'.[12]

The United States is distinctive in that it launched the most serious threat to the arm's-length method. Two levels (i.e. federal and state) have to be considered in this respect. In the Congress the revolt against the arm's-length method is championed by Senator Byron Dorgan. His opinion is that the calculations required by the method produce an extra burden on public administration and permit manipulations which unduly subtract revenue. In his own words 'Our current system is a huge bureaucracy that can't keep up with sophisticated transnational companies that juggle income to calculate how much tax is owed in each state or country'.[13] Not only did Dorgan persuade the Senate to pass a non-binding resolution against the arm's-length method; more importantly still, he has successfully driven the Congress to postpone ratification of essential double tax treaties. The way for Senate ratification was cleared only in August 1995, when the US Treasury promised to overhaul the criteria of the international tax system. In fact, the Treasury has only promised to hold a conference for probing alternative methods to the arm's-length, but commentators were worried about this concession to Dorgan and his allies in the Senate.[14]

Given the federal structure of the American political system, it is interesting to investigate whether political pressure against the arm's-length method extends to the state level. At the federal level, as already mentioned, the American President and the US Treasury (see Grubert *et al.* 1993) criticise foreign transnational companies for abusing the arm's-length method, but at the state level things are even worse for these companies. A number of states, such as North Dakota, Montana and, most notably, California, have abandoned the arm's-length method and have consequently opted for the unitary method or formula apportionment. The essence of the method is to substitute complicated calculations and almost endless tax disputes for a formula for distributing taxable income in different jurisdictions. According to the unitary method, a company's taxable income in a given state is calculated by multiplying the total world-wide company's income by a factor based on some mix of property, payroll and sales located within that state. The unitary system is hence based on the idea of apportioning the taxable income by means of a formula which reflects the activity of the transnational company in a given jurisdiction. As such, it presents clear benefits (from the revenue's point of view) for taxing foreign firms.[15] Under the arm's-length method foreign transnational companies can disguise their profits in one way or another; by contrast, when unitary methods are applied, there is no way to conceal the fact that an extensive market presence (as measured by property, payroll, and sales) must be reflected in substantial taxable income within that jurisdiction.

The flip side of the coin, however, is that the unilateral resort to formula apportionment leads to double taxation because it conflicts with arm's-length rules used elsewhere. For corporations, the breaking up of consensus on the arm's-length rule is a major problem. The divergence between US rules and other countries' rules in transfer pricing means double taxation. Transfer pricing is therefore an area in which companies prefer homogeneous rules to a loose policy integration. This is the fundamental issue that has spawned the seventeen-year legal battle by the UK Barclays Bank against California's world-wide unitary method. The legal confrontation ended in 1994 with a decision of the Supreme Court in favour of Californian methods, but the political consequences were not trivial. Governments were involved in the row, and Kenneth Clarke, the UK Chancellor, went to the point of saying that 'the government has strongly opposed the imposition of worldwide unitary tax on UK-owned companies and supported Barclays throughout the litigation'.[16] Not only did governmental relations between the US and the UK deteriorate, but new pressure groups mushroomed during the battle, such as the Unitary Tax Campaign and the Organization for International Investment. Thus a cross-border fiscal problem has now become fully politicised and the idea of UK retaliatory measures against California was aired during the climax of the Barclays case.[17] It is easy to see how detrimental to international trade a UK retaliatory action would be. To conclude, criteria for settling tax disputes have to be consensually agreed by nations if such a thing as a tax order has to emerge. A breach of arm's-length criteria – even though justified in terms of economic analysis – inevitably produces international tax entropy.

Given the current state of uncertainty on transfer pricing assessments and the lengthy procedures of legal tax controversies, companies look towards advance pricing agreements, a relatively new policy tool (in the US and elsewhere). Through these agreements companies receive advance approval from tax authorities of the pricing methods employed. However, the diffusion of advance agreement does not proceed swiftly. By 1993 nine agreements only had been concluded and it seems that the number of companies able to get an agreement will remain limited in the foreseeable future.

In addition, serious concerns have been put forward concerning this procedure. Sven-Olof Lodin, an influential author in corporate tax policy,[18] has noticed that the advance pricing agreement procedure is based on secret negotiations outside court control, but the outcome of these negotiations ultimately affects later applicants and the remaining companies which do not have an agreement 'although they have had no opportunities to influence the guiding agreements or even gain an insight into what has been going on'. Besides, the procedure 'may have the effect that tax considerations rather than business reasons will influence transfer pricing principles as the advantages of getting an advance pricing agreement overshadow the advantage of basing transactions on purely business reasons' (Lodin 1995: 243).

This argument has some merit as the planning of transfer pricing is an ordinary aspect of business strategies. Accordingly, the 1979 OECD guidelines contained the following statement: 'The consideration of transfer pricing problems should not be confused with the consideration of problems of tax fraud or avoidance, even though transfer pricing policies may be used for such purposes' (OECD 1979). However useful they may be, particularly in terms of avoiding long tax conflicts, advance pricing agreements are still a limited solution to transfer pricing problems.

In conclusion, empirical evidence does not corroborate the hypothesis of American institutions being captured by business interests. Yet it might be observed that the reassertion of American institutions refers only to foreign companies. If this were true, the point argued in this chapter, i.e. that institutions have become more autonomous from private interests, would inevitably lose potential. This is not the case, however: Hufbauer (1992) indicates several aspects of US tax policy that penalise US-based transnational companies. Further, tax disputes on transfer pricing practices involve US-based transnational companies as well,[19] as typified by the fact that the legal row with the state of California included a similar case brought by Colgate-Palmolive. Whilst Barclays, backed by the UK government and business pressure groups, challenged unitary taxation on the ground of double taxation arguments, Colgate made the case that exempting foreign but not domestic companies from unitary taxation[20] would be unfair and distortionary. As mentioned above, the decision of the Supreme Court was not harmful to California.

Double tax treaty policy

The discussion of transfer pricing issues will be completed in the following section, in which recent American tax policies will be situated in the wider international context. At this point it must be observed that the US 'tough line' has gone beyond transfer prices. A second area of dynamism concerns double tax treaties. As mentioned earlier in this chapter, the network of nearly 2,000 tax treaties is one of the very few elements of structuration of the international tax system. After decades of steady development of the treaty network, earlier under the aegis of the League of Nations and later under the OECD guidelines, several treaties could now be ripped to shreds as the US aims at harsh revisions of certain treaties with the final objective of getting more income from international business operations. The clearest example of the new tax treaty policy is the revision of the United States–Dutch treaty. This time-honoured treaty (it was drafted in 1948) had become widely used for channelling investment from the Middle East, Hong Kong, and Latin America to the US via the Netherlands.

The fact is that the above mentioned countries do not have any tax treaties with the US, and hence income flowing from those countries to the US can be subject to double taxation. Instead, by using the Netherlands as an intermediary, investment in the US was entitled to benefit from favourable anti-double taxation clauses contained in the

United States–Dutch treaty. The route through the Netherlands therefore saved 20 per cent of taxes on investment from countries such as Hong Kong (Doggart 1993). This triangulation explains why the Netherlands appears each year as the third largest foreign investor in the US. Presumably with some reluctance, the Dutch tax negotiators, under the threat of termination of agreement,[21] were forced to revise the treaty and the current treaty (signed on 18 December 1992) contains rigorous anti-abuse provisions (described by Kaplan 1993 and Spector 1993).

The treaty policy of the US towards developing areas is also unique. For developing countries, the existence of tax treaties represents an important indication of fiscal stability and therefore a tax treaty encourages investment in these countries. The economic policy of developing countries is usually targeted towards foreign investment and not surprisingly tax incentives abound. However, the economic benefit from tax incentives can be lost when income is repatriated to the home country. This does not happen if a mechanism called tax-sparing is applied. Tax-sparing treats income from investment which has benefited from tax incentives (i.e. income which has not been taxed) as if it had been taxed. Accordingly, the headquarters of a transnational company is entitled to apply the foreign tax credit. Many countries have agreed to tax-sparing provisions, but not the US, and it is not likely that this position will change soon. This creates a fiscal disadvantage for US-based transnational companies which compete in developing countries with, say, Japanese or German transnational companies which benefit from tax-sparing credits (Hufbauer 1992: 132). It can be concluded that US treaty policy shows a relative independence from the interests of transnational companies.

Controlled foreign company policy

After transfer pricing and double tax treaties, a third thorny issue in international taxation concerns controlled foreign company legislation. In this case, again, the US administration has taken the lead in cracking down on abuse by companies established in low tax jurisdictions for the sole reason of avoiding the payment of taxes due by US residents. A number of leading countries have already enacted controlled foreign company provisions,[22] which follow, more or less, the same pattern: 'the undistributed income of a controlled foreign company is taxed in the hands of its domestic shareholders on a current basis' (Sandler 1994: 19). The introduction of controlled foreign company legislation in 1962, following proposals put forward by President Kennedy in 1961, was strongly opposed by US transnational corporations (Sandler 1994: 19). Their pressure succeeded in watering down the most radical suggestions, but could not thwart enactment of legislation. It is important to observe that the current US legislation in this area denies deferral, which instead is commonly employed elsewhere. Through deferral, payment of tax is delayed until profits of foreign companies are distributed to resident shareholders. US legislation aims at avoiding the possibility that payment of taxes could be continuously postponed through systematic use of deferral rules. Accordingly, US legislation employs the concept of deemed distribution: even though profits are not distributed, under certain parameters (which indicate the possibility that the foreign company is nothing but a tax shield used by US residents) revenue authorities 'deem' that the profits constitute shareholders' taxable income.

Another characteristic of recent US tax policy is the idea of disregarding intermediate entities when they are judged to be mere conduits for tax avoidance. This problem is associated with the previously mentioned abuse of tax treaties. The revision of the US–Dutch treaty did in fact have the aim of cracking down on conduit companies employed for 'treaty shopping' (Kaplan 1993). It should also be noted that the US has considered the interaction of controlled foreign company legislation and double tax treaties in a very drastic manner. Whilst countries agree to Article 1 of the OECD model convention (1992) which stipulates that tax treaties cover residents of both countries, the US has always held the view that treaties are only for the benefit of non-resident aliens.[23] Consequently, the US entered a reservation on Article 1 of the model convention. The implication is that the US holds the right to tax its residents as if the treaty did not exist.

To sum up then, in the three tax policy areas under examination (i.e. transfer pricing, double tax treaties, and controlled foreign company legislation) electoral incentives and the political economy of budgetary choices have enabled American institutions to curb the political pressure of corporations, thus confirming the assertion of diffuse interests brought about by the 1986 tax reform. This empirical result is consistent with new research on public policies and shows a political system which is still able to cope with powerful interests. Yet an important question arises: can domestic tax policies be assessed without a consideration of their international impacts?

INTERNATIONAL TAXATION: ENTROPY OR INSTITUTIONALISATION?

In this section three arguments are presented and subsequently challenged: first, US transfer pricing policy renders the institutionalisation of principles and policy fora more problematic. Second, the consequence of aggressive tax policies – not necessarily US tax policy – against foreign companies transforms tax policy into a segment of trade policy, but this happens in a world in which there are no institutions with a remit to tackle the trade implications of international taxation. Therefore tax issues become more intractable. Third, the network of bi-lateral treaties caves in as a consequence of the US effort (in itself extremely laudable) to challenge and possibly stop abuse of tax treaties.

As will appear clear, it is contended here that these three arguments shed light on recent events – and therefore are useful – but fail to consider the essence of institutionalisation. The structural politics of creating order (i.e. institutionalisation) is inherently conflictual. Innovation and 'entrepreneurial projects' (DiMaggio 1988; Powell and DiMaggio 1991) in international taxation, given the low institutionalisation of this policy domain, originate conflict precisely because imposing order upon a turbulent international tax world is all about using and creating power. There are winners and losers in any process of institutionalisation and whilst some actors actively promote their project for the future tax world, others will resist. The current situation of international taxation is so dynamic that it is impossible to draw neat conclusions. Both entropy and the emergence of a still fragile consensus are simultaneously present in different tax issues. Whatever the conclusion may be, in the first instance attention must be drawn to empirical evidence.

The destabilisation of international consensus: the transfer pricing row

In the previous section the various political forces leading to a tougher line on transfer pricing in the US were presented. There is evident political pressure on the Treasury to abandon or at least challenge the arm's-length principle. The formulary tax constituency (which advocates world-wide taxation with formulary apportionment) is small but extremely combative. Political pressure for suppressing transfer pricing abuse does not come from isolated, though pugnacious, Senators or just from California. Indeed, an amendment to Section 482 of the Internal Revenue Code voted by the Congress in 1986 (known amongst the pundits as the 'commensurate with income' standard) obliged the US Treasury to draft new proposals. The Treasury, caught between the Scylla of some belligerent Senator (not to mention the daring promises made by President Clinton during his electoral campaign) and the Charybdis of a mandate from the Congress, has decided to go down the very sensible road of condemning the formulary approach (Samuels 1995). At the same time, the Treasury issued no less than three waves of regulations: the 1992 proposed regulations, the 1993 temporary regulations and eventually the 1994 final regulations.

It is impossible to understand these hectic movements without taking into account both the substantive content of the proposals and the international reaction to them. As mentioned, the Treasury did not espouse the cause of formulary taxation, but nevertheless the 1992 proposed regulations struck a lethal blow to the arm's-length principle. At least, this is what was perceived by some commentators, as shown below. The bone of the contention at that time was the appearance in the proposed regulation of the 'comparable profits interval' method. The latter, unlike the arm's-length method, is not based on transactions: this means the revenue authorities can make adjustments of transfer prices without looking at specific transactions but considering overall profit indicators of the controlled company and comparing them with the profit indicators of comparable companies. To some commentators, for example the Baker & McKenzie North American Tax Practice Group, it appeared that the comparable profits interval method had became '*the* most important method, as it had a role both as a primary pricing method and as a required check on most of the other methods' (1994: 546, emphasis in original).

The reactions to the 1992 proposed regulations were – as noted in the Baker & McKenzie briefing report (1994: 547) – 'vociferous and often critical'. Lodin stated that the choice of a profit method 'represents a major deviation from the internationally accepted concept of the arm's-length principle, which moreover will be impossible to apply in a wider international context' (Lodin 1995: 240). International concern became so high as to force the OECD to set up a special task force composed of nine member countries. The remit of the task force was to examine in a very thorough manner the content of the proposed regulations.

The subsequent document of the US Treasury (the 1993 temporary regulations) was influenced by this climate of international concern. The report issued by the OECD task force recommended several amendments to the US proposals. The 1993 temporary regulations eliminated part of the emphasis on profit methods,[24] but worries remained, and the OECD task force had to issue a second report in 1993 in which further amendments were suggested (OECD 1993). Another contentious matter was represented by the 1993 proposed penalty regulations, which included strict provisions in terms of the documentation indispensable in order to escape from 20 per cent to 40 per cent tax penalties. Finally, the 1994 final regulations were issued by the Treasury. These regulations reaffirm the arm's-length as a standard rather than as a method. Accordingly, more than one method becomes acceptable. The best method is the one that, given certain facts and circumstances, comes closer to arm's-length results. Profit methods are not given priority; yet they are still considered valid in cases of last resort.

A director of a thriller film could not have set a better scene for the presentation of the 1994 draft regulations. Suspense was administered in the right doses and the effect was worthy of a great show. On 28 June 1994 the OECD presented the draft of its new guidelines on transfer pricing in which the use of profit methods was considered appropriate when data did not exist or was so poor as to flaw transaction methods. Furthermore, the OECD openly invited submissions: this unusual choice of consultation was presumably dictated by the anticipation of angry reactions. To put it bluntly, the OECD, knowing that the material was really 'hot stuff', tried to cover its back by presenting to every affected interest the possibility of having a say through the consultative procedure.

The tax world had just a few days to swallow the OECD argument when the US Treasury unveiled its final regulations in July 1994. Not unlike a good movie in which different stories converge towards the principal scene of the film, influential OECD officers hastened to affirm that the US regulations 'are consistent with the spirit – and in some cases use languages which are strikingly similar to the OECD draft guidelines' (Hay, Horner, and Owens 1994: 425). In turn, Leslie B. Samuels, assistant secretary for tax policy at the US Treasury, praised the OECD 'for making an extremely important contribution to tax administration'. He went on to say:

> This is why revised OECD guidelines are so important. They represent broad acceptance by all our major trading partners of the reality that the traditional methods are appropriate when the data to apply them is adequate. But the traditional methods must be supplemented by new methods when the data is not adequate.
>
> (Samuels 1995: 66)

For such a smooth and discreet world as the tax world is (or used to be) it was quite astonishing to read the following expressions in the editorial of a sober professional journal – *Intertax*:[25]

> It is an open secret that this procedure (i.e. submitting guidelines in a draft form) on the part of the OECD gave way to American pressure. The USA was in a hurry because it wanted to obtain the blessing of the OECD for its highly problematical regulations on transfer pricing, which were being revised at the same time as the OECD was conducting its deliberations. Thus we already hear from official American sources that the new American regulations have been endorsed by the OECD, and that the latter's guidelines were in line with the regulations of the US. . . . Instead of standing by valuations which have always been accepted in the past, the OECD is now declaring these profit approaches to be methods under the arm's length standard, though admittedly with a great many ifs and buts. This is as erroneous as it is dangerous.
>
> (Ritter 1994: 312)

Unfortunately the tax scene is not as exciting as a good movie and there is no intriguing plot to be discovered. Truly, it is an 'open secret' that the US tax authority and the OECD worked together.[26] The US officers were aware of the potentially destabilising impact of their ideas and hence they attempted to minimise the divergence between the US and the OECD. The latter, which had independently decided to revise its guidelines on transfer pricing, could not disregard the fact that the US is a tremendously important part of the tax system: therefore the OECD policy process had to convey at least part of the US concerns. All in all, the tax world is interdependent and co-existence has to be pursued under any circumstances. Moreover, the formulary tax constituency had to be marginalised in order to avoid more serious dangers. Indeed, an international tax official from the Treasury explicitly warned businesses that, had the new OECD guidelines been rejected by the US, double taxation caused by 'inconsistent approaches' to transfer pricing would have been increased.[27]

Notwithstanding this search for a compromise, a row was not averted. During 1995 European governments (France and Germany being the most active countries), professional associations (such as the Fédération des Experts Comptables Europeénns (FEE) 1995), and pressure groups (for example, the International Chamber of Commerce (ICC) 1995) insisted on the same point: profit methods could not be considered – as the OECD draft guidelines maintained – arm's-length methods. The outcome of the row is the current situation in which disagreement persists even though an open war has been prevented. A compromise was reached – and this is an important element of stabilisation – but German officials were still unhappy with some parts of the 1995 OECD guidelines and Mr Jim Marshall, head of the KPMG European transfer pricing network, stated: 'This gives the US an umbrella under which it can work. Behind the consensus the transfer pricing battle will go on – but it has avoided a transfer pricing war'.[28] The final guidelines issued by the OECD in July 1995 contain an extremely qualified acceptance of profit methods: indeed they are not banned, but they have to be based on transactions and used only as a last resort. The idea is that profits arising from controlled transactions are compared to profits arising from comparable transactions between independent entities. The final guidelines reject the possibility of comparing overall profit indicators: instead of profits with profits, transactions are compared with their respective profits (Becker 1995: 387; OECD 1995).

The trade implications of tax policy

Turning now to the interaction between trade and taxation, it has already been noted (Owens 1993) that tax policy is part of trade policy. What is new is the degree of tension present in the relations between trade partners. Tax authorities have become more aggressive in their transfer pricing adjustments. In 1994 Nissan was compelled to agree to a considerable refund to the US authority and the following year Japanese tax authorities imposed an almost identical adjustment on Coca-Cola. Commentators did not hesitate to link the two events and indicated that tax had become an issue of the wider trade dispute between the US and Japan (Otsuka 1994). Similar cases are not restricted to US transnational companies operating in Japan: Roche and Ciba-Geigy from Switzerland, and Hoechst from Germany have faced similar difficulties in Japan. The nub of the problem is not US behaviour, but a lack of institutionalisation. Tax policy is trade policy; yet there is not a policy forum or an institution in which trade disputes involving the retaliatory use of transfer pricing policy can be settled. Trade has become global trade but first the General Agreement on Tariffs and Trade and recently the World Trade Organisation have assisted the internationalisation of trade. Taxation has become international taxation but this new dimension is not covered by appropriate fora or organisations.[29]

Tax treaties under pressure

Finally, the treaty network is put under strain in the current tax world. Not only is the treaty network incomplete and subject to abuse (Picciotto 1992), but two novel elements of the tax scene put in jeopardy the stability of the network. First, the US threatened existing tax treaties: either abused treaties were revised, or the US was prepared to terminate them, or to override with national legislation certain clauses subject to abuse. Admittedly, the position of the US is quite correct: it might be better not to have a double tax treaty than to have a treaty which is systematically abused. For the tax payer, however, a world with fewer tax treaties is inevitably a world with more double taxation. An efficient scenario is one in which the US threat generates treaty revisions that close the door to tax avoidance and at the same time protect the diligent tax payer against double taxation. Empirical evidence points towards this direction: if the US and the Netherlands were able to revise one of the most controversial treaties, perhaps other less controversial treaties can be revised in the near future.

Unfortunately, even in this optimistic (though not unrealistic) scenario the treaty network would not be secure. In fact controlled foreign company legislation is inherently incompatible with tax treaties (Sandler 1994). This legislation is perfectly sensible from the point of view of domestic tax policy as it chases and eradicates tax avoidance and tax evasion. But in an international context controlled foreign company legislation implies that a state taxes the profit of a company which is resident in another state, for example imputing all profits (distributed or not) to a resident shareholder. This is literally in contrast with the provisions of the OECD model conventions (OECD 1992) which are enshrined in tax treaties. For this reason Sandler (1994), concluding his acute analysis of controlled foreign company legislation, asserts that this legislation represents tax treaty overriding. A recent OECD study on controlled foreign company regimes (OECD 1996b) provides a more benign interpretation of this policy instrument. It should also be observed that the commentary to the OECD model tax treaty has been modified in order to minimise the clash between tax treaties and controlled foreign company legislation. Yet the problem remains that controlled foreign company regimes entail high costs in terms of administration, compliance, and, more generally, uncertainty and complexity, as the OECD itself acknowledges:

> In many of the countries concerned, the provisions dealing with controlled foreign companies in the income tax legislation are probably the most complex within an already very complex revenue

> code. Certain countries, such as France, have very broadly worded provisions which leave much to uncertainty.
>
> (OECD 1996b: 21).

Another problem with controlled foreign company legislation is that its implementation would need, ideally, a multi-lateral, or, at least, bi-lateral approach to information gathering. But, of course, countries targeted by controlled foreign company provisions (e.g. tax havens) more often than not do not have any agreement with countries imposing this type of legislation. The OECD concludes on this issue that

> While progress is being made in the area of international cooperation, its impact on the ability of a country to effectively enforce its controlled foreign company measures is extremely limited, primarily due to the lack of available information from target territories.
>
> (OECD 1996b: 91)

Accordingly, the existence of controlled foreign company regimes increases the demand for policy co-operation and for co-ordination across different policy instruments (i.e. tax treaties and controlled foreign company legislation). To anticipate a point to be developed below, it can be argued that there is an asymmetry between the demand and the supply for institutionalisation.

CONCLUDING REMARKS: INTERNATIONAL TAXATION IN SEARCH OF INSTITUTIONALISATION

This chapter has considered empirical evidence of the reassertion of institutions against business interests in tax policy. The impact of domestic tax policies on the tax order, however, cannot be considered efficient. Choices which, at the domestic level, are politically rational, and quite often ethical and sensible, increase the overall level of entropy in the international tax order. Time-honoured principles have been destabilised, respectable international organisations have been accused of being the instrument of one state, and companies have been dragged into a trade war that uses direct taxes as a new weapon.

It is argued here that the cause of entropy is *not* American tax policy *per se*. As stated, American tax policy is legitimate and somewhat prudent: the formulary tax constituency has been marginalised, at least for the time being. Moreover, it could be argued that the US is the only country that has decided to take action against the most evident cases of tax avoidance: controlled foreign company legislation, tax treaty revision, and qualified use of profit methods are all examples of innovation. The understanding of the US role becomes clearer if the whole market for institutionalisation is taken into account. It is to this question that we now turn.

The real problem is that the market for institutionalisation is profoundly asymmetric and in this highly imperfect market policy innovation is inherently conflictual. How can demand and supply for institutionalisation be assessed? Let us begin with the demand. The latter has to do with private actors, i.e. firms and individuals. It could be argued that firms prefer tax avoidance and unbridled tax competition to the creation of an international tax order. Accordingly, in this interpretation there would be no demand for order and stability on the part of private actors. However, it is difficult to see how firms could be better off in a tax world in which controlled foreign company legislation chases the profits of foreign-owned companies; tax treaties, which are supposed to mitigate double taxation, are put in jeopardy; and revenue authorities' rules for assessing transfer pricing diverge, thus creating double taxation of corporate income, until finally trade war becomes tax war. Current developments in international taxation originate uncertainty. As shown by economic theory (Heiner 1983), radical uncertainty leads to an increased demand for rules, stability and order, not to a demand for entropy.

The demand for institutionalisation, fuelled by increased radical uncertainty, does not encounter an adequate supply of institutionalisation in the tax world. The uncertainty about 'what can be done' is a radical form of uncertainty as it implies the question 'which institutions for which problems?' And in fact *formal institutions* capable of governing international taxation have not as yet emerged, with the partial exception of the OECD, whose status as neutral tax policy forum was questioned during the transfer pricing controversy. However, the OECD provided the forum in which the 1995 guidelines on transfer pricing were agreed upon. The OECD has shown that it can still play the role of policy broker. In 1994 its credibility was questioned, but during the following year the OECD was able to forge a compromise. Thanks to the OECD, the US revised the initial radical proposals on transfer pricing. The OECD itself was able to learn from the angry reactions to the 1994 OECD draft guidelines and succeeded in producing a final text that has been agreed. In conclusion, the OECD can still manage to co-ordinate the process. This does not mean that the OECD is an agenda-setter: a process co-ordinator plays the limited role of guarding the process and securing a final outcome. For the time being, states have not withdrawn their legitimacy in the

OECD: the transfer pricing row reached a climax in 1994, when it seemed that legitimacy was to be questioned, but the deal struck in 1995 confirmed that the policy forum provided by the OECD still works. However, these events also show how difficult it is to generate consensus in international taxation. The cost of producing consensus (in terms of OECD legitimacy and concessions from member states) has dramatically increased in the 1990s and the compromise reached in 1995 is fragile, given that commentators have argued that fundamental differences remain between the US and the rest of the world.

In conclusion, the degree of institutionalisation provided by formal institutions is relatively low and extremely difficult to achieve. However, another notion of institutionalisation, based on *meaning* rather than formal institutions (March and Olsen 1989; 1995), needs to be assessed. If institutions are examined in this respect, the picture does not improve much. Controversies surrounding fundamental principles of international taxation (i.e. the residence principle, world-wide taxation, and the taxation of capital income as part of progressive taxation of personal income) are symptoms of a de-structuration of meaning. The transfer pricing controversy discussed here attests that the foundations of international taxation are shaky. Time-honoured principles are threatened and new principles (e.g. the formulary approach) are ostensibly opposed by too many actors to qualify as a realistic alternative for the foreseeable future.

The crisis of the arm's-length principle is crucial in this scenario. As shown by new institutionalism, institutionalisation consists of taken-for-granted rules and 'ways of doing things' which appear normal and natural to participants in political life.[30] In the past, the arm's-length principle performed the function of 'framing' inter-jurisdictional problems of transfer pricing as technical problems (Picciotto 1993). The reference of the principle to 'natural' market mechanisms was essential in this respect. The current difficulties of the arm's-length method have shown the political dimension of inter-jurisdictional allocation of taxable income, which can no longer be considered a technical and de-politicised affair.

At this point an important question has to be raised: can institutional entrepreneurs fill the gap between supply and demand in the 'market for institutionalisation'? The supply of stability and order, in fact, can be guaranteed by institutional entrepreneurs, provided that their institutional projects satisfy the demand of institutions by providing rules, norms, cognitive maps, and shared meanings (DiMaggio 1988). However, the politics of tax institutionalisation explains why, when institutional entrepreneurs appear, conflict, consensus and power are inevitably blended. Institutionalisation requires the mobilisation of power resources and, at the same time, institutionalisation itself is a source of power. It is through institutionalisation that an institutional entrepreneur influences the models which actors employ for interpreting their social role and for defining their interests.

Indeed, the emergence of policy innovation on the part of the US can be understood as a project of institutionalisation. Transfer pricing policy and treaty policy seem to sustain this interpretation. To begin with transfer pricing, the 1979 OECD guidelines were no longer up to the job: the proliferation of intangible resources and the advent of the information society had made a substantial revision of rules and principles necessary. In the 'real world' the application of the arm's-length principle had become increasingly problematic and revenue assessors were in search of new ways of coping with new products, new industries and new dilemmas. In this scenario, the United States took the leadership in innovation. Although aggressive, American ideas on transfer pricing have stimulated a revision of the OECD rules. The fact that a compromise was eventually struck with the 1995 OECD guidelines is proof that international order and consensus – although more fragile than in the past – have been achieved.

As far as treaty policy is concerned, the network of bi-lateral treaties is under stress, but is not withering away. Perhaps it can be argued that the US is playing the role of institutional entrepreneur by stimulating a new generation of tax treaties, which will be more efficient in dealing with tax treaty abuse. The signature of a new treaty between countries with such strong structural divergencies as the US and the Netherlands provides empirical evidence that American policy innovation is producing some results, and not mere havoc in the tax world.

The current scenario of international taxation is characterised by ambiguities: on the one hand, US policy has dissipated entropy and destabilised the scene. On the other, there was an objective need to revise rules and principles of international taxation. Only in the future will it become clear whether order or entropy will prevail. For the time being, it can be said that the cost of producing and generating consensus has increased and that the overall institutionalisation of international tax policy remains poor. Conflictual institutionalisation and power will be the fundamental ingredient of future developments. Blaming the US for attempting to increase its power through the institutionalisation of new principles is a contradiction in terms. The process of institutionalisation *is* a process in which power is created and employed. This is why, in conclusion, the creation of an international tax order is a political process.

Part III

Conclusions and perspectives

9 Conclusion

Knowledge, institutions and policy change

> The reason for this lack of action on the part of the national [tax] authorities may owe more to the uncertainty and disagreement among experts and policymakers on what to do than to political inertia, although the latter undoubtedly has played a role.
>
> (Tanzi 1995: 66)

In this chapter the main results of the research are discussed in light of their theoretical implications. This book draws upon three different literatures which deal with the role of knowledge in the policy process, the politics of tax reform, and European public policy. The three literatures are usually considered as distinct. However, the idea of considering them jointly has revealed potential for generating empirically testable hypotheses on the politics of international corporate tax policy. The hypotheses, discussed in detail in the previous chapters, relate to the explanation of policy change, the characteristics of European direct corporate tax policy, and the Europeanisation of domestic tax policy.

The question to be explored now is the following: given the theoretical framework and the empirical results of this research, is there any theoretical innovation which stems from our analysis? It is true that the policy processes considered here (i.e. the European direct corporate tax policy process and the corporate tax policy processes in Italy and the UK) do not allow for a statistical generalisation of a 'universe' of policies: it is not possible to generalise case studies in this way. However, case studies are particularly fertile for developing theoretical knowledge. In this respect an argument can be made for the case study as a method of 'theoretical generalisation' (Yin 1994). Is it then possible to suggest theoretical implications that expand the understanding of public policy, with the aim of building up cumulative knowledge in political science? With this question in mind we now turn to three issues: the cognitive structure of public policy, the regulative dimension of European tax harmonisation, and the problematic institutionalisation of international tax policy.

THE COGNITIVE DYNAMICS OF PUBLIC POLICY

Empirical research is particularly suitable for tackling controversies over the role of knowledge in the explanation of policy change. Indeed, whilst at the more abstract level the dimensions of power and knowledge can be treated as distinct, this distinction does not hold at the empirical level. It is not an easy task to show that a particular policy choice observed in the real world has been caused by cognitive dynamics, and not by power variables (Goldstein 1993; Jacobsen 1995).

A closer examination of the literature on the political role of knowledge provides insights for elaborating upon this point. As shown in Chapter 2, the main thrust of this literature is to pin down the inadequacies of policy change models that are based exclusively on power dynamics. The theoretical attack on these models proceeds along two alternative tracks. Authors such as P. Haas (1992) take a radical position in the debate and argue that, under conditions of uncertainty, interests (for example, state interests on a given policy agenda) cannot be defined without interpretative paradigms. The latter provide causal assumptions, prescriptions, and ultimately make sense of a complex reality, thus enabling action. Knowledge – not power – covers the bridge between actors, their interests, and action. Actors' preferences are shaped and moulded by knowledge.

The second route is less radical and is epitomised by authors such as Goldstein. Indeed, she concedes that interests can be defined by actors with a certain precision. However, given that a set of preferences is normally compatible with more than one policy choice, only the cognitive dimension can cover the bridge between the given set of preferences in a policy area and the particular choice that is observed. Ideas and policy paradigms are 'lenses' which focus interests upon a particular choice. Or, to use another metaphor introduced by Goldstein, ideas provide 'road maps' that direct interests along a particular track when more tracks are available for the satisfaction of actors' preferences.

Given these two positions, our theoretical argument revolves around an intermediate position and can be articulated in two propositions. First, knowledge and power are hardly distinguishable in empirical analysis (see Chapter 2, and D. Stone 1996: 113), so much so that we are able to turn to the metaphor of Yin and Yang for describing these two poles, which are theoretically distinct but indispensable one to the other in political action. Second, it can be argued that the crucial point is explaining knowledge transmission in the policy process. Instead of asking what comes first (knowledge or power), it is more useful to understand when, how, and why knowledge is transmitted into policy choices. Given this intermediate position, the advocacy coalition approach developed by Sabatier and Jenkins-Smith (1993) comes in handy. To begin with, the approach draws attention to a fundamental element of structuration, i.e. coalitions which amalgamate interests, ideas, and knowledge. Second, the approach provides a series of causal propositions that can be tested empirically. However, the advocacy coalition approach is not fully satisfactory when it explains non-incremental change as a consequence of environmental change. Policy change, in fact, is ultimately explained exogenously by Sabatier and Jenkins-Smith. In other words, when the policy environment changes, the resources available to actors are modified and this triggers different games between one coalition and another. However, the EU policy change examined in Chapter 6 suggests a more in-depth consideration of endogenous elements of policy change.

It is necessary to clarify this proposition by analysing the causal structure of policy change models and in particular the choice of independent and dependent variables. Confining our attention to policy change models in which knowledge plays a role, the individuation of independent variables relies ultimately on two strategies. The point to be emphasised here is that in both strategies the explanation of policy change has to do with elements that are exogenous to actors directly involved in the system of interaction that originates policy. It is precisely in this sense that a drive towards exogeneity can be detected and criticised.

But what are the above mentioned two strategies? Put succinctly, and perhaps at the cost of over-simplification, the former strategy is typical of the advocacy coalition approach, whilst the other strategy pertains to a second class of models. It has already been shown that for Sabatier and Jenkins-Smith coalitions alternate in their control of policy areas when environmental changes alter the availability and the value of resources controlled by different actors. The search for independent variables leans therefore towards the policy environment. A different strategy is pursued by other authors who seek independent variables within the cognitive domain of policy. The following are examples. Weiss (1979) posits that gradual enlightenment produced by the development of social sciences originates the diffusion of new policy paradigms. This, in the long term, causes non-incremental change. Goldstein (1993) and P. Hall (1989) argue that policy paradigms and their institutionalisation activate change. Finally, P. Haas (1992) analyses epistemic communities as the primary force in international policy co-ordination.

What is wrong with these strategies? The crucial flaw appears to be the exclusion of endogenous elements. More precisely, both strategies overlook how the system of actors' interaction can in itself produce policy change. The core of the two strategies, however nuanced and multi-faceted they may be, is contained in the proposition that more often (or almost invariably) variables that are exogenous to the system of interaction produce non-incremental policy change. It is this proposition that can be challenged, using the empirical evidence presented in this study.

EU tax policy shows that the 'exogenous view' of policy change is correct, but it should be complemented by the consideration of how learning *within* the policy process produces policy change. Surely, the Single European Act and the '1992 initiative' modified the resources available to actors involved in the EU direct tax policy process; not so much in terms of formal legal procedures (EU taxation remained subject to unanimity voting) but, more fundamentally, in terms of the drive towards the establishment of the single market. Hence environment has played an important role in forging the political context in which tax proposals became plausible and necessary. In this sense the insights provided by the advocacy coalition framework are of invaluable help. Moreover, policy change was facilitated by the emergence of an embryonic epistemic community of international taxation. The policy discourse on tax neutrality put forward by this epistemic community brought about a new interpretative paradigm that was employed by the Commission, member states, and pressure groups. Gradual enlightenment (more precisely, the paradigm of tax neutrality) closed the gap between the 'inter-governmental' coalition – centred upon member states – and the 'supra-national' coalition, led by the Commission. Therefore it was concluded (in Chapter 6) that the exogenous development of an embryonic epistemic community was a necessary pre-condition of policy change.

Nevertheless, however important policy environment and epistemic communities might have been, policy change in EU direct corporate taxation occurred only when actors in the 'supra-national' coalition (most crucially, the Commission) became capable of reflecting critically upon their interpretative paradigm, and were able to exploit the favourable environmental change produced by the '1992 initiative'[1] thanks to the action of purposeful policy entrepreneurs (Kingdon 1984) such as Commissioner Madame Scrivener, and actively pursued a different representation of policy problems, i.e. engaged in a problem re-definition exercise. Therefore learning and frame reflection are endogenous elements that have to be carefully considered in the explanation of policy change. Models based on social interaction (Lindblom 1990) and frames (Schön and Rein 1994) have potential in locating the sources of change. Actors involved in policy controversies can and sometimes do discover innovation directly, via a learning process. A conclusion can be drawn at this point. In order to gain explanatory power, knowledge-based explanations of policy change must include both exogenous and endogenous elements. Rather than contrasting endogenous elements of the policy process with the exogenous elements in which contingent choices are entrenched, it is useful to stress the interaction between the two. The epistemic community approach and the advocacy coalition model shed light on important pre-conditions of policy change, but they tend to underestimate the importance of learning and frame reflection within the policy process: hence the necessity to include endogenous elements in the explanation of policy change.

This does not necessarily mean that the literature on economic policy paradigms or the study of epistemic communities should be neglected. Instead, the argument outlined here leads towards the rejection of a view implicit in these threads of research, i.e. the 'anthropomorphic' view of knowledge. Or, better, it is the tendency to define knowledge in relation to certain actors (e.g. experts, consultants, academics or even the 'normal' discourse in social sciences, in the Kuhnian sense) that ought to be challenged. To posit a one to one correspondence between the political role of knowledge and the participation of specific actors to the policy process is not fruitful. True, it is thanks to this correspondence that previously neglected actors have been discovered by the policy sciences (epistemic communities being a case in point). Nevertheless, the 'knowledge perspective' on the policy process cannot be reduced to the insertion of one or more actors into analytical models used by political scientists. On the contrary, *it can be argued that knowledge has less to do with specific actors than with the structure in which actors act.*[2] Actors operate in the knowledge structure of the policy process, taking for granted certain rules and norms and using shared paradigms. At the same time, through their actions actors modify the cognitive resources available in the policy process.

There is a crucial similarity between the power structure and the knowledge structure of the policy process. The power structure is composed of formal institutions, power relations, decision rules, constraints and opportunities related to asymmetrical opportunities to influence behaviour. The institutionalised elements of the power structure are taken for granted by actors involved in the policy process, but policy evolution itself can bring about a modification of structure. By the same token, the cognitive structure of the policy process provides interpretation, representations of political events, learning opportunities and 'lenses' that give focus to interests and behavioural codes. In turn, learning can be a powerful catalyst for a modification of the cognitive structure and, ultimately, for policy change. The cognitive structure contains professional knowledge produced by the social sciences, but it also includes interactive knowledge, i.e. knowledge one actor has about other actors' strategies. Knowledge is produced – not only reproduced – through the interaction in the policy process. This is the deeper meaning of knowledge endogeneity in the policy process. More importantly still, this explains why preferences are not exogenous in political analysis. Preferences are defined and modified through social interaction.

The relationship between agency and structure is dialectic. At a given moment in time, actors are literally immersed in the cognitive structure, but the latter comes to life only through actors' behaviour. Put differently, structure has to be enacted and interpreted (Giddens 1984; Wendt 1987: 359). This has important implications. Indeed the cognitive component of public policy is reproduced and institutionalised (i.e. acquires stability and impacts on public policy) only if it is reproduced by policy-makers who, say, conform to shared interpretative paradigms, stick to a common view of political, social and economic realities, and perceive the same meaning attached to action. But it is exactly through action that actors contribute to the development of the cognitive structure, for example by modifying an interpretation, or, alternatively, by discovering previously unforeseen meanings of public policy. The cognitive structure is constant only in a static perspective. This is tantamount to saying that in a given moment the cognitive structure is taken for granted by actors because it is institutionalised. However, it becomes variable when the analysis shifts from the static mode to a dynamic perspective. In a given moment the institutionalisation of knowledge has constitutive value in respect to action as it provides meaning attached to action. But 'the individual (unlike the behaviourist's rats) shapes the maze while running it' (Thompson, Ellis and Wildavsky 1990: 22).

Giddens' notion of 'duality of structure' is extremely useful here (Giddens 1984). Structure is both the medium and the unintended outcome of social practices, Giddens asserts. Actors draw on elements of the structure (e.g. rules or resources)[3] in the enactment of social practices, and by using these elements simultaneously contribute to the reproduction of structure. Social structures do not exist independently of agents, but require agents in order to be reproduced. As Wendt, drawing upon Bhaskar and Giddens, has put it,

> social structures have an inherently *discursive* dimension in the sense that they are inseparable from the reasons and self-understandings that agents bring to their actions. . . . Social structures are ontologically dependent upon and therefore constituted by the practices and self-understandings of agents.
>
> (Wendt 1987: 359, emphasis in original)

Accordingly, at each point of the process of structural reproduction, actors have potential for change. These notes on structure and agency chime with the argument presented above about the necessity to integrate endogenous and exogenous elements. In conclusion, it is not by isolating and contrasting exogenous structures and endogenous agency, but by looking at their interaction, that knowledge-based explanations of policy change gain theoretical leverage.

THE REGULATIVE DIMENSION OF EU TAX HARMONISATION

The analysis of policy change can be carried out by taking into consideration another dimension of the research, i.e. European public policy. The basic question can be articulated as follows: is the policy approach useful for understanding the policy under examination here? What can be discovered through this approach that could not have been discovered by other 'mainstream' approaches, such as neo-functionalism, or liberal inter-governmentalism, or realism?

It has been argued already that the most valuable insight provided by the application of the policy approach is the examination of the cognitive dynamics of the European corporate tax policy process. Similarly to what has been observed in relation to agency and structure, it is more useful to combine the insights provided by the policy approach with other theoretical approaches to European integration rather than highlighting stark contrast. Inter-governmental approaches to European integration (Moravcsik 1991; 1993) can explain without difficulty the long period of inaction in European direct corporate tax policy. Why should states agree to lose revenue for mitigating double taxation? Why should they delegate power to the Commission in a policy which is a bastion of statehood? When, however, the limits to policy integration highlighted by inter-governmentalist approaches are combined with a consideration of the cognitive dimension of public policy the interpretative model can explain both inertia *and* policy change and hence has more theoretical potential.

The necessity to integrate the insights provided by knowledge-based explanations of policy change with the inter-governmentalist emphasis on the constraints on delegation of power becomes clear if the question of 'what is learnt' is raised. What is the object of the learning exercise in which the 'supra-national' coalition was engaged in the second half of the 1980s? The previous examination of frame reflection and more generally of endogenous policy change has shown that learning processes enabled actors to 'discover' the web of inter-governmental relationships and consequently to modify their frames of reference, thus producing policy change. The consideration of agency – in other words – has shed light on how the 'supra-national' coalition guided by the Commission 'learned' the structural power of member states in European taxation and the peculiarities of this regulatory policy. At the end of the 1980s, after two decades of elusive attempts to produce a European corporate tax system, the Commission learned that direct tax harmonisation was deeply entrenched in the symbolic power of direct taxation (i.e. the link between taxation and representation) and in revenue authorities' institutional mission of guarding the revenue base. In this sense, agents learned about the deep structure of the policy game. At that moment, the supra-national coalition embraced a new frame, withdrew the old proposal, and achieved limited but significant success, thus generating change in an inertial process. The tough constraint of inter-governmental relations was relaxed, at least in the 1990 'policy window' in which three corporate tax measures were agreed upon by the Council.

As for the future, the next chapter will examine whether this constraint could be relaxed or even removed by the development of the cognitive structure of the corporate tax policy process. Now attention is drawn again to the object of learning, and precisely to the above mentioned 'peculiarity' of European tax policy as regulatory policy. To begin with, the analysis of policy types – which is in itself a valuable analytical perspective provided by the policy approach[4] – has fostered the conclusion that EU direct tax policies have nothing to do with the emergence of a European welfare state. On the contrary, European direct taxation is a regulatory policy, and accordingly it should be interpreted as a component of the 'quasi-federal' regulatory polity that characterises the EU (Majone 1994a). Direct tax harmonisation does not reflect equitable goals and is not targeted towards social citizenship. On the contrary, it reflects the efficiency rationale typical of regulatory policies.

But why is tax policy a peculiar example of regulation? Harmonising corporate taxes in Europe means that taxes on cross-border trade and investment have to be eliminated. Domestic revenue – not companies or citizens – suffers the consequences of tax harmonisation. Therefore the cost structure of corporate tax harmonisation is not opaque, but indeed extremely clear to member states taking decisions in the Council of Ministers. Perhaps this is the single most important reason for the complexity of corporate tax regulatory policies, as opposed to other forms of regulations in the EU.

This chimes with what has been noted by authors dealing with the politics of domestic tax reform, most notably Mucciaroni (1992). In his critique of Kingdon, Mucciaroni has asserted that change in tax policy is less indeterminate than Kingdon believes, precisely because tax policy solutions are filtered by 'structures' such as (a) policy-makers who defend the relationship between taxation and representation, and (b) tax administrations whose remit is to guard the revenue base. The analysis of EU direct corporate tax policy has shown how the question of 'who bears the cost of regulation' is a crucial characteristic of corporate tax policy change in the EU. The visibility of the cost structure strengthens the inter-governmental grip on European corporate tax harmonisation: in this respect, the finding that knowledge-driven explanations of policy change and 'supra-national' choices are possible in corporate taxation is valuable because this challenges the *prima facie* hypothesis that concessions cannot be made by the Council.

In other regulatory policies – as explained by Majone (1993a; 1994a) – the cost structure is more opaque and 'supra-national' choices less constrained. Majone – whose analysis does not cover direct taxation – has contended that the production of regulation does not entail high costs for the regulator. Following his analysis, only a small 'internal' cost, that is the rule-making cost, is borne by the regulator. The more substantial costs of regulations are borne by firms and individuals who have to comply with them. It is true that in the long term member states 'discover' their own costs associated with the implementation of EU regulations, but the fact remains that at the decision-making stage of the policy process, i.e. when a decision is taken by the Council, the opacity of the cost structure facilitates adoption of EU regulatory policy. Quite the opposite can be said of direct corporate tax policy.

The analytical puzzle is that direct corporate tax policy is a regulatory policy, yet it does not fit the regulatory ideal-type proposed by Majone. The slow progress of corporate tax co-ordination in the EU, as opposed to the growth of regulation in other areas of EU policy, is an empirical proof of the fundamental peculiarity, related to the cost structure, of the policy area examined in this study. The central point argued here is that Majone's ideal-type is not exhaustive: it covers the core aspects of *certain* regulatory policies, but other regulatory policies can be processed in different ways. The point can be generalised by arguing that the ideal-type of EU regulation can be broken down into different types of regulatory policy, each characterised by distinct political dynamics. In other words, each form of regulatory policy has its distinctive politics attached: the politics of policy-making varies according to the peculiarities of different regulatory policies.

Following Gormley (1985–1986), who suggested a typology of regulatory policies for the analysis of the American political system, further analysis could be done on the games played in different regulatory arenas.[5] Gormley presented a four-fold typology based upon two dimensions, i.e. salience and complexity. In order to add clarity to the otherwise elusive concept of salience, it could be argued that the former dimension does not refer to salience *per se* (every policy is 'salient' in the eyes of some actors) but, more pertinently, to the public visibility of a policy. A highly salient policy is therefore a policy in which public opinion, mass media, political parties and mass movements are active: put succinctly, it is a policy 'with a public'. By contrast, more 'technocratic' policies are processed in relative isolation from the public debate. Turning to the EU, although professional bodies are active in EU corporate tax policy, certainly there is not the same 'hot' public debate aroused by, for instance, the proposal to regulate media concentration with EU law (Harcourt 1996). Briefly, EU tax policy, like standardisation and other regulatory policies described by Majone, is a policy 'without a public'.

Is there a second important element of differentiation, apart from salience? All EU policies tend to be rather 'complex' and, accordingly, the second dimension suggested by Gormley is not very useful for the analysis of EU regulatory policy. However, a crucial dimension that separates tax policy from the policies examined by Majone has been indicated already: the question of 'who bears the cost' makes a difference in the politics of regulatory policy-making. This leads to the four-fold typology suggested in Table 9.1.

Table 9.1 Regulatory policies in the European Union

	Low salience	*High salience*
Costs borne by states	Direct corporate tax policy	EU – rest of the world trade tariffs Common energy policy
Costs borne by societal actors	Standardisation	Media ownership regulation

In Table 9.1, the two dimensions that alter the dynamics of regulatory policy games refer to the presence of a public debate (i.e. policies are distinguished as policies 'with a public' and policies 'without a public') and to the actors who bear the cost in the first instance. In EU direct corporate tax policy costs are borne in the first instance by state structures, whilst in other regulatory policies costs are borne by societal actors. Table 9.1 portrays different regulatory games: the game of regulation is more easily played in policy areas such as standardisation wherein there is no public debate and state structures do not bear the cost of regulation. The presence of high saliency can facilitate the policy process by forcing EU policy-makers to accept an issue onto the agenda, provided that costs fall upon societal actors. This is most probably the case with media policy. The latter reached agenda status[6] thanks to the initiatives of the European Parliament which conveyed and amplified a widespread public concern with the issue of media ownership (Harcourt 1996). However, when high saliency is combined with costs falling upon state structures the regulatory game is easily stymied, as shown by the difficulty of regulating tariffs on trade between the EU and the rest of the world. The internal market for energy, and more generally the common energy policy, is representative of a policy area which has gradually gained visibility because of its repercussions on security and environmental policy (Haaland Matlary 1996). Not surprisingly, progress has been slow on this policy, characterised by an increasing degree of salience, in which economic costs are borne by public-owned industries (with the exception of countries in which the energy market has been liberalised) and political costs (in terms of security) borne by states. In conclusion, the point emphasised here is that the political structure of regulatory policy in the EU deserves more attention. The typology proposed here is nothing more than an initial step in this direction, and should be considered as a device for stressing the need to explore different regulatory arenas in the EU rather than as a fully-fleshed proposal.

INTERNATIONAL TAXATION: A POLICY IN SEARCH OF INSTITUTIONALISATION

The analysis of policy change will soon be completed with the consideration of the impact of Europeanisation on domestic taxation of international income. This raises the issue of the relevance of international phenomena in domestic taxation. Accordingly, two questions arise. First, has corporate tax policy become an international policy, or can it still be studied as a domestic policy? Second, why is international taxation of interest to political scientists?

The international tax order: a waste land?

The former question will be tackled briefly below, but the second question has wide implications for the research agenda of political science. It is to this question that we first turn. International taxation is inherently political because it revolves around a political problem. In a closed economy, taxation is a matter of political choice as it is embedded in the political dialectic between citizenship and state, or representation and resource extraction. In open economies the political problem of taxation becomes how to choose between different mechanisms for governing tax policies: is 'multi-level' governance (Hooghe 1996; Marks 1993) possible in international taxation? The challenge of multi-level governance in international taxation is political as international tax problems, in order to be solved, require a successful search of conditions for the emergence of institutions beyond the nation state.

An elaboration of this argument is needed at this point. The political implications of international taxation stem from actors, problems and choices in search of institutionalisation. As shown by Chapter 8 and by the quotation that introduces this section, the uncertainty about 'what can be done' is a radical form of uncertainty in the search for multi-level governance. Formal mechanisms (e.g. international organisations) of multi-level governance have not as yet appeared, with the partial exception of the OECD. Trade has become an international policy, but at the same time international rules were provided by such institutions as GATT and, more recently, by the World Trade Organisation. It does not matter whether GATT was systematically abused or not. The point to stress is that GATT represented an institutional device for coping – more or less efficiently, and with abuses – with trade globalisation. Taxation has undergone the same globalisation drive as trade, and is perhaps now part of global trade (Owens

1993). However, there are no *formal institutions* wherein international tax problems are treated. In international taxation, OECD status goes beyond that of a 'talk-shop': its position is influential, yet its contribution to the construction of an international tax order has serious limitations.[7] However, it is useful to explore the typical 'OECD method' of coping with international tax problems before considering its limitations. The main contribution of the OECD to the construction of the international tax order consists of the elaboration and dissemination of rules and principles to follow for the negotiation of bi-lateral tax treaties. Rules and principles devised by the OECD have spawned a tax treaty network that nowadays includes nearly 2,000 treaties (Arnold and McIntyre 1995). Thus the initial effort undertaken by the League of Nations in the creation of a treaty network (Picciotto 1992) has been continued by the OECD since the Second World War.

Today the network of bi-lateral tax treaties, albeit incomplete and subject to abuse, is still the major element of order in the international tax system. Double tax treaties have the following three goals: to remove, or at least mitigate, international juridical double taxation (and this is the goal most appreciated by companies), to fight tax evasion and to set up non-discrimination principles (OECD 1992). The method employed by the OECD is extremely interesting for its 'soft' political characteristics, particularly if compared with such a 'hard' method as EU directives. OECD guidelines are enshrined in the OECD model tax convention. The latter is literally a model made up of articles and a detailed commentary. The model allows for a good deal of flexibility. States can make observations on single articles of the convention. These observations establish how a country will interpret and apply the provisions of a single article. Therefore states can restrict the implementation of articles to what they consider to be the most desirable interpretation.

A more relevant element of flexibility is the possibility of making reservations on single articles. A state can hence decide that it will not stick to a certain article of the convention. As seen previously, the United States made a reservation to nothing less than Article 1 of the OECD model tax convention. Whilst the other countries agreed to Article 1 of the OECD model convention (1992), which stipulates that tax treaties cover residents of both countries, the US has always had the view that treaties are only for the benefit of non-resident aliens. Consequently, the US entered a reservation on Article 1 of the model convention. The implication – as shown in Chapter 8 above – is that the US holds the right to tax its residents as if the treaty did not exist. It is evident at this point that the 'soft' approach of the OECD has a flip side: the institutionalisation of principles is in fact inherently incomplete, given that states can and do make reservations and use observations in order to steer the process of interpretation and implementation.

Moreover, it should be noted that the OECD strategy is not a multilateral strategy: the OECD model tax convention is employed for the negotiation of bi-lateral treaties. Only in recent years did the OECD seek to promote a multi-lateral (as opposed to bi-lateral) strategy, with an OECD–Council of Europe convention on the exchange of information (OECD 1994). This is an important step, but it is confined to exchange of information between tax administrations.[8] In addition, countries outside the OECD tend to prefer another model tax convention proposed by the United Nations (United Nations 1980). Whilst the OECD model opts for the residence principle, the United Nations model gives negotiators the possibility of using the residence principle or the territorial taxation principle.[9] As a consequence, the institutionalisation of a unique set of international tax principles is hindered.

Finally, three recent dynamics in the taxation of international income – analysed in Chapter 8 – have put the consolidation of OECD principles in jeopardy. No more than a succinct summary of these dynamics is needed here. To begin with, the OECD has always had a 'relative specialisation' in the area of transfer pricing. Observers and policy-makers interviewed for this study regard the OECD as *the* policy forum for transfer pricing issues. However, the most astonishing tax controversy of the last few years has involved transfer pricing, thus undermining the influential role of the OECD. The publication of new OECD guidelines on transfer pricing (OECD 1995) is a healthy sign as it shows that the OECD is still able to forge consensus, but the cost of producing consensus has increased dramatically. The road towards convergence between the US and European countries in transfer pricing policy has become steeper. A second threat to the consolidation of OECD principles comes from the diffusion of controlled foreign companies legislation (Sandler 1994); this legislation is to a certain extent incompatible with the OECD principles. The third threat is represented by the need to revise tax treaties: a new generation of tax treaties is needed in order to cope with tax treaty abuse, but this requires an immense effort of institutionalisation.

Taken together, these three threats represent both a source of entropy and opportunities for the institutionalisation of a tax order. As explained in the previous chapter, the process of institutionalisation in international tax policy originates conflict and is a long way from completion. In this scenario, the major institutional entrepreneur is represented by the US, but American projects for new tax principles have not yet gained legitimacy. Currently, the OECD is the only policy forum wherein legitimacy is produced. It must however be stressed that the OECD is more a policy broker than an agenda-setter: it presides over the process of co-ordination rather than putting new issues onto the agenda.

The OECD role in the politics of international taxation was examined to this extent because there is not another organisation that can compete with it. Neither the United Nations nor the International Monetary Fund, which, through its executive board, monitors the developments of international taxation, play similar roles.[10] And the EU is notable for its absence from the international tax debate. For example, there is only limited synergy between the European Commission and the OECD.

If institutionalisation is considered in terms of *meaning* rather than formal institutions (March and Olsen 1989), the overall assessment of multi-level governance does not change much. On the one hand, the institutionalisation of international taxation as a matter of tax neutrality has progressed enormously, and the EU tax regime, centred on a rigorous application of tax neutrality principles, has contributed to the affirmation of this meaning. At least there is a general consensus, within the EU and in the rest of the world, on what international taxation should seek in terms of its ultimate goals. On the other hand, the consensus on tax neutrality as a benchmark for international business taxation, although important, does not lead to unequivocal policy choices. Indeed, if one tries to operationalise neutrality in terms of capital export neutrality (CEN) and capital import neutrality (CIN), the trade-off between the two concepts crops up and complicates policy choice: as shown in Chapter 5, CEN and CIN are both achieved only through identical tax systems, bases and rates (Devereux and Pearson 1989: 24). This generates a political paradox in European corporate taxation: the completion of the single market requires both CEN and CIN (Devereux and Pearson 1989: 24), but achieving both (if that would ever be possible) would imply huge administrative and political costs (in terms of sovereignty). Therefore any operationalisation of neutrality must ultimately be chosen on the basis of political and administrative choice.

Authors such as Devereux and Pearson (1989) believe that economic theory can help policy-makers, in particular by selecting CEN as the most relevant principle of neutrality. However, economic theory has not reached a unanimous agreement on the meaning of neutrality. Indeed, economists who model neutrality in a world in which portfolio flows and R&D make a competitive difference have argued that CEN is obsolete (Grubert and Mutti 1995; Hufbauer 1992). Economists themselves are in search of a new language for international business taxation, thus revealing the difficult path towards the institutionalisation of meaning. Slemrod (1995: 471) has pointed out this problem by arguing that 'the traditional objectives of international tax policy, such as capital export neutrality, are no longer relevant for today's economy' and sets out the agenda of future research in terms of seeking 'new insight – indeed a new language – for international tax policy'.[11]

More importantly, evidence of current controversies surrounding fundamental principles of international taxation (i.e. the residence principle, world-wide taxation, the taxation of capital income as part of progressive taxation of personal income) does not indicate a structuration of meaning. The transfer pricing controversy discussed in Chapter 8 attests that the foundations of international taxation are currently being challenged. Old principles are threatened as they no longer cope with the new political economy of international taxation, but new principles (e.g. the formulary approach) do not qualify as realistic alternatives for the foreseeable future.

To conclude on the point of institutionalisation, it can be argued that the problem of institutionalisation affects the supply of institutionalisation more than the demand. Tax entropy and tax degradation boost the demand for stable rules. Radical uncertainty fuels the demand for institutionalisation. At the same time, institutional entrepreneurship on the part of the US has triggered more conflict than consensus and overall the supply of institutionalisation remains poor. A problematic process of institutionalisation implies conflict and even entropy because it is a political process wherein power is created and gains and losses are allocated.

Capital income taxation: still a domestic policy?

At this point we can turn to the first question introduced at the beginning of this section: to what extent has taxation become an international policy? We have now seen that international taxation is a policy in search of institutionalisation. However, it could be objected that the impact of poor institutionalisation is not so dramatic as it seems. If only the international dimension of taxation were a marginal, additional component of domestic tax structures, the fact that an international tax order does not as yet exist would not cause great trouble. Unfortunately, the internationalisation of taxation can be compared to an earthquake that violently shakes the fundamentals of domestic tax structures. This is particularly true in three areas: the taxation of corporate income, the taxation of portfolio income, and the taxation of skilled labour (Tanzi 1995). The principles that have cemented the very idea of progressive and fair taxation, i.e. the residence principle and the world-wide taxation of income, are difficult to sustain in the current scenario of tax globalisation.

Without institutions that manage exchange of information between tax authorities and given the presence of tax havens, bank secrecy laws and deferral rules,[12] some countries have already abandoned progressive taxation – *de facto* if not *de jure* – and are moving towards schedular taxation (Sorensen 1994). Looking at the near future, the choice is not between a reliance on progressive and equitable tax principles or the accommodation of increasingly mobile capital's preferences, thus dismantling the essence of the welfare state. The real choice is between a *de facto* internationalisation with the current, obsolete tax structures still in place, thus generating avoidance, inefficiencies, distortions, and a heavier tax burden on less skilled labour (Commission 1996; Razin and Sadka 1989), and a major re-design of fiscal structures based upon more realistic principles and their institutionalisation at the international level. In this scenario, the relationships between the EU and international organisations in the rest of the world are more important than the relationship between the Commission and its member states.

Is there a role for the EU in tax globalisation?

Presumably, tax policy in the EU has to be re-framed as a problem of external relations rather than as an item falling exclusively under the rubric of the single market. The EU has been fraught with huge difficulties in building up an embryonic EU regime. Accordingly, it has not as yet assigned priority to the globalisation of taxation. In Chapter 5 it was argued that international tax problems in the EU can be 'framed' in different ways, globalisation being one of these. It was also concluded that the politics of tax problem definition in the EU is dominated by a narrow definition of tax policy problems. Now we can see what the implications of this narrow definition are. The EU is not a major player in the attempt to govern the globalisation of taxation and it is forced to play the role of a passive spectator, taking international tax dynamics as given constraints. In the scenario of tax globalisation, the EU is a policy-taker, not a policy-maker.

A different assessment of EU corporate tax policy stems from the consideration of the relationship between the EU tax regime and domestic taxes in member states. Put differently, we are now shifting our attention from the 'EU–rest of the world' tax relationships to the 'EU–member states' ones. The analysis of two national cases has shed light on the impact of the European tax regime on domestic taxation. What has been defined in Chapter 7 as the 'top-down' or 'immediate' effect of Europeanisation has touched upon domestic legislative styles. Moreover, a complicated and incomplete set of provisions regulating the cross-border taxation of dividends has been substituted by a more rational mitigation of international double taxation, thanks to the 1990 'parent–subsidiaries' directive. And the convention on transfer pricing controversies has been considered by American commentators as an example of efficiency and fairness, to be imitated in other parts of the world (Hufbauer 1992).

However, in all probability the 'bottom-up' or indirect effect of Europeanisation is the most striking consequence of EU tax policy upon domestic taxation. The paradigm of tax neutrality contemplated by the 1990 directives has become a benchmark in the domestic tax policy discourse, both in the UK and in Italy. In addition, the Europeanisation of the domestic tax policy discourse has brought about a change of tax policy instruments in the UK. This indirect effect of Europeanisation is important because it shows that domestic policy can change when the policy discourse becomes Europeanised: policy-makers employ a European frame of reference and consequently alter domestic policy in order to make it compatible with European concepts, paradigms, and policy goals, even though there is not a direct compulsion (for example a directive) from the EU. Europeanisation of the tax policy discourse has therefore had an important 'bottom-up' impact on domestic policy in the UK, mediated by the political role of influential policy fora and professional bodies.

As for the future, Europeanisation of domestic corporate tax policy could proceed thanks to the action of the European Court of Justice (ECJ). The latter has recently taken a number of decisions on the taxation of residents in one country who work in another.[13] Three points must be emphasised. First, the recent ECJ jurisprudence has been developed along the same line of 'non-discrimination' suggested by the Commission in its recommendation on cross-border taxation of individuals (21 December 1993), thus showing that 'soft' and non-compulsory measures such as recommendations can increase their political salience when taken into account by the ECJ. Second, although ECJ decisions refer to individuals, they have important implications for major components of the tax system, such as the fiscal treatment of pensions and the fiscal relationship between employer and employee. This could stimulate a pre-emptive change in national tax law, in order to avoid the challenge of the ECJ on the basis of discrimination. As noted in Chapter 7, in countries such as the UK policy-makers have already considered lists of domestic tax issues that may need a pre-emptive 'Europeanisation' (Nias 1995). Third, and more generally, companies have started challenging domestic corporate tax law in courts by arguing that national tax provisions are incompatible with the fundamental principles of EU law, such as non-discrimination and the basic principles of freedom established by the treaties (Gammie and Brannan 1995). In conclusion, although the degree of Europeanisation remains limited and progress at the Council level is currently stymied, the transformation of national tax systems could proceed indirectly, through the Europeanisation of frames of reference employed by policy-makers, and pre-emptively, through the Europeanisation of national taxes in order to bring them into line with ECJ jurisprudence.

Finally, the Commission has recently sought to promote a wider debate on direct taxes by arguing that the lack of progress in EU tax policy is generating unbridled tax competition among member states. When direct taxes are not co-ordinated at the EU level, tax competition leads to a 'race to bottom' in capital income taxes and to an increased tax burden on workers. Inertia in EU tax policy aggravates the problem of unemployment in Europe, via increased tax burden on workers (Commission 1996). The new strategy of the Commission shows that EU tax policy should be redefined within a more salient discourse in order to persuade reluctant member states. In the next chapter the pre-conditions for a new discourse will be considered.

10 Corporate tax policy development in the EU

The 'fiscal federalism' argument

> The features of arguments . . . and the way arguments are utilised by the various actors will play a crucial role in the choice of instruments and influence their effectiveness. This does not mean that arguments are regarded as substitutes of power relations; rather they are powerful resources in the policy process.
>
> (Liberatore 1995: 55)

A chapter that stretches the constitutive elements of a book beyond the conclusions is admittedly somewhat peculiar. Why then is further analysis needed? Simply put, whilst in the previous chapter the theoretical conclusions of this study were presented, the question of whether the EU policy process will develop in the future still requires assessment. This is why attention is turned in this chapter to the examination of European tax policy development. The latter can be analysed by projecting the conclusions of this study onto conjectures relating to the future. As such, the analysis of policy development represents more a reflection on 'how things ought to be and could be in the future' than a study of 'how things are'. The shift from the current state of the 'EU direct corporate tax policy process' (labelled TP, for 'tax process', as in Chapter 6) to the assessment of policy evolution suggests therefore a separate treatment. This explains why policy development is analysed here: all in all, this chapter is a way of looking into the future and making policy suggestions.

Policy development is analysed in stages, as follows. First, the potential of arguments as catalysts for policy change is briefly discussed in the first section, which represents the logical consequence of the theoretical underpinnings illustrated at the beginning of this book. Given that it has previously been argued that the cognitive structure of public policy is a crucial element in the analysis of the TP, logically the assessment of policy evolution should proceed along the same theoretical tracks, by seeking to explore the potential of the cognitive structure for the development of corporate tax policy in the EU. The conceptual dimensions of federalism and the main arguments of fiscal federalism are discussed in the subsequent section, and the potential of fiscal federal arguments as a catalyst for policy dynamics is assessed in the final section, which combines the analysis of the policy process with the examination of arguments.

ARGUMENTS AS CATALYSTS FOR POLICY CHANGE

As shown in Chapter 6, two hallmarks typify the TP: first, the presence of inaction and change has produced policy reversals. There is no inexorable movement in one direction, for instance towards substantial harmonisation, or, alternatively, towards complete tax differentiation. Second, the very presence of European direct taxation on the agenda of European integration is now threatened. Recent decisions of the European Court of Justice on the cross-border taxation of individuals and a consultative paper of the Commission (see Commission 1996 and Chapter 9) have re-launched the debate on EU direct tax policy. But the fact remains that since 1990 no directive has been agreed upon by the Council. Put differently, the TP suffers from the *political problem of low salience* rather than from the *technical* problem of how tax harmonisation ought to come about. Indeed, interaction is relatively scarce: few dossiers are currently open and some tax proposals have been withdrawn. Quite correctly, the Commission argues that EU tax policy should be considered within a wider discourse able to account for the consequences of tax competition in terms of unemployment (Commission 1996). This chapter takes a similar position and raises the question whether a more salient discourse on EU tax policy could be activated by federal arguments.

The conventional explanation of the current situation underlines the lack of institutional innovation: the TP – this explanation argues – is hampered by the presence of unanimity voting in the Council (Vanistendael 1993). The bottom line of this interpretation is that the TP is 'under-developed' because taxes, which are a significant part of the single market project, have not been up-graded to qualified majority voting. By contrast, the core policy areas of the single market have been assigned qualified majority voting rule since the Single European Act. This aspect will become extremely important, of course, especially if, as Mazey and Richardson (1996a) indicate, pressure groups increasingly lobby for more qualified majority voting. Thus, a change in voting procedures cannot be ruled out, even though the current low political salience of EU corporate taxation represents a major hurdle in this direction. However, the conventional explanation is suited to understanding parameters and constants, whereas it is at odds with policy variation. The TP, as already mentioned, is indeed characterised by policy reversals, not by perennial stalemate.

In this chapter an alternative explanation, based upon the cognitive component of politics, is suggested. It argues that the TP is underdeveloped in a more subtle sense: *it is not underdeveloped just in terms of voting rules, but in terms of its narrow cognitive component*. The EU tax policy discourse revolves around neutrality but it is insulated by other much more politically salient 'universes of discourse' such as the one generated by the debate on fiscal federalism. Almost twenty years ago, Dunsire (1978) observed clusters of activity in public administration forming an 'order of comprehension'. The latter is characterised by distinctive 'universes of discourse' which separate that 'order' from other clusters of activity. A similar occurrence takes place within the TP: the 'universe of discourse' of EU corporate direct tax policy does not communicate with the contiguous (yet definitively separated) discourse on fiscal federalism in the EU.

It is important to observe that it is precisely this aspect – i.e. the cognitive component of the policy process – that is deemed to be underdeveloped. Other aspects of the TP have in fact improved throughout the years: most importantly, two rival advocacy coalitions have emerged. To reiterate the findings of our analysis, these coalitions are the 'inter-governmental' coalition, centred around member states (politicians and public administrations), and the 'supra-national' coalition, composed of the Commission, experts with policy-relevant knowledge and corporate actors. The Commission is in a pivotal position within the 'supra-national' coalition as it has been active in brokering ideas and interests, and, occasionally, in mobilising policy-oriented expertise (Easson 1992). The participation of corporations and peak employers' federations in the supra-national coalition has become increasingly important as the emergence of a common European market has progressively underlined the importance of removing tax obstacles to facilitate the spread of European businesses. Taxes became a relevant source of distortion following the gradual suppression of other barriers to the free movement of capital, labour and goods. The presence of peak employers' federations and multinational firms as actors in the TP is yet another example of the increasing importance of business groups in the politics of EU policy-making (Green Cowles 1995; Mazey and Richardson 1996b).

As shown by Sabatier (1988) and Sabatier and Jenkins-Smith (1993) the presence of advocacy coalitions provides structure to a public policy. A policy develops when actors become engaged in coalitions that promote alternative causal beliefs, ideas, and policy solutions, and in so doing coalitions provide a form of institutionalisation, here defined as a process by which a policy process acquires stability, legitimacy, and ultimately political salience. More precisely, coalitions provide a dual centre of gravity, that is, two important poles around which actors amalgamate and policy choices emerge.

A similar process of structuration cannot be observed in terms of the cognitive component of the TP. Indeed, the 'menu' of arguments has not developed substantially. However, the gulf between the two advocacy coalitions has been partly bridged by the emergence of a new policy paradigm, centred around the concept of tax neutrality, which asserts that taxes should be neutral to international economic choices, and consequently should be harmonised only when they distort cross-border economic trade and investment. Therefore a limited process of cognitive evolution can be detected. However, such an important theme as fiscal federalism has not yet reached agenda status. The key questions then become: can the lack of political importance currently characterising the TP be the result of an underdeveloped cognitive component, and do policy arguments have potential for policy change in European taxation?

The importance of arguments in the policy process has been highlighted by Majone (1989) and, more recently, Liberatore (1995).[1] Arguments, indeed, can be catalysts for policy change (Majone 1989) and their content represents a fundamental aspect of the policy process. The public policy literature on the cognitive dimension of politics is vast (see Chapter 2) but relatively few studies explore the way arguments 'soften-up' and are constructed (Kingdon 1984 being a notable example) or the relationship between arguments, interests and policy development, that is to say, the relationship between knowledge and action. Drawing upon this literature, it will be argued that the policy implications of arguments, and, more precisely, the 'politics of issue-framing' (Rein and Schön 1991; Schön and Rein 1994) are extremely useful in the explanation of inaction and change.

Of course, it is not advisable to espouse a causal determinism that goes from framing to policy change. However, given that EU policy-making is characterised by shifting agendas (Peters 1994) and radical uncertainty,[2] there is room for arguing that the adoption of a certain frame is not without political consequences. Those who view Euro-politics from the 'inside', such as the Commission *fonctionnaires* interviewed for this study, are deeply convinced that most of their work consists of finding the most persuasive argument within which their preferred proposals could be encased. There is no such thing as a 'genuine' issue of European taxation: for example, tax rates can be considered an EU tax issue or not, depending on the frame employed. As a consequence, this chapter investigates the cognitive component of the TP and considers the implications of adopting a frame in which fiscal federal arguments play a large part. On a more theoretical note, the point argued here concerns the *theory of the European policy process*. Instead of interpreting the dynamics of European integration exclusively in terms of structural variables, such as the relative power of member states and voting rules in the Council, it is argued here that the rather unexplored cognitive dimension of EU dynamics deserves more attention because there is a causal relationship between conceptual frames and the choice of policy instruments and policy strategies. Issue-framing (i.e. the way facts are filtered and perceived within cognitive frameworks) is a vital pre-condition of policy development: without the appropriate frame, certain instruments will not be discovered and certain strategies will not be envisaged by policy-makers.

FEDERALISM AND FISCAL FEDERALISM

Whither federalism?

It is surprising to observe that the arguments of fiscal federalism are absent from the TP. Fiscal federalism has long had a presence in key areas of European integration (such as monetary union and the EU budget: see Commission 1977; De Grauwe 1994, MacDougall 1992) but does not appear in the system of interaction between the two coalitions considered here. Fiscal federalism – which obviously deals with taxation – is not a central theme within the frames of the two rival coalitions, even though both the UK-based Institute for Fiscal Studies (Gammie and Robinson 1989) and the Ruding Committee (Commission 1992) sought to make a case for fiscal federalism in the debate on EU taxation. However, what are the implications of fiscal federalism for the EU? And what is the potential of fiscal federalism for the development of the TP?

Fiscal federalism is an important feature of federal systems. Consequently, it is useful to highlight the political meaning of 'federalism' in the first instance, and then turn to 'fiscal federalism'. As shown by Elazar (1987) and Ostrom (1991), federalism is all about diversity. There is a striking convergence between federalism and the theory of democracy which stems from public policy analysis. Nothing illustrates this better than the insistence, typical of policy scholars such as Lindblom (1990) and Wildavsky, on social interaction and mutual adjustment among different partisan actors as the most satisfactory ways to build up acceptable collective decisions. To quote from Wildavsky:

> In a federal regime, states and localities are disobedient. The operational meaning of federalism is found in the degree to which the constituent units disagree about what should be done, who should do it, and how it should be done. In a word, federalism is about conflict. It is also about cooperation. . . . A federal regime, therefore, cannot be co-ordinated from the center. . . . Coordination . . . does not necessarily imply a coordinator. Under an operative federalism, coordination occurs by interaction among many governments, not by intellectual cogitation by a single one.
>
> (Wildavsky 1979: 142)

Federal systems exhibit a consistent degree of integration, but one of their main characteristics is non-centralisation. There is a subtle and crucial difference between non-centralisation and decentralisation. Decentralisation is typical of non-federal systems, where a central authority agrees to a diffusion of power. By contrast, contractual non-centralisation is defined by Elazar (1987: 34) as 'the structured dispersion of power among many centres'. This is relevant for the political discourse on the EU because the latter, as Ward has observed (drawing upon post-modern authors such as Lyotard and Derrida), 'is defined by its difference' and 'integration presumes difference' (I. Ward 1995: 28).

Elazar has made it clear also that the very core of federalism is not found in a specific set of institutions; rather, the core of the federal principle consists of a system of institutionalised relationships between participants in political life. Hence federal relations can be consistent with a broad variety of political structures (Elazar 1987: 11–12). This is particularly important, given that EU institutions do not resemble the political structure of a fully fledged nation state (see Sbragia 1992, Chapter 8; Scharpf 1994b for a more detailed analysis). Indeed, the EU emerging polity is peculiar in that it represents a case of welfare 'laggard'. Whilst the development of nation states has been characterised by the expansion of taxing and spending policies, the EU budget is limited and severely constrained. Therefore the EU cannot provide its citizens with large spending programmes along the lines of the welfare states (e.g. education, labour, pension, and housing policies) and demand the payment of EU taxes in exchange for EU public expenditure. This raises the following question: if EU direct tax policy does not represent the 'revenue side' of the EU welfare state – simply because the latter does not exist – what type of policy is it?

Here Majone's notion of regulatory federalism is useful once again. Majone (1994a) has pointed out that the European state has gradually grown developing regulatory policies. Whilst the policies of the welfare state are concerned with distribution (e.g. a public programme for housing), redistribution (e.g. a progressive income tax) and equality (e.g. free access to education), the purpose of regulatory policies is to tackle market failures, thus enhancing efficiency.

However, why should EU states, given the presence of market externalities, delegate power to a supra-national regulator? After all, if national regulators were willing and able to operate under the conditions established by the Coase theorem (which establishes that co-ordination among independent actors removes externalities provided that there are no barriers to contract: see Coase 1960), negative cross-border externalities 'could be managed in a co-operative fashion without the necessity of delegating regulatory powers to a supra-national level' (Majone 1991: 23). EU taxation provides an answer to this puzzle. The rationale for EU tax policy (as for other forms of supra-national regulation: see Majone 1991) is regulatory failure rather than market failure. For a national regulator, it is logical to regulate tax avoidance and tax evasion by, for instance, levying a tax of 15 per cent on dividends paid to a foreign citizen. The residence country of the tax payer will probably acknowledge, through a bi-lateral mechanism such as a tax treaty, the payment of the tax by giving a tax credit. However, the credit will not exceed the amount of tax that would have been levied in the residence country. If the residence country levies taxes at 10 per cent on its residents, the citizen will be granted a tax credit of the same amount. Governments are in fact reluctant to encourage foreign investments of residents by paying their foreign taxes in excess of the domestic rate (Giovannini and Hines 1991: 185). As a consequence, the extra 5 per cent of tax paid will not be recovered, thus creating a case of regulatory failure: in fact domestic and foreign investments will be taxed at different rates. This example can be generalised by arguing that (a) national tax authorities are not willing to take into account the international implications of their choices; (b) the amount of information exchanged among tax authorities is far from the amount needed for effectively regulating tax avoidance through co-operation (see Tanzi 1995); and (c) the costs of organising and monitoring tax policy co-ordination are high (Giovannini and Hines 1991). These are precisely the three conditions which, according to Majone (1991), justify the recourse to supra-national regulation.

Existing federal tax systems and lessons for the EU

Turning now to the theory of fiscal federalism: this identifies two economic criteria for conferring tax powers at the federal level. First, the attribution of a tax to a certain governmental unit should be chosen in relation to the fiscal base: if the tax base cannot be defined at the state level, there is an economic rationale for centralising tax competencies. Second, central taxes are a sensible economic response to cross-border tax externalities. These are the essential characteristics suggested by the theory. However, Walsh (1993) points out that the theory of fiscal federalism is far from being of immediate interest to the EU. Indeed, this theory is mainly concerned with mature federations with a developed democratic polity, in which no problem of democratic deficit exists. Also, the theory assumes less heterogeneity than exists in the EU, where strong differences in citizens' preferences suggest that the attribution of supra-national functions could impose excessive uniformity.

If we need to be cautious in applying fiscal federal theory to the EU, what can we learn from the practice of fiscal federalism in the USA, Canada, Germany, Australia, Switzerland, and, more recently, Belgium? At the cost of over-simplification, there are four broad lessons.[3] First, it is impossible to draw simple tax assignment lessons from current federal practices, because 'virtually every sort of tax is used somewhere by each sphere of government' (Walsh 1993: 36). Second, it is customary to find a variety of rates between one state and another. A general case can therefore be made for tax competition, with due qualifications (see McLure 1986). One author even observes that in North America 'neither the base nor the rates have been the object of any formal harmonisation' (Reichenbach 1993: 84). Third, the mitigation of socio-economic differences among states is assured by equalisation grants, geared by a formula which differs from one federal country to another. Also, asymmetric shocks affecting regions of economic and monetary union are absorbed via federal stabilisation mechanisms. Sala-i-Martin and Sachs (1992) have estimated that a one dollar reduction in a United States region's per capita income triggers a decrease in federal taxes of about 34 cents, and an increase in federal transfers of about 6 cents. Fourth, after a period of general centralisation (the 1950s and the 1960s) in a number of federal systems the pendulum is currently shifting towards greater autonomy for the periphery (Benz 1989: 218–219; Brosio 1994; Daly 1992: 391–392).

Turning now to corporate taxation in particular, further elements have to be taken into account: the most common feature is the existence of federal corporate income taxes, which do not exist at the EU level. Most crucially perhaps, convergence among jurisdictions has been directed primarily at the suppression of inter-jurisdictional double taxation (Commission 1992: 186). No withholding taxes are levied on inter-jurisdictional capital income flows. This is of significance because from 1989 onwards the Commission has identified this issue (i.e. the suppression of inter-jurisdictional double taxation) as the main priority of EU tax harmonisation. Moreover, in federal systems such as Canada, the USA and Switzerland the historical trend is not towards the harmonisation of rates, but is more oriented towards the harmonisation of the tax base. Canadian Tax Collection Agreements are a case in point, where provincial tax rate differentials are combined with a common base. According to Boadway (1989: 55), differences in tax rates are acceptable because at the same time there is an extensive set of federal–provincial transfers.

IS THERE AN OPPORTUNITY FOR FISCAL FEDERALISM IN EU CORPORATE TAXATION?

The policy implications of a fiscal federal frame

Although it is clear that many of the features of existing federal systems cannot be transferred to the EU, a case can be made for fiscal federal arguments as catalysts for policy development. This section therefore tackles the following two questions: does the previous analysis of federalism and fiscal federalism shed light on the limits of the current strategy of the supra-national coalition? And what instruments could be devised through the possible adoption of a frame sensitive to fiscal federal arguments?

To begin with, diversity and tax competition are vital aspects of federal practice: thus every move towards EU harmonisation which does not respect these essential features is doomed to failure. The need for tax harmonisation must be justified on a case by case basis, with a rigorous application of the subsidiarity principle. Some federal countries have exhibited an historical trend towards the achievement of common tax bases, whilst tax rate uniformity has turned out to be a more ambitious policy goal. Hence, the focus of the Commission on rates and systems,[4] and the very late attempt to set the policy agenda in terms of tax base,[5] can be criticised.

In any case, tax harmonisation in federal countries stems from historical evolution (Commission 1992: 190). In this process of evolution, the network of fiscal relations between the centre and the periphery was built up through negotiation and shifting equilibria, not by means of planned development. Federalism is a mechanism for elaborating different solutions in tune with socio-economic and political dynamics. It does not provide a formula or a stable, ultimate solution in terms of the balance of power in inter-governmental relations. From the supra-national coalition's perspective, this means that *building up an embryonic 'federal environment' is more important than getting a single directive through the policy process*: for example, by using the Commission as a policy forum for debate and mutual adjustment; by employing the facilitatory role of EU institutions; by promoting policy-oriented research, brokering and disseminating new tax ideas; by supporting the implementation of the 1977 directive on mutual collaboration among national fiscal administrations; and by trying to establish a role for European institutions in tax treaty negotiations, wherein transnational European companies might appreciate the possibility of facing an increasingly integrated North America with a 'single voice'. The general idea is to involve interest groups and member states in a more intense system of interaction, thus creating a 'centre of gravity' for international taxation around EU institutions.

Despite this, prospects for the TP appear low, because three common features of federal countries are absent in the EU: a single currency, a federal corporate tax , and 'compensatory measures' such as equalisation grants and other side payments. Compensatory measures are indispensable in order to mitigate economic differentials, thus obtaining wide support from federal units. A fiscal federal structure includes *explicit side payments* necessary for building consensus among the members. Side payments are, of course, an important aspect of many EU decisions (see Lange 1993; Marks 1992). Therefore the most striking limit of the current strategy pursued by the supra-national coalition is that it imposes political costs (e.g. concessions in terms of sovereignty) and economic costs (e.g. revenue losses, when taxes affecting investment abroad are suppressed) on member states without explicit compensatory measures. In all probability, it was a mistake to elaborate tax proposals which allocate losses, without including side payments, which allocate benefits. Therefore in any future attempt to persuade member states to adhere to a fiscal federal structure, the supra-national coalition would need to be extremely sensitive to the political logic of side payments, bearing in mind that in EU tax harmonisation, economically strong countries (for example, Holland and the UK) would need to receive compensatory benefits.

Fiscal federalism has potential in widening and strengthening the frame of the supra-national coalition in another sense. Scholars of fiscal federalism have emphasised that specific measures of tax assignment and tax harmonisation in federal systems have to be assessed taking into account the broader issue of the federal budget. Yet the 'universe of discourse' of EU tax harmonisation does not as yet include a consideration of the federal budget issue. Put differently, the two rival coalitions in the TP are engaged in a rather narrow debate on tax neutrality but their discourse does not consider EU tax policy problems within the more politically salient issue of the EU budget. This can be a result of the internal organisation of the Commission, in which two distinct Directorates-General deal with corporate taxation and the budget. Hence this can be another example of the thorny issue of policy co-ordination in Brussels. Indeed, to use Dunsire's notions once again, budget and direct taxation are processed by two distinct 'orders of comprehension' in which the 'universes of discourse' do not communicate. Proof of this is that an important policy study on the EU budget, entitled *Stable Money, Sound Finances* (Reichenbach 1993), has been conducted under the aegis of the Commission's Directorates-General for Economic and Financial Affairs and for Budget, but this report has not as yet had any impact on the discourse of the two rival coalitions considered in this chapter. Yet *Stable Money, Sound Finances* strongly supports a greater Community involvement in capital income taxes, corporate taxes, and environmental taxes. The report recommends, *inter alia*, corporate tax base harmonisation and a minimum statutory rate. It is worth stressing that a new 'window of opportunity' for EU tax harmonisation could therefore appear as a consequence of broader considerations relating to the Community budget. This means that there is the possibility of increasing the political salience of EU direct tax harmonisation, by fuelling the TP with new political and economic arguments. Therefore fiscal federalism, by drawing attention to the EU budget and breaking the wall which separates the discourse on EU direct taxes from budgetary issues, has potential in terms of policy development.

The relationship between arguments and instruments

Turning now to the relationship between arguments and instruments, could a frame built around fiscal federalism help the supra-national coalition in the discovery of a strategy for selecting policy instruments? Scharpf, who has considered the federal characteristics of the EU polity (1994b) has underlined that policy instruments in the EU have more success when they represent 'saddle-point' solutions. A 'saddle-point' is minimally adequate and efficient from a technical point of view and represents the maximum sacrifice of political autonomy that can be voluntarily reached by member states. What are the implications of this for the TP? Can the supra-national coalition devise 'saddle-point' instruments in this field?

The Commission has always been extremely cautious in proposing new tax instruments, presumably preferring solutions that represent more or less the average of existing tax systems. However, as mentioned in Chapter 5, if this strategy makes sense where powerful, credible and desirable 'anchors' exist (for example, in the case of monetary union, it can be argued that German monetary institutions possess the characteristics of an 'anchor'; see Dyson 1994), there is not a similar 'anchor' as far as domestic tax institutions are concerned. No one has as yet argued that the 'policy credibility' of, say, French tax institutions is greater than that of Swedish tax institutions. We do not know what is the optimal (or most desirable) tax system which could play the role of the driving force for harmonisation (Tanzi and Bovenberg 1990). Harmonising around existing tax systems means selecting an average of non-optimal systems, and this average will not necessarily be optimal or desirable.

In addition, it can be argued that the Commission achieved its most striking successes by brokering interests and disseminating new ideas (Mazey and Richardson 1994). Then why not re-launch a policy process in which no new ideas have emerged within the past five years or so by proposing a debate on new tax instruments? On this point the supra-national coalition could benefit from some recent ideas floating around the embryonic epistemic community of international taxation. It is surprising that the Commission has not as yet promoted anything, not even a conference, on new types of corporation tax. This is an area in which the relationship between the supra-national coalition and the underlying embryonic epistemic community could be strengthened.

For example, in the UK, experts working under the aegis of the Institute for Fiscal Studies have devised a new tax which could 'accommodate' a variety of different direct tax systems. This type of corporation tax, entitled Allowance for Corporate Equity (ACE) (Devereux and Freeman 1991; Gammie 1991b; IFS 1994), has the political advantage of providing a neutral international tax environment without the need to harmonise the tax base across member states. A solution such as ACE potentially offers three advantages. First, it could trigger a new debate on EU direct taxation, thus permitting the opening of new dossiers. Second, it could be presented as an option favoured by the Commission and available to member states. There is no need to 'impose' an ACE solution on all member states at the same time: member states could be persuaded gradually by a policy discourse which underlined the benefits and the long-term economic implication of a more efficient tax environment. The supra-national coalition could act as a purposeful policy entrepreneur, facilitating the so-called lesson-drawing effect (i.e. the cross-national transmission of ACE tax reforms from one country to another; see Rose 1991 on the lesson-drawing effect). With the passing of time a critical mass of ACE countries would gradually emerge. Third, by setting the policy game in terms of new solutions, the supra-national coalition could avoid the criticism that it was trying to adopt a national solution which lacked any real 'anchor' power. To sum up then, a more active role by the Commission in structuring the policy agenda in terms of new alternatives with saddle-point properties could result from the adoption of a fiscal federal frame. Supra-national policy brokers such as the Commission do not merely react to co-ordination problems in the EU but can purposefully set the agenda and re-structure policy games.

However, is there a *political drive* to fiscal federalism in the EU? A potential drive is represented by the Economic and Monetary Union (EMU) process. In existing monetary unions – such as the USA and Canada – the absence of flexible exchange rates (which are useful for responding to regional problems) is associated with a fiscal federal structure. According to some economists (De Grauwe 1994; Eichengreen and Frieden 1994; MacDougall 1992), the well-known EMU troubles are a result of the absence of fiscal federalism in the EMU policy process. The institutionalisation of a single monetary policy in the EU, if not accompanied by some elements of fiscal federalism, could originate both technical problems and a new area of democratic deficit (Verdun 1996). It is not inconceivable to argue, in conclusion, that the road to monetary union, will require, at some point, an explicit consideration of fiscal federalism as a complementary aspect of EMU.

Appendix A

Chronology: corporate tax harmonisation in the EU

1962 Neumark Committee. The Committee proposes a common system for the taxation of profits. The preferred system is the split-rate system, which taxes distributed and retained profits with different rates.

1966 Segrè Committee. The Committee examines the fiscal pre-conditions for the creation of a common market for capital. European tax harmonisation and capital market liberalisation are thought of as two complementary aspects of the single market.

1967 Action Programme of the Commission for tax harmonisation. The Commission argues for the introduction of a value added tax in all member countries of the Community and for a common general tax on profits. In turn, the path towards a general tax on profits – the Commission points out – could be made easier by an approximation of the tax base in Europe.

1969 Commission proposal for two directives on the cross-border taxation of dividends paid between parents and subsidiaries and on the fiscal treatment of mergers and acquisitions between companies of different EC countries.

1970 Werner Report on economic and monetary union in Europe. According to the Report, tax harmonisation should accompany the creation of a monetary union.

1970 Van den Tempel completes an independent study on behalf of the Commission. His Report suggests a common system for the taxation of profits based upon the absence of fiscal links (e.g. tax credits) between corporate taxation of profits and personal taxation of income. This system is referred to as 'classic' (see Messere 1993a).

1971 Following to the Werner Report, the Council gives prominence to fiscal harmonisation as an indispensable aspect of monetary union with a Resolution (22 March) on the economic and monetary union.

1972 A Council Resolution (21 March) reiterates the necessity to proceed with fiscal harmonisation in conjunction with the implementation of the Werner Report on economic and monetary union.

1973 Organisational change within the Commission. The journal *European Taxation* (1973) hints that this change could slow down the activity of the Commission in tax harmonisation policy.

1975 Commission Programme on tax harmonisation and proposal for a directive on corporate taxation. The proposed directive recommends minimum and maximum corporate tax rates and a common system for the taxation of profits. Whilst the Neumark Committee opted for a split-rate system of profit taxation and Van den Tempel suggested a classic system, the 1975 proposal argues for an imputation system in which corporate taxes on profits and personal income taxation are linked.

1976 The Commission proposes a directive on the fiscal treatment of transfer pricing.

1977 The Council adopts a directive on mutual assistance among tax administrations of member states. The main aim of the directive is to curb tax evasion through exchange of information and multi-lateral initiatives for monitoring portfolio investment in the EC.

1978 Following a Dutch suggestion, the 1976 proposed directive on transfer pricing is transformed into a proposed convention.

1979 The European Parliament does not come up with a resolution on the 1975 proposed directive on a common system of corporate taxation, but prefers to issue an interim Report (Nyborg Interim Report) in which the Commission is invited to look at tax base harmonisation before submitting proposals, such as the 1975 draft directive, dealing with corporate tax rate and tax system harmonisation.

1980 The Commission releases a Report on corporate tax harmonisation and withholding taxes on dividends. The 1975 proposed directive remains the official policy of the Commission.

1983 The European Parliament reiterates its 1979 position. The EP refuses to issue an opinion on the 1975 proposed directive in the absence of specific proposals on tax base co-ordination. Accordingly, the Commission is invited to submit proposals concerning the tax base.

1984 The Commission restructures the proposal on transfer pricing, by changing the role of the independent commissions that should decide upon international transfer pricing controversies. In the earlier proposal, these commissions were supposed to substitute tax administrations, whereas in the 1984 new draft they are assigned a consultative role. The new draft is therefore more palatable to member states.

1984 Proposal of the Commission for a Council Directive on the harmonisation of the laws relating to tax arrangements for the carry-over of losses of undertakings.

1985 White Paper of the Commission on the single market. Only two paragraphs are dedicated to corporate taxation; essentially, they announce new initiatives of the Commission.

1985 (July) Communication of the Commission to the Council. The Commission focuses upon tax measures dealing with parent–subsidiary flows of dividends, the fiscal treatment of cross-border mergers and acquisitions, and transfer pricing.

1988 The Commission seeks to accommodate the European Parliament requests (made in 1979 and 1983) suggesting measures for harmonising the tax base across Europe. An informal draft directive is circulated, but severely hostile reactions of some member states bring the Commission to withdraw the proposal before formally submitting it to the Council.

1988 Directive 88/361/EEC on capital movement liberalisation. Article 6 of the directive stipulates that new tax measures will be presented by the Commission.

1989 Further to the directive on capital movement liberalisation, the Commission proposes a directive on a common withholding tax on interest income in the EC. The proposal is deemed to avoid the risk of tax degradation and widespread tax avoidance by introducing a common withholding tax on savings. Luxembourg and the UK express a negative opinion on this proposal.

1989 Christiane Scrivener begins her mandate as Commissioner with the tax portfolio. She drastically limits the scope of the Commission's initiatives in EC tax harmonisation. Subsidiarity and limited intervention of the Commission in direct tax policy become the key-words of her speeches. According to Scrivener, the Commission's initiatives should aim at mitigating double taxation rather than advocating the harmonisation of rates and tax systems.

1990 The Commission withdraws its 1975 proposal on a common system of profit taxation and on minimum and maximum corporate tax rates.

1990 Document of the Commission, entitled 'Guidelines on Company Taxation'. The Document underlines the new pragmatic approach of the Commission. The 1975 grandiose plan for tax harmonisation is shunned, and at the same time the Commission focuses upon a coherent, although limited, package of tax measures against double taxation. The Document announces the formation of a group of independent experts in the near future.

1990 (July) For the first time the Council agrees upon direct corporate tax proposals. Three measures are approved, namely the parent–subsidiary directive (90/435/EEC), the merger and acquisitions directive (90/434/EEC), and the convention on transfer pricing arbitration (90/436/EEC). Article 20 of the arbitration convention on transfer pricing provides for a limited duration of five years (starting from the entry into force of the convention).

1990 (November) The Commission launches a proposal for a directive on cross-border taxes on interest and royalties. The proposal aims at eliminating double taxation.

1990 (December) The Commission issues a proposed directive to provide a cross-border loss relief. The proposed measure considers both permanent establishments and subsidiaries. With the 1984 proposal, the 1990 proposed directive comprises the 'loss package' of the Commission.

1991 The Ruding Committee is formed and initiates proceedings.

1991–1992 The scope of the proposed directive on interest and royalty payments is progressively widened by the Commission and the European Parliament.

1992 The Ruding Report is published. A partially negative reaction to the Report comes from the ECOFIN meeting of November, convened under the British Presidency of the EC.

1992 At the 19 December ECOFIN meeting, Luxembourg blocks an agreement upon a Council resolution on the removal of bank secrecy laws in cases of alleged tax fraud.

1993 The Commission proposes to the Council to widen the scope of the two 1990 tax directives. Notwithstanding a favourable opinion of the European Parliament (19 April 1994, OJC128, 9 May), this relatively simple proposal has not been adopted.

1993 Working Document of the Commission 'Towards a Strategic Programme for the Internal Market'. In this document the Commission draws attention to the fiscal problems of small and medium size enterprises and to the role of tax policy in affecting the free movement of persons.

1993 Germany re-launches the idea of a common EC withholding tax on savings. The Commission re-considers its 1989 proposal and lowers the suggested tax rate from 15 per cent to 10 per cent. However, even the new proposal is rejected by the Council. In addition, Article 73 D(1) (a) of the EU Treaty 'authorises member states to continue to apply certain national tax provisions distinguishing between tax payers who are not in the same position with regard to the place of investment of their capital' (CFE 1996: 63).

1994 The convention on transfer pricing (also known as arbitration convention) is ratified by all member states, Portugal being the last state to deposit the instrument of ratification at the office of the Secretary-General of the European Council (28 October 1994). The Convention comes into force on 1 January 1995.

1994 Recommendation of the Commission on the taxation of small and medium size enterprises.

1994 (November) The proposed directive on interest and royalties is officially withdrawn by the Commission.

1995 Mario Monti is the new Commissioner with the tax portfolio. Throughout 1995 there is no initiative of the Commission in the field of direct corporate taxation.

1995 Two decisions of the European Court of Justice (i.e. the Schumaker case, ECJ of 14 February 1995, C-279/93, and the Wielockx case, ECJ of 11 August 1995, C-80/94) spawn a debate on tax obstacles to the free movement of persons. The main problem, originally addressed by the Bachmann case (ECJ of 28 January 1992, C-204/90), concerns the link between pensions, tax policy, and free movement of persons.

1996 (April) During the Italian presidency, at the Verona informal ECOFIN meeting, EU economy and finance Ministers discuss the

Commission's paper on 'Tax Policy in the EU'. The document examines tax policy in a broad conceptual framework. In the document the Commission argues that the lack of tax co-ordination (in personal taxes, excise duties, VAT, and corporate taxation) 'slows down the realisation of the single market, jeopardises tax revenues, and denies member states the freedom to restructure their tax systems'. ECOFIN ministers decide to appoint their personal representatives to a high level reflection group on tax policy in the EU (chair: Commissioner Mario Monti).

1996 In his memorandum on 'Action for employment in Europe: a confidence pact', the President of the European Commission, Jacques Santer asserts that 'taxation policy plays an increasingly important role in the strategy for employment. A tax environment which stimulates enterprise and job creation needs to be created. The Commission is very gratified at the favourable reception given to its background paper [tax policy in the EU] advocating a comprehensive approach to the question and the establishment of a high-level group headed by the Commission'.

1996 (21–22 June) The European Council discusses the confidence pact for employment put forward by the Commission's President: although the Council agrees with the strategy outlined by the confidence pact, it stresses that 'high and sustained non-inflationary economic growth over the medium term is essential to significantly and durably reduce the Community's unacceptably high level of unemployment', thus assigning priority to sound public finance over EU initiatives for tackling unemployment. As far as tax policy is concerned, the European Council requests 'a report on the development of tax systems within the Union, taking account of the need to create a tax environment that stimulates enterprise and the creation of jobs and promote a more efficient environmental policy'.

1997 (March) The high-level group on tax policy devotes its meeting to the problem of 'damaging tax competition'. It is agreed at the meeting that the Commission will discuss with the group the possibility of establishing a 'code of conduct' to be respected by member states.

Appendix B

EU corporate tax law and proposed directives

Treaty principles

- Article 48: free movement of people
- Article 52: right of establishment
- Article 59: free provision of services
- Article 67: free movement of capital
- Article 220: abolition of double taxation within the Community.

EU law on direct corporate taxation

- Mutual Assistance Directive (77/99/EEC)
- Mergers Directive (90/434/EEC)
- Parent–Subsidiary Directive (90/435/EEC)
- Arbitration Convention (90/436/EEC).

Recommendations

- Commission recommendation on the taxation of non-residents (21 December 1993).
- Commission recommendation on the taxation of small and medium-sized enterprises (25 May 1994).

Pending proposals for Council directives:

1 Corporate taxes:
Proposal on tax arrangements for the carry-over of losses of undertakings, COM 84 (404), Final
Proposal on cross-border loss tax relief, applicable to subsidiaries and permanent establishments, COM 90(595), Final

Proposals for extending the scope of the merger and parent–subsidiary directives, COM 93 (293), Final

2 Taxation of interest income:

Proposed directive on a common system of withholding tax on interest income, COM 89(60), Final

3 Pending measures regarding company law that have implications for the implementation of the 1990 directive on the fiscal treatment of cross-border mergers and acquisitions (90/434/EEC):

Amended proposal for a Council regulation on the statute for a European Company, COM 91(174), Final

Amended proposal for a Council directive complementing the statute for a European Company with regard to the involvement of employees, COM 91(174) Final

Proposal for a tenth Council directive concerning cross-border mergers of public limited companies, COM 84(727), Final.

Withdrawn corporate tax proposals

- Proposed directive on the taxation of interest and royalty payments, COM 90(571), Final
- Proposed directive concerning the harmonisation of systems of company taxation and of withholding taxes on dividends, COM 75(392), Final
- 1988 Preliminary draft proposal for a directive on the harmonisation of rules for the determination of taxable profits of enterprises. This proposal was withdrawn before formal submission to the Council. The text is commented by Kuiper (1988).

Appendix C
Interviews (1994–1996)

Pietro Adonnino (Professor of tax law, Rome; formerly MEP, President of the International Fiscal Association)

Julian S. Alworth (Tax consultant; Lecturer in economics of taxation at Bocconi University, Milan)

Roberto Artoni (Professor of public economics, Bocconi University, Milan; formerly President of CONSOB, the Italian Stock Exchange Commission)

Samuel Brittan (*Financial Times*, London)

Mario Burgio (Commission, DG XXI; formerly in the cabinet of Commissioner Raniero Vanni d'Archirafi)

Angelo M. Cardani (Commission, cabinet of the Commissioner Mario Monti, 1995 to the present; Professor of economics at Bocconi University, Milan)

David Carr (Commission, DG XV, until 1995; formerly member of the Ruding Committee Secretariat)

Gaetano Casertano (Assonime, Rome)

Vieri Ceriani (Banca d'Italia, adviser to the Minister of Finance, Rome; in 1996 member of the high level group set up by the Commission on tax policy in the EU)

John Chown (John Chown Company Ltd; founding member of Institute for Fiscal Studies (IFS), London)

Antonio Colombo (Confindustria, Rome)

Michael Daly (OECD, Paris; formerly Secretary of the Ruding Committee)

Giuseppe de Angelis (Assonime, Rome)

Michele del Giudice (Servizio relazioni internazionali, Ministry of Finance, Rome)

Michael Devereux (Professor and Head of Department at Keele University; member of the Institute for Fiscal Studies (IFS), London; Director of fiscal studies; Consultant to the Ruding Committee)

Andrew Dilnot (Director, Institute for Fiscal Studies (IFS), London)

Tommaso Di Tanno (International tax lawyer, Rome)

Franco Gallo (Professor of tax law and tax lawyer; formerly Italian Minister of Finance, 1993–1994)

Malcolm Gammie (Linklaters and Paines; IFS; Institute of Taxation)

Silvia Giannini (Professor of public economics at University of Bologna; participant in the project 'Ipotesi di riordinamento dell'attuale apparato normativo in materia fiscale' launched by the Ministry of Finance and conducted by CNEL in 1992–1993; participant in the advisory commission on tax reform launched by Minister Tremonti in 1994)

Robert Goergen (Commission, Honorary Director, DG XV)

Giorgio Guarneri (Commission, member of Commissioner Christiane Scrivener's cabinet 1989–1994)

Maria Cecilia Guerra (Professor of public economics at University of Modena and Bocconi University, Milan; participant in the advisory commission on tax reform launched by Minister Tremonti in 1994)

Tony Hughes (Coopers & Lybrand, London)

John Kilby (Touche Ross, London)

Margaret Lamb (Lecturer in corporate taxation, University of Warwick)

Peter Lewis (International Tax Division, Inland Revenue, London)

Giansandro Locatelli (Fédération des Experts Comptable Européens (FEE))

Giovan Battista Lombardo (IRI, Rome)

Guglielmo Maisto (Tax lawyer, formerly consultant to the business industry advisory committee at the OECD; consultant to ECOSOC)

Giuseppe Marino (Lecturer in international tax law at University Bocconi, Milan; tax lawyer at 'Studio Uckmar', Milan)

Ken Messere (OECD, Paris, 1971–1993; formerly member of the Ruding Committee)

Adrian Ogley (Confederation of British Industry (CBI), London)

Jeffrey Owens (Head, Fiscal Affairs Committee, OECD)

Philippe Pelle (Commission, DG XV; formerly member of the Ruding Committee Secretariat)

Patrizio Pesci, Marco Felisati (Confindustria, EU unit, Brussels)

John Rienstra (International Bureau of Fiscal Documentation, Amsterdam)

Bill Robinson (London Economics; past Director IFS; member of the Ruding Committee in 1991; special advisor to N. Lamont, Chancellor of the Exchequer 1991–1992)

Igino Rossi (Servizio relazioni internazionali, Ministry of Finance, Rome)

Vincenzo Russo (Professor at the University of Rome; adviser to the Minister of Finance, Franco Gallo, 1993–1994)

Dierk Schelpe (Commission, DG XV, Brussels)

Peter Short (HM Treasury, London)

Andrea Simoni (ENI, Rome)

Geoff Snaydon (International Tax Division, Inland Revenue)

Iain Stitt (Arthur Andersen, Brussels)

Marco Tucci (Fiat, Turin; member of the Ruding Committee)

Mario Usellini (formerly MP and member of the Parliamentary Finance Committee, Italy)

Frans Vanistendael (Professor at Leuwen University, Belgium; formerly member of the Ruding Committee)

Claudio Venturato (Civil servant, research and documentation unit of the Italian Chamber of Deputies – Finance Committee)

Vincenzo Visco (Professor; MP; Minister of Finance in the Prodi government)

Roy Warden (Corporate Tax Division, Inland Revenue)

Peter Wardle (International Tax Division, Inland Revenue)

Willem Wijnen (Director of research, International Bureau of Fiscal Documentation, Amsterdam)

Notes

1 INTRODUCTION

1 See Picciotto (1992) on international taxation; IFA (1994) and Easson (1980; 1993) on European taxation.

2 See Alworth (1988) for an economic analysis of the impact of taxation on multinationals; Hufbauer (1992) on US international tax policy; Devereux and Pearson (1989) and Giovannini (1989) on European taxation and Sinn (1990) on tax competition in Europe; Bird (1988), and Tanzi (1995) on the international tax system.

3 Notable exceptions are Garrett (1995), Hallerberg (1996), Hallerberg and Basinger 1997, forthcoming) and Hocking (1993). This does not mean that political scientists have disregarded taxation in general. See *inter alia* Peters (1991).

4 Economists such as Gordon (1992) and political scientists engaged in comparisons between the European Union and earlier examples of monetary unions (Hallerberg 1996) observe that tax competition represents a prisoner's dilemma in which states prefer to defect (by lowering tax rates on capital) rather than co-operate. However, Gordon and Hallerberg argue – the former with economic arguments, the latter by dint of historical comparison – the presence of a 'Stackelberg' leader provides a 'lowest common denominator' tax rate. Accordingly, states will not lower tax rates on capital to zero, but will stop lowering their tax rates at the level set by the 'Stackelberg' leader.

2 THE ROLE OF KNOWLEDGE IN THE POLICY PROCESS

1 The expression 'autonomous element' denotes a theoretical perspective in which the cognitive dimension of politics is not ultimately reduced to other elements of the policy process, such as, for example, interests. As shown below, this does not prevent knowledge from being transmitted into the policy process in conjunction with interests and other elements of political life.

2 The reference for the third quote – the lyrics by the rock group King Crimson – breaks with the orthodoxy in academic language. However, it

can be argued that this type of source has now become part of the culture of this *fin de siècle* and therefore should be accepted.

3 The term 'rules' should be considered in a broad sense here, from legal rules to rules of intersubjective meaning.

4 The 'perverse' effects of learning are illustrated by Lindblom (1990: 206) and Weiss (1986). March and Olsen (1995: 97) observe that 'learning by doing . . . leads political institutions to become over-committed to what they have done and are doing'.

5 Peters and Barker (1993: 17) describe a pragmatic decision as one in which 'it is believed that an effective "solution" or "cure" is available for a problem – even when the etiology of the problem or "disease" is not certain or accepted'.

6 Yee observes that 'just as institutions govern the entry of ideas into the policy-making process, they also effect the access of policy-makers to those ideas. Ideas percolate up to decision makers, but decision makers also search down into the bureaucracy for ideas. Both processes occur within and are shaped by institutions' (Yee 1996: 92).

7 Rein and Schön's model focuses upon policy controversies (Schön and Rein 1994). A discussion and empirical analyses based upon this model are contained in the monographic issue of *Knowledge and Policy* edited by Kleiboer and Hart (1995–1996), and the response provided by Rein and Schön (1996) .

8 The construction of problems may also lead to the creation of target populations in the so-called policy design stage. The target population model has been developed in an attempt to integrate power and cognitive variables in the analysis of public policies (Schneider and Ingram 1993): here political power and social constructions are two dimensions of a fourfold typology of target populations (which includes the advantaged, the contenders, the dependents, and the deviants). Not only does the target population model integrate power and knowledge dimensions, but it also shows how the design of public policy can shape and funnel various patterns of participation in the policy process. Thus public policies, instead of being the conclusion of the policy process (as outputs), acquire an important role at the outset of the process in that their design can either hamper or bolster participation of specific categories of actors.

9 For some, even post-modernist: see Fishman (1992), Rosenau (1993), and Yee's review of post-modern international relations theorists (Yee 1996: 95–104).

10 Hall argues that a paradigm change could occur as a result of critical reflection on a paradigm's past performance. It must be stressed that Hall posits a distinction between paradigm change, dubbed 'third order' policy change, and less radical policy change, which alters either the settings of policy instruments ('first order' policy change) or the instruments, without however modifying the overall policy goals ('second-order' change). See Hall (1993) and the discussion of Europeanisation in Chapter 7.

11 The Adam Smith Institute. See *inter alia* Gaffney (1991) and Stone (1996) on British think-tanks in comparative perspective.

12 This explains why the criticism raised by Jacobsen (1995) misses the target. Indeed, his implicit yardstick for measuring the benefits of policy

studies based upon the cognitive dimension of politics is the feasibility of research designs in which independent variables are not correlated.

13 The Advisory Group advising the Prime Minister in New Zealand, with two-thirds of its members coming from outside the public sector, is a case in point (Boston 1988). The basic idea in setting up non-bureaucratic advisory structures is that career public servants, for a variety of reasons, cannot adequately supply the kind of advice required by a prime ministerial role. As a consequence, business and academic communities are selectively brought into the governmental machine.

14 According to neo-functionalist models of European integration, the collaboration of elites in specific European policy projects triggers an important mechanism of cognitive change. In fact 'a mutual sense of confidence and *engrenage* – the sense of professional empathy, understanding and trust that facilitates effective joint responses to common problems – follows on from intense cooperation in joint policy making' (O'Neill 1996: 42). Neo-functionalist writers such as E. B. Haas predicted change in political values as a consequence of *engrenage*.

3 POLICY-MAKING IN THE EUROPEAN UNION

1 The Treaty on the European Union introduced this new denomination (i.e. European Union). The EU includes three pillars: the European Community, the foreign and security common policy, and the home and justice affairs policy (Nugent 1994). Tax policy-making in the EU pertains to the first pillar, i.e. to the European Community. Therefore it is possible to refer to European taxation either using the EC denomination (in order to indicate that tax policies are processed within the first pillar) or the EU one, to underline the new polity which has emerged since the Treaty on the European Union came into force.

2 Many reviews and readers on theories of European integration (Caporaso and Keeler 1995; Hodges 1972; Marks *et al.* 1996; Nelsen and Stubb 1994; O'Neill 1996) are available. As this chapter is not concerned with reviewing theories of European integration, the discussion of theories and models will be highly selective.

3 See Risse-Kappen 1996a; Puchala first noted how difficult it is to assess the nature of the beast in his 1972 article.

4 On functionalism and neo-functionalism see Haas (1958), Lindberg (1963), and Tranholm-Mikkelsen (1991).

5 Tranholm-Mikkelsen (1991); see also the criticisms reviewed by O'Neill (1996: 48–49) and the qualifications advanced by Schmitter (1996).

6 Which have recently been revisited and refined, thus creating a *déjà-vu* effect: see O'Neill (1996).

7 In addition, change in the EU is iterative: change at a given point in time feeds into the sources of future change. See Marks *et al.* (1996: vii).

8 For an illustration of the approach see Richardson (1996) and Wallace and Wallace (1996).

9 Regulation is defined here as a policy type concerned with the authoritative determination of behaviour (of the regulated actors). The rationale

for regulation is efficiency and not fairness or equality (the typical rationales of redistributive and distributive policies).

10 Following Caporaso (1996), who draws upon Benjamin and Duvall, the state refers to a stable structure of governance and rule. The state is a political structure that includes formal rules and norms, shared understandings, standard operating procedures and other socially accepted 'ways of doing things'.

11 Regulatory policy has its main rationale in the attempt to correct market failures, such as externalities and natural monopolies. See Breyer (1982) for a description of the most important regulatory rationales.

12 See however Caporaso (1996) on the implicit redistributive dimension of regulatory policy.

13 This is a limit of the theory of liberal inter-governmentalism (Moravcsik 1991; 1993) which seems unable to go beyond the nonetheless crucial constitutional decisions. For a typology of decisions and their impact on actors and decision-making styles see Peterson (1995).

14 This paragraph draws entirely upon Cram (1995, 1997). See also Bulmer (1994).

15 However, their ultimate thrust is to integrate ideas and interests.

16 To be precise, Garrett and Weingast focus upon the political role of the European Court of Justice.

17 On this point see Eichenberg and Dalton (1993) and the initiative of the Commission for 'selling' the Economic and Monetary Union to the public.

18 See however Richardson (1996). Risse-Kappen (1996a) has argued that comparative policy analysis, in combination with international relations, provides a useful conceptual framework for the understanding of European integration.

4 THE POLITICS OF TAX REFORM

1 As witnessed by the 1996 presidential campaign in the USA.

2 This point is elaborated by Mucciaroni, who draws upon Wilson (1980). See Mucciaroni (1990).

3 Hood (1994) discusses the differences between incremental models of tax policy and inertial models.

4 See Wilson (1980) for the political properties of these choices.

5 It is not an exaggeration to consider the US tax reform of 1986 extraordinary: in 1985 Witte, commenting upon the plan for tax reform, argued that '*there is nothing, absolutely nothing in the history or politics of the income tax that indicates that any of these schemes have the slightest hope of being enacted in the forms proposed*' (Witte 1985: 380, emphasis in original).

6 See Chapter 2 for the characteristics of this model.

7 The assumption is made here that radical uncertainty originates a demand for policy co-ordination. See Heiner (1983).

5 PROBLEM DEFINITION IN EU DIRECT CORPORATE TAX POLICY

1 By contrast, the source principle states that income should be taxed where it is produced. The source principle therefore leads to territorial taxation, as opposed to worldwide taxation.
2 Deferral indicates 'the practice of subjecting the profits derived from foreign investment through foreign corporations to taxation only when the profits are repatriated to the country of residence of the investor' (Arnold and McIntyre 1995: 129). A company can use deferral systematically in order to avoid payment of domestic taxes (Giovannini 1989: 352).

6 CORPORATE DIRECT TAXATION IN THE EUROPEAN UNION

1 This is a well-known tenet of policy studies: see Kellow (1988) and Lowi (1964; 1972).
2 Action Programme for Taxation, Communication from the Commission to the Council, 23 July 1975, Doc. Com. (75) 391 final.
3 Com. (75) 392 final, 23 July 1975. Withdrawn by the Commission on 10 April 1990.
4 A detailed analysis of the implementation of the two corporate tax directives is provided by IBFD (1995).
5 The Commission has proposed, so far without success, to extend the list of entities to which the parent–subsidiary and merger directives would apply. See Com. 93/293 final, OJ C225, 200893, and the favourable opinion of the European Parliament (OJ C128, 9 May 1994).
6 The future of the convention is however unclear. The convention has a limited validity of five years, after which member states will have to decide whether to continue or terminate it. The CFE has noted that member states could be tempted 'to use the argument that only limited use has been made of the convention as a reason not to renew it' (CFE 1996: 61).
7 See Chapter 2 above for the concept of epistemic community.
8 The role of the IFS is investigated further in Chapter 7.
9 An example of the way the CFE intervenes in the EU policy process is provided by the document submitted to DG XV and DG XXI at the beginning of 1996 (CFE 1996). In its document, the CFE lamented 'the absence of a long-term strategic plan for direct taxation' (CFE 1996: 61) and on several occasions stressed that CFE positions corresponded to the preferences of the business community as a whole. It is also interesting to observe that the CFE document was followed by a consultative paper of the Commission (1996) which placed EU direct taxation within a long-term strategic plan.
10 Cf. Darolles and Tucci (1992), Gammie (1992), Messere (1993b), Vanistendael (1992; 1993). The following organisations sent comments to the Report: UNICE, CFE, Association of Co-operative banks of the EC, CNFP (Patronat Français), and Banking Federation. See also Commission (Communication to the Council and the European

Parliament, June 1992, SEC (92)-1118 Final), ECOFIN (November 1992), ECOSOC (Report of Mr Pelletier, CES 1332–1392 sf], European Parliament (Report of Mr Cox).

7 EUROPEANISATION AND POLICY CHANGE: ITALY AND THE UK

1 See the discussion in Chapter 2.

2 See the survey of MPs commented by Radaelli (1988).

3 And Labour MPs are somewhat in trouble on this issue: see Baker *et al.* (1996).

4 Tremonti and Uckmar being notable exceptions; see their recent views in Tremonti (1993) and Uckmar (1993).

5 On the attempts to reform tax administration see Lupi (1996) and Russo (1989; 1995). According to these authors, even the belated reform of the *Ministero delle Finanze* (1991) was ineffective. Indeed, Lupi maintains that the 1991 reform made things worse (Lupi 1996: 42–43).

6 Physically, the Ministry is comprised of one huge building, divided into 'towers', on the outskirts of Rome, in the EUR administrative district: EUR architecture is still reminiscent of its fascist legacy.

7 The majority of tax experts are also tax consultants.

8 Lupi (1996: 59) observes that the role of Parliament in tax policy as a whole has been extremely constrained and that during the last ten years no single tax reform bill presented by MPs or opposition parties has even been discussed by the two chambers.

9 In 1994 a law (No. 945) was passed by the Danish Parliament. The law withdrew exclusive power to ratify treaties from the Minister of Taxation and restored the power of the Parliament. See Weizman (1995).

10 The so-called Legge La Pergola, described by Giuliani (1996).

11 The delay was caused by the indecision of the Berlusconi government on whether to give the opposition the right to select one Italian Commissioner or not.

12 See Gaffney (1991) and D. Stone (1996) for comparative analyses of the role of think-tanks in the UK political system.

13 The imputation system gives a credit for taxes paid by a company when profits are distributed; see Chapter 6.

14 See Kingdon (1984) for the difference between agendas and alternatives.

15 See data on the economic relevance of this perverse effect in Bond, Chennells and Devereux (1995) and Freeman and Griffith (1993).

16 See Gammie (1991b) and IFS (1994) for more details. See also Chapter 10 of this volume on the role of ACE in the development of fiscal federalist arguments for EU corporate tax co-ordination.

17 It is, however, interesting to observe that Professor Vincenzo Visco, a few days after he took up his job as Minister of Finance in the Prodi government (June 1996), addressed the Italian Parliament with a speech underlining the necessity to re-think tax design in terms of 'dual income tax', which is precisely what the Scandinavian countries have done recently (Sorensen 1994). At the end of 1996, the Italian government took on board Visco's suggestion and presented a proposal for a *sui*

generis dual income tax. This spawned a debate between experts and policy-makers on the structure of dual income taxes and the concept of neutrality in corporate tax policy. The government's proposal was accepted in broad terms by the parliament: with law no. 662–1996, the parliament delegated power to the government for formulating a legislative decree on the dual income tax. However, the main goal of the dual income tax 'Italian-style' is not to cope with the consequences of tax globalisation (this being the main aim in Scandinavian reforms instead), but to sustain the capitalisation of firms. Hence the role of internationalisation in Italian tax policy remains limited.

8 INTERNATIONAL TAX COMPLEXITY

1 See Bird (1988), Owens (1993), Picciotto (1992) and the primer by Arnold and McIntyre (1995).
2 Epitomised by the classic work of Macridis (1961).
3 See Sinn (1990) and Chapter 1 of this volume.
4 For example, Vogel (1995) argues that non-governmental organisations have been instrumental in protecting diffuse interests in trade globalisation. By contrast, international tax policy is still firmly in the hands of governments and governmental organisations. The case of EU tax policy – where professional bodies participate in the policy process – is however different, as contended in Chapter 6.
5 Throughout this chapter, the argument of institutional autonomy refers to strategies, initiatives, and broad political trajectories pursued by American institutions. The argument does not go so far as to claim that the impact of recent American tax policies has been economically adverse to corporations. Indeed, only an accurate evaluative research design could assess the policy impact.
6 'Going, going . . . America's balanced budget shambles', *Economist*, 4 March 1995; 'Setback for a "revolution": the defeat of an attempt to make a balanced budget a constitutional requirement in the US', *Financial Times*, 4 March 1995; 'Spotlight is on North Dakota Senators whose votes could tip the balance on budget amendment', *Wall Street Journal*, 24 February 1995.
7 According to economists at the Treasury Department, President Clinton's 1994 proposals would imply a decrease in revenue of around US$ 60 billion over five years. The contract would cost US$ 197 billion over the same period. See 'The year of cutting dangerously. US tax cuts unlikely to satisfy voters', *Economist*, 7 January 1995.
8 In fact, the concern with abusive transfer pricing rules is not limited to Clinton's electoral campaign. Congress passed the Revenue Reconciliation Act of 1990 containing provisions to curb abuses. A scholarly study tried to explain the low taxable income of foreign-controlled companies in the US and found considerable empirical evidence of transfer pricing distortions (Grubert, Goodspeed and Swenson 1993). The Internal Revenue Service elaborated upon this study and presented in Congress an estimate of US$ 3 billion annual revenue shortfall due to non-compliance (Hufbauer 1992: 116–118).

9 The literature on transfer pricing is vast. Amongst the others see E. King (1994), Pagan and Scott Wilkie (1993), Picciotto (1992, Chapter 8), and the empirical analysis presented by Grubert, Goodspeed and Swenson (1993). Hufbauer (1992) puts forward specific recommendations for US transfer pricing policies. Arnold and McIntyre (1995) provide a plain introduction to transfer pricing issues. The text of transfer pricing provisions contained in national legislation and in official texts issued by international organisations is contained in the four loose-leaf volumes published in various years by the IBFD.

10 The economic importance of transfer pricing is a result of growing intra-company trade. In 1989, 89 per cent of US parent-company exports went to foreign affiliates, and 86 per cent of US parent-company imports came from foreign subsidiaries (data quoted by Hufbauer 1992: 108).

11 Shirley D. Peterson, Commissioner of Internal Revenue, stated in the sub-committee on oversight, House Committee on Ways and Means (1992), that the Internal Revenue Service employed 582 international examiners of transfer pricing practices, 68 economists, and 125 international attorneys. Quoted in Hufbauer (1992: 119).

12 The quote is from the *Financial Times*, 'Survey or world taxation – Long arms of the revenue collectors', 20 May 1994. Another interesting quote is from John Fairley of Ernst and Young (London): 'Transnational companies face increased scrutiny of their transfer pricing practices as many jurisdictions demand their "fair share" of the global revenue pie', in an article entitled 'Tax authorities take tougher line over transfer of profits', *Financial Times*, 17 July 1995.

13 Quote from 'California faces huge revenue refund', *Financial Times*, 28 March 1994.

14 The announcement of the conference prompted an alarmed reaction. See 'US tax move alarms international groups', *Financial Times*, 15 August 1995.

15 This statement should not be exaggerated, however. Formula apportionment based on factors such as payroll, sales, and property could negatively affect the United States because significant income generated by US transnational companies is not attributable to the three factors, but to intangible property. In other words, it is not clear at all whether the United States as a whole would benefit from the application of formula apportionment on a world scale or not. At the same time, it is evident that from the point of view of American states which host foreign companies, formula apportionment presents advantages.

16 'US judges dismiss Barclays' challenge on unitary tax law', *Financial Times*, 21 June 1994.

17 It appears that the use of retaliatory measures on the part of the UK was avoided, *inter alia*, by the passage of new Californian legislation in 1993. In that year, California allowed tax payers to choose between world-wide unitary taxation and a 'water's edge election', that is a method confining the over-reach of Californian tax powers to the US borders. Before the 1993 change, companies were allowed (by a 1986 law) to opt for the 'water's edge', but they had to pay an election fee which was considered unfair and discouraging by the business community. The then UK Chancellor, Kenneth Clarke – in a letter to Secretary of the Treasury

Lloyd Bentsen dated shortly after the passage of the California legislation (14 September 1993) – stated that 'the UK government will defer the implementation of retaliatory measures. . . . [T]he UK will retaliate only if it becomes clear that the legislation is being applied in a way that damages UK companies by imposing tax in violation of the arm's length principle.' However, in the same letter the Chancellor stated that 'if Barclays is not successful in its litigation, the UK will have to retain its retaliatory power in reserve against the possibility that states might re-introduce unitary taxation at some time in the future', thus retaining a preservation of options. The letter is quoted from the *Wall Street Journal*, 14 April 1994.

18 Lodin's assessment of the expenditure tax is considered a cornerstone in the tax debate. See Lodin (1978).

19 In 1989, the Internal Revenue Service proposed US$ 4 billion in transfer pricing adjustments involving US-controlled firms (Hufbauer 1992: 118).

20 In the event of a Supreme Court decision in favour of Barclays.

21 Indeed, the US had a third option, i.e. unilaterally overriding with national legislation the clauses of the treaty that were considered subject to abuse. Interviews conducted for this study confirm that this third option was utilised for putting pressure on the Dutch negotiators.

22 See the systematic review conducted by the OECD (1996b). The best treatment of controlled foreign company legislation can be found in Arnold (1986) and Sandler (1994).

23 As noted by Sandler (1994: 107) this position explains the US objections to tax sparing provisions in treaties with developing countries.

24 In the 1993 temporary regulations, instead of the comparable profit interval the comparable profit method was chosen. The latter was not considered a mandatory check on other methods and therefore lost part of its primacy over other methods.

25 The editorial was written by Professor Ritter in his capacity of Vice-Chairman of the Tax Commission of the International Chamber of Commerce.

26 See also Deloitte, Touche, Tohmatsu International (1995: 2).

27 The opinion of the high-ranking Treasury official John Guttentag is quoted by Turro (1995).

28 'Global deal averts threat of transfer pricing war', *Financial Times*, 28 July 1995. A sympathetic comment on the OECD guidelines came from the US: see 'US Council welcomes approval of OECD transfer pricing guidelines', US Council for International Business, press release, 29 June 1995.

29 Many authors in the past lamented the absence of a GATT for taxation; see Owens (1993), Tanzi and Bovenberg (1990). The latest book written by Tanzi contains a thorough analysis of this problem (Tanzi 1995). However, Fischer-Zernin (1987) argued that double tax treaties are not compatible with the multilateral, non-discriminatory, most favoured nation system of GATT. Using the GATT method for tackling tax issues – Fischer-Zernin's argument goes on – would require an extremely critical consideration of the existing networks of double tax treaties.

30 For the 'old' institutionalism the cognitive forms of institutionalisation were values and norms. By contrast, for the 'new' institutionalism the key

forms of cognition are classifications, routines, schema, and scripts (Powell and DiMaggio 1991).

9 CONCLUSION: KNOWLEDGE, INSTITUTIONS AND POLICY CHANGE

1 The consideration of the capability to exploit environmental changes has led Jenkins-Smith and Sabatier to a slight modification of the advocacy coalition framework. See Jenkins-Smith and Sabatier (1994).
2 This was the intuition offered by Susan Strange (1994b), i.e. the knowledge structure has now become one of the fundamental structures of international political economy. I am grateful to Kenneth Dyson for having drawn my attention to this point.
3 Indeed, Giddens considers three main elements: structure, resources, and morality.
4 See Majone (1994a) and Pollack (1994) for the analysis of policy types in the EU.
5 On the analysis of different types of regulatory policy see Wilson (1980).
6 Although no directive has as yet been agreed upon by the Council.
7 It is in this sense that the long-standing quest for a 'tax GATT' can be interpreted (Owens 1993; Tanzi 1995; Tanzi and Bovenberg 1990).
8 The multi-lateral convention entered into force on 1 April 1995. At that time, parties to the convention included Denmark, Finland, Norway, Sweden, and the United States.
9 The difference between the OECD model convention and the United Nations one stems from a divergence in the structural interests of advanced countries and developing countries which import capital in order to expand their growth. For a capital-import developing country the adoption of the residence principle makes it impossible to tax income produced by foreign multinationals therein. By contrast, territorial taxation (i.e. the source principles) allows capital-import developing countries to tax income generated locally by foreign multinationals.
10 Although international organisations have not produced a world tax order, there is evidence of regional tax regimes. The Nordic Mutual Assistance Treaty, signed in 1972, then amended in 1976, 1981 and 1987, and eventually revised in 1989, is a case in point.
11 In particular, Slemrod (1995: 471) proposes to recast international tax policy 'in parallel with the theory of international trade'.
12 See Chapter 5 above.
13 For the complete list of relevant decisions see IBFD, *EC Corporate Tax Law*, Binder 2, section on 'decisions of EU court'.

10 CORPORATE TAX POLICY DEVELOPMENT IN THE EU: THE 'FISCAL FEDERALISM' ARGUMENT

1 The emphasis on arguments is of course part of the more general interest in the cognitive perspective on the policy process described in Chapter 2.

2 See *inter alia* Mazey and Richardson (1996a), and Chapter 3 of this volume.
3 See Benz (1989); Fisher (1987). On business taxation in federal countries see Boadway (1989); Commission (1992: Chapter 9); McLure (1989); OECD (1991).
4 For instance, in the 1975 draft directive, Com. 75 (392), Final, subsequently withdrawn in 1990.
5 An informal proposal was circulated in 1988 (Kuiper 1988) and withdrawn before formal submission to the Council. Later some recommendations were advanced in the Ruding Committee Report (Commission 1992).

Bibliography

Aaron, H. J. (1989) 'Politics and the professors revisited', *American Economic Review: Papers and Proceedings*, 79(2) May: 1–15.

—— (1990) 'Lessons for tax reform', in J. Slemrod (ed.) *Do Taxes Matter? The Impact of the Tax Reform Act of 1986*, Cambridge, MA: MIT Press, 321–331.

Adler, E. and Haas, P. M. (1992) 'Conclusion: epistemic communities, world order, and the creation of a reflective research program', in P. M. Haas (ed.) 'Knowledge, Power and International Policy Coordination', *International Organization*, Special Issue, 46(1): 367–390.

Alworth, J. S. (1988) *The Finance, Investment and Taxation Decisions of Multinationals*, Oxford: Basil Blackwell.

Argyris, C. and Schön, D. (1978) *Organizational Learning: A Theory of Action Perspective*, Don Mills: Addison-Wesley.

Arnold, B. J. (1986) *The Taxation of Controlled Foreign Corporations: An International Comparison*, Toronto: Canadian Tax Foundation.

—— and McIntyre, M. J. (1995) *International Tax Primer*, Den Haag: Kluwer Law International.

Arthur Andersen (1993) *Corporate Taxation in the EC*, London: Arthur Andersen.

Ashford, D. (1982) *British Dogmatism, French Pragmatism*, London: Allen & Unwin.

—— (1992) (ed.) *History and Context in Comparative Public Policy*, Pittsburgh: Pittsburgh University Press.

Axelrod, R. (1976) (ed.) *Structure of Decision. The Cognitive Maps of Political Elites*, Princeton: Princeton University Press.

Backer & McKenzie – North American Tax Practice Group (1994) 'The final section 482 regulations', *Intertax*, 12: 544–554.

Baker, D., Gamble, A., Ludlam, S., and Seawright, D. (1996) 'A "rosy" map of Europe? Labour Parliamentarians and European integration', *Paper prepared for the PSA annual conference*, Glasgow, April.

Barker, A. and Peters, G. B. (1993) (eds) *The Politics of Expert Advice. Creating, Using and Manipulating Scientific Knowledge for Public Policy*, Edinburgh: Edinburgh University Press.

Baumgartner, F. R. and Jones, B. D. (1991) 'Agenda dynamics and policy subsystems', *Journal of Politics*, 53(4): 1044–1074.

—— (1993) *Agendas and Instability in American Politics*, Chicago: University of Chicago Press.

Becker, H. (1995) 'Highlights of the new OECD report on transfer pricing', *Intertax*, 8–9: 387–388.

Beer, S. (1977) 'Political overload and federalism', *Polity*, 10(1) Fall: 5–17.

Beighton, L. J. H. (1994) 'The Finance Bill process. Scope for reform?', *Second Philip Hardman Memorial Lecture*, London: Institute for Chartered Accountants in England and Wales.

Bennett, C. J. and Howlett, M. (1992) 'The lessons of learning: reconciling theories of policy learning and policy change', *Policy Sciences*, 25: 275–294.

Benz, A. (1989) 'Inter-governmental relations in the 1980s', *Publius. The Journal of Federalism*, 19: 203–220.

Bernardi, L. (1989) 'Per un'introduzione al dibattito sul sistema tributario italiano e alle proposte di riforma', in A. Pedone (ed.) *La questione tributaria. Analisi e proposte*, Bologna: Il Mulino, 25–89.

Beyer, J. and Trice, H. M. (1982) 'The utilization process. A conceptual framework and synthesis of empirical findings', *Administrative Science Quarterly*, December: 589–621.

Bhaskar, R. (1986) *Scientific Realism and Human Emancipation*, London: Verso.

Bird, R. M. (1987) 'Corporate–personal tax integration', in S. Cnossen (ed.) *Tax Coordination in the European Community*, Daventer-Antwerp and London: Kluwer, 227–251.

—— (1988) 'Shaping a new international tax order', *Bulletin for International Fiscal Documentation*, July: 292–299.

Birnbaum, J. and Murray, A. (1987) *Showdown at Gucci Gulch. Lawmakers, Lobbyists, and the Unlikely Triumph of Tax Reform*, New York: Random House.

Blumer, H. (1971) 'Social problems as collective behavior', *Social Forces*, 18: 298–306.

Boadway, R. (1989) 'Corporate tax harmonisation: lessons from Canada', in M. Gammie and B. Robinson (eds) *Beyond 1992: A European Tax System*, London, IFS Commentary No.13: 52–57.

Bond, E.W. and Samuelson, L. (1989) 'Strategic behavior and the rules for international taxation of capital', *Economic Journal*, 99: 1099–1111.

Bond, S., Chennells, L. and Devereux, M. (1995) 'Company dividends and taxes in the UK', *Fiscal Studies*, 16(3), August: 1–18.

Boston, J. (1988) 'Advising the prime minister in New Zealand: the origins, functions and evolution of the prime minister's advisory group', *Politics*, 23(1): 8–20.

Bradford, D. F. (1986) *Untangling the Income Tax*, Cambridge, MA: Harvard University Press.

—— and Stuart, C. (1986) 'Issues in the measurement and interpretation of effective tax rates', *National Tax Journal*, 39(3): 307–316.

Brean, D. (1993) 'Policy perspectives on international taxation', in C. Sandford (ed.) *Key Issues in Tax Reform*, Bath: Fiscal Publications, 238–262.

Brennan, G. and Buchanan, J. (1980) *The Power to Tax. Analytical Foundations of a Fiscal Constitution*, Cambridge: Cambridge University Press.

Breyer, S. (1982) *Regulation and its Reform*, Cambridge, MA: Cambridge University Press.

Brooke, P. (1989) 'The Government's approach to the Community: some myths dispelled', in M. Gammie and B. Robinson (eds) *Beyond 1992: A European Tax System*, London, IFS Commentary No.13: 35–38.

Brosio, G. (1994) *Equilibri instabili*, Torino: Bollati Boringhieri.

Buchanan, J. M. (1995) 'Clarifying confusion about the balanced budget amendment', *National Tax Journal*, XLVIII, No. 3, September: 347–355.

—— and Wagner, R. E. (1977) *Democracy in Deficit: the Political Legacy of Lord Keynes*, London: Academic Press.

Bulmer, S. (1994) 'The governance of the European Union: a new institutionalist approach', *Journal of Public Policy*, 13(4): 351–380.

Burgio, M. (1990) 'L'imposizione sulle società: orientamenti recenti della Comunità europea', in A. Majocchi and G. Tremonti (eds) *Le imposte del 1992. Aspetti fiscali del completamento interno europeo*, Milan: Angeli, 195–216.

Burley, A. M. and Mattli, W. (1993) 'Europe before the court: a political theory of legal integration', *International Organization*, 47(1), Winter: 41–76.

Campbell, D. T. (1969) 'Reforms as experiments', *American Psychologist*, 24 (4) now in E. L. Struening and M. B. Brewer (eds) (1983) *Handbook of Evaluation Research*, London: Sage.

Caplan, N., Morrison, A. and Stambaugh, R. J. (1975) *The Use of Social Science Knowledge in Policy Decisions at the National Level*, Ann Arbor: Institute for Social Research of the University of Michigan.

Caporaso, J. (1996) 'The European Union and forms of state: Westphalian, regulatory or post-modern?', *Journal of Common Market Studies*, 34(1), March: 29–52.

—— and Keeler, J. (1995) 'The European Union and regional integration theory', in C. Rhodes and S. Mazey (eds) *The State of the European Union, Vol. 3: Building a European Polity?*, Boulder: Lynne Rienner, and London: Longman, 29–62.

Casertano, G. (1995a) 'Riflessioni in merito alla gerarchia delle norme tributarie alla luce della recente evoluzione del diritto interno, comunitario e convenzionale', *Rassegna Tributaria*, 38(3): 441–478.

—— (1995b) 'La direttiva madri–figlie, le norme interne e le convenzioni contro le doppie imposizioni', *Rassegna Tributaria*, 38(5): 804–819.

Cecchini, P., with Catinat, M. and Jaquemin, A. (1988) *The European Challenge 1992: the Benefits of a Single Market*, Aldershot: Wildwood House.

Ceriani, V. and Giannini, S. (1994) 'Il concetto di neutralità fiscale: Aspetti positivi e ipotesi di riforma', in CNEL (ed.) *Ipotesi di riordinamento dell'attuale apparato normativo in materia fiscale (Progetto Fisco Ordinato)*, CNEL, Rome, typescript.

——, Frasca, V. and Monacelli, D. (1992) 'Il sistema tributario e il disavanzo pubblico: problemi e prospettive', in Ente Einaudi (ed.) *Il disavanzo pubblico in Italia: natura strutturale e politiche di rientro*, Bologna: Il Mulino, 601–819.

Chown, J. (1984) 'The 1984 Budget, the Finance Bill and corporate finance', *Fiscal Studies*, 5(2): 73–81.

—— (1994) Company Tax Harmonisation and Public Policy in the European Community, London, European Policy Forum Discussion Draft, London, 20 April, unpublished.

—— and Hopper, W. (1982) 'Company tax harmonisation in the European Economic Community', *Intertax*, 8: 275–284.

Clayson, M. (1992) 'Government implements the merger directive (or some of it anyway)', *European Taxation*, 32(11): 370–375.

Cnossen, S. (1990) 'The case for tax diversity in the European Community', *European Economic Review*, 34: 471–479.

——(1993) 'What kind of corporation tax?', in C. Sandford (ed.) *Key Issues in Tax Reform*, Bath: Fiscal Publications.

Coase, R. (1960) 'The problem of social cost', *Journal of Law and Economics*, 3: 1–44.

Cobb, R., Ross, J. K. and Ross, M. H. (1976) 'Agenda building as a comparative political process', *American Political Science Review*, 70: 126–138.

Cohen, M., March J. and Olsen, J. (1972) 'A garbage-can model of organizational choice', *Administrative Science Quarterly*, 17: 1–25.

Colander, D. and Coats, A. W. (1989) (eds) *The Spread of Economic Ideas*, Cambridge: Cambridge University Press.

Collingridge, D. and Reeve, C. (1986) *Science Speaks to Power. The Role of Experts in Policy Making*, London: Pinter.

Collins, R. (1992) 'The romanticism of agency-structure versus the analysis of micro-macro', *Current Sociology*, 40(4), Spring: 77–97.

Commission (1966) *Le développement d'un marché européen des capitaux* (Segrè Report), Brussels: November.

—— (1970) *Impot sur les sociétés et impot sur le revenu dans les Communautés européennes* (Van den Tempel Report), Commission, Etudes – Serie Concurrence, 15.

—— (1977) *Report of the Study Group on the Role of Public Finance in European Integration* (MacDougall Report), Brussels.

—— (1980) *Report from the Commission to the Council on the Scope for Convergence of Tax Systems in the Community*, Bulletin-Supplement 1.

—— (1990) *Guidelines on Company Taxation*, Commission Communication to Parliament and Council, 20 April.

—— (1992) *Report of the Committee of Independent Experts on Company Taxation* (Ruding Report), Luxembourg: Office for Official Publications.

—— (1996) 'Tax policy in the EU', Consultative Paper, Brussels, 20 March.

Confédération Fiscale Européenne (CFE) (1996) 'Future progress on the harmonization of taxation within the European Union', Paper submitted by the CFE to DG XV and DG XXI of the European Commission and to Finance Ministries of EU member states', *European Taxation*, 36(2): 61–66.

Conlan, T. J., Wrightson, M. T. and Beam, D. R. (1990) *Taxing Choices. The Politics of Tax Reform*, Washington, DC: Congressional Quarterly.

Coopers & Lybrand (1992) *EC Initiatives in Direct Taxation and the National Responses*, Deventer: Kluwer.

Cosciani, C. (1950) *La riforma tributaria. Analisi critica del sistema tributario italiano*, Florence: La Nuova Italia.

Council-Commission (1970) *Interim Report on the Establishment by Stages of Economic and Monetary Union* (Werner Report), Supplement to Bulletin 7.

Cram, L. (1993) 'Calling the tune without paying the piper? Social policy regulation: the role of the Commission in European Community social policy', *Policy and Politics*, 21(2): 135–146.

—— (1995) 'Policy-making and the integration process. Implications for integration theory', *Paper prepared for the Fourth ECSA Conference*, Charleston: May.

—— (1997) *Policy-making in the European Union. Conceptual Lenses and the Integration Process*, London: Routledge.

Cronbach, L. J., Ambron, S. R., Dornbusch, S. M., Hess, R. D., Hornik, R. C., Phillips, D. C., Walker D. F. and Weiner S. S. (1980) *Toward Reform of Program Evaluation*, San Francisco: Jossey-Bass.

Crozier, M. and Friedberg, E. (1977) *L'acteur et le Système*, Paris: Editions du Seuil.

Daly, M. (1992) 'Tax coordination and competition in Canada: some lessons for the European Community', in Commission (1992) *Report of the Committee of Independent Experts on Company Taxation* (Ruding Report), Luxembourg: Office for Official Publications, 383–395.

Darolles, Y. and Tucci, M. (1992) 'The Ruding Report. A business point of view', *EC Tax Review*, 1: 39–46.

De Grauwe, P. (1994) 'The need for real convergence in a monetary union', in C. Johnson and S. Collignon (eds) *The Monetary Economics of Europe*, London: Interpublishers, 269–279.

Deloitte, Touche, Tohmatsu International (1995) *The OECD Transfer Pricing Guidelines: A Commentary*, London: DTT International Transfer Pricing Unit.

Dente, B. (1995) *In un diverso stato*, Bologna: Il Mulino.

Derthick, M. and Quirk, P. (1985) *The Politics of Deregulation*, Washington, DC: Brookings Institution.

Dery, D. (1984) *Problem Definition in Policy Analysis*, Lawrence: University Press of Kansas.

Deutsch, K. W. (1966) *The Nerves of Government*, New York: The Free Press.

Devereux, M. (1986) 'The IFS model of the UK corporation tax', *IFS Working Papers*, No. 84, London: Institute for Fiscal Studies.

—— and Freeman, H. (1991) 'A general neutral profit tax', *Fiscal Studies*, 13(3): 1–15.

—— and Mayer, C. P. (1984) 'Corporation tax. The impact of the 1984 budget', *IFS Report Series*, Report No. 11, London: Institute for Fiscal Studies.

—— and Pearson, M. (1989) 'Corporate tax harmonisation and economic efficiency', London, *IFS Report Series* No. 35.

—— (1995) 'European tax harmonisation and production efficiency', *European Economic Review*, 39: 1657–1681.

DiMaggio, P. (1988) 'Interest and agency in institutional theory', in L. Zucker (ed.) *Institutional Patterns and Organizations*, Cambridge, MA: Ballinger, 3–21.

Di Tanno, T. (1993) 'Le direttive comunitarie sulla fiscalità delle imprese: stato di emanazione e di attuazione', *Rivista di Diritto Tributario*, I: 181–199.

Dobuzinskis, L. (1992) 'Modernist and postmodernist metaphors of the policy process: control and stability vs chaos and reflective understanding', *Policy Sciences*, 25(4): 355–380.

Doggart, C. (1993) *Tax Havens and Their Uses*, London: The Economist Intelligence Unit.

Dolowitz, D. and Marsh, D. (1996) 'Who learns from whom: a review of the policy transfer literature, *Political Studies*, XLIV: 343–357.

Dror, Y. (1980) 'Think tanks: a new invention in government', in C. H. Weiss and A. H. Barton (eds) *Making Bureaucracies Work*, London: Sage, 139–152.

Dryzek, J. (1992) 'How far is it from Virginia and Rochester to Frankfurt? Public choice as critical theory', *British Journal of Political Science*, 22: 397–417.

Dudley, G. and Richardson, J. J. (1996) 'Why does policy change over time? Adversarial policy communities, alternative policy arenas, and British trunk roads policy, 1945–1995', *Journal of European Public Policy*, 3(1): 63–83.

Dunn, W. (1980) 'The two-communities metaphor and models of knowledge use. An explanatory case survey', *Knowledge: Creation, Diffusion, Utilization*, 1(4), June: 515–536.

—— (1981) *Public Policy Analysis: An Introduction*, Englewood Cliffs: Prentice Hall.

Dunsire, A. (1978) *Implementation in a Bureaucracy*, Oxford: Martin Robertson.

Dyson, K. (1994) *Elusive Union*, London: Longman.

—— and Featherstone, K. (1996) 'Italy and EMU as "Vimcolo Esterno": empowering the technocrats, transforming the state', *South European Society and Politics*, 1(2): 272–99.

Easson, A. J. (1980) *Tax Law and Policy in the EEC*, London: Sweet and Maxwell.

—— (1992) 'Harmonization of direct taxation in the European Community: from Neumark to Ruding', *Canadian Tax Journal*, 40(3): 600–638.

—— (1993) *Taxation in the European Community*, London: The Athlone Press.

Edwards, J. and Keen, M. (1996) 'Tax competition and Leviathan', *European Economic Review*, 40: 113–134.

Eichenberg, R. and Dalton, R. (1993) 'Europeans and the European Community: the dynamics of public support for European integration', *International Organization*, 47(4): 507–534.

Eichengreen, B. and Frieden, J. (1994) (eds) *The Political Economy of European Monetary Unification*, Boulder: Westview Press.

Elazar, D. J. (1987) *Exploring Federalism*, Tuscaloosa: University of Alabama Press.

Elliott, P. (1993) 'United Kingdom', *EC Tax Review*, 1: 43–51.

Escalar, G. (1995) 'Il rimborso di imposte a soci non residenti tra normativa "madri–figlie" e accordi bilaterali', *Rassegna Tributaria*, I: 66–82.

Etzioni, A. (1976) *Social Problems*, Englewood Cliffs: Prentice-Hall.

European Taxation (1969) 'Proposed directives concerning a common system of taxation applicable to merger-type transactions and parent–subsidiary relationships between corporations of different member states', *European Taxation*, 9(7), July: 147–165.

European Taxation-Editorial (1973) 'Damocles and the enlarged common market', *European Taxation*, 13(1): 3–4.

Evans, P., Rueschemeyer, D. and Skocpol, T. (eds) *Bringing the State Back In*, Cambridge, MA: Cambridge University Press.

Fantozzi, A. (1993a) 'L'attuazione della direttiva Cee madre–figlia in Italia. Confronto tra la direttiva Cee e la legge italiana di attuazione', *Rivista di Diritto Tributario*, I: 521–547.

—— (1993b) 'Italy welcomes further EC harmonization', *Bulletin for International Fiscal Documentation*, September: 474–479.

—— and Manganelli, A. (1993) 'Italy', *EC Tax Review*, 1: 32–39.

Fédération des Experts Comptables Européens (FEE) (1995) 'FEE comments on discussion draft of part I of the OECD transfer pricing guidelines', *Intertax*, 2: 104–105.

Feldman, M. S. and March, J. (1981) 'Information in organizations as signal and symbol', *Administrative Science Quarterly*, 26(1), March: 171–186.

Fischer, F. (1990) *Technocracy and the Politics of Expertise*, London: Sage.

Fischer-Zernin, J. (1987) 'GATT versus tax treaties? The basic conflicts between international taxation methods and the rules and concepts of GATT', *Journal of World Trade Law*, 21(3): 39–62.

Fisher, R. (1987) *State and Local Public Finance*, Glenview: Scott, Foresman and Company.

Fishman, D. B. (1992) 'Postmodernism comes to program evaluation. A critical review of Guba and Lincoln's fourth generation evaluation', *Evaluation and Program Planning*, 15: 263–270.

Freeman, H. and Griffith, R. (1993) 'Surplus ACT – a solution in sight?', *Fiscal Studies*, 14(4): 58–73.

Frenkel, J. A., Razin, A. and Sadka, E. (1991) *International Taxation in an Integrated World*, Cambridge, MA: Cambridge University Press.

Frey, B. S. and Eichenberger, R. (1996) 'To harmonize or to compete? That's not the question', *Journal of Public Economics*, 60: 335–349.

Fullerton, D. (1986) 'The use of effective tax rates in tax policy', *National Tax Journal*, 39(3): 285–292.

Furner, M. O. and Supple, B. (1990) (eds) *The State and Economic Knowledge. The American and British Experiences*, Cambridge, MA: Woodrow Wilson International Center for Scholars and Cambridge University Press.

Gaffney, J. (1991) 'The political think-tanks in the UK and the Ministerial cabinets in France', *West European Politics*, 14(1): 1–17.

Gamble, A., Olson, M., Barry, N., Seldon, A., Hartwell, M. and Melnyk, A. (1989) *Ideas, Interests and Consequences*, London: Institute of Economic Affairs.

Gammie, M. (1984) 'Has Nigel Lawson really reformed business taxation?', *Fiscal Studies*, 5(3), August: 82–92.

——(1990) 'The process of tax reform in the United Kingdom', Discussion Paper, London: The Law Society of England and Wales.

—— (1991a) 'Imputation systems and foreign income: The UK surplus ACT problem and its relationship to European corporate tax harmonisation', *Intertax*, 12: 545–560.

—— (1991b) 'Corporate tax harmonisation: an "ACE" proposal. Harmonising European corporate taxation through an allowance for corporate equity', *European Taxation*, August: 238–242.

—— (1992) 'The Ruding committee: an initial response', London: Institute for Fiscal Studies.

—— (1993) 'Solutions to the UK surplus advance corporation tax problem?

Budget changes and proposals for foreign income dividends', *Intertax*, 8: 340–350.

—— (1994) 'Foreign income dividends: the UK response to surplus advance corporation tax', *Intertax*, 6–7: 250–258.

—— and Robinson, B. (1989) (eds) *Beyond 1992: A European Tax System*, IFS Commentary No. 13, London: Institute for Fiscal Studies.

—— and Brannan, G. (1995) 'EC law strikes at the UK corporate tax: the death knell of UK imputation?', *Intertax*, 8–9: 389–405.

Garrett, G. (1995) 'Capital mobility, trade, and the domestic politics of economic policy', *International Organization*, 49(4), Autumn: 657–687.

—— and Weingast, B. R. (1993) 'Ideas, interests, and institutions: constructing the European Community's internal market', in J. Goldstein and R. O. Keohane (eds) *Ideas and Foreign Policy. Beliefs, Institutions, and Political Change*, Ithaca and London: Cornell University Press, 173–206.

Giannini, S. (1994) *Imposte e mercato internazionale dei capitali*, Bologna: Il Mulino.

Giddens, A. (1984) *The Constitution of Society: Outline of the Theory of Structuration*, Cambridge: Polity Press.

Giovannini, A. (1989) 'National tax systems versus the European capital market', *Economic Policy*, 9, October: 346–386.

—— (1990) 'Reforming capital income taxation in the open economy: theoretical issues', in H. Siebert (ed.) *Reforming Capital Income Taxation*, Tubingen: J. C. B. Mohr, 3–18.

—— and Hines, J. (1991) 'Capital flight and tax competition: are there viable solutions to both problems?', in A. Giovannini and C. Mayer (eds) *European Financial Integration*, Cambridge: Cambridge University Press, 172–210.

Giuliani, M. (1992) 'Il processo decisionale italiano e le politiche comunitarie', *Polis*, 6, August: 307–342.

—— (1996) 'Italy', in D. Rometsch and W. Wessels (eds) *The European Union and Member States. Towards Institutional Fusion?*, Manchester: Manchester University Press, 105–133.

Goldstein, J. (1993) *Ideas, Interests, and American Trade Policy*, Ithaca: Cornell University Press.

—— and Keohane, R. O. (1993) (eds) *Ideas and Foreign Policy. Beliefs, Institutions and Political Change*, Ithaca and London: Cornell University Press.

Gordon, R. H. (1981) *The Taxation of Controlled Foreign Corporations: an International Comparison*, Toronto: Canadian Tax Foundation.

—— (1992) 'Can capital income taxes survive in open economies?', *The Journal of Finance*, 47(3), July: 1159–1180.

Gormley, W. T. Jr (1985–1986) 'Regulatory issue-networks in a federal system', *Polity*, 18: 595–620.

Gourevitch, P. (1978) 'The second image reversed: the international sources of domestic politics', *International Organization*, 32(4): 881–911.

—— (1984) 'Breaking with orthodoxy: the politics of economic responses to the depression of the 1930s', *International Organization*, 38, Winter: 95–130.

Green Cowles, M. (1995) 'Setting the agenda for the new Europe: the ERT and EC 1992', *Journal of Common Market Studies*, 33(4): 501–526.

Grubert, H. and Mutti, J. (1995) 'Taxing multinationals in a world with portfolio flows and R&D. Is capital export neutrality obsolete?', *International Tax and Public Finance*, 2(3): 439–457.

——, Goodspeed, T. and Swenson, D. (1993), 'Explaining the low taxable income of foreign-controlled companies in the United States', in A. Giovannini, G. R. Hubbard and J. Slemrod (eds) *Studies in International Taxation*, Chicago: University of Chicago Press, 237–270.

Guba, E. and Lincoln, Y. (1989) *Fourth Generation Evaluation*, London: Sage.

Guerra, M. C. (1993) 'Tax policies in the 1980s and 1990s: the case of Italy', in A. Knoester (ed.) *Taxation in the United States and Europe. Theory and Practice*, London: St Martin's, 328–354.

Haaland Matlary, J. (1996) 'Energy policy: from a national to a European framework?', in H. Wallace and W. Wallace (eds) *Policy-Making in the EU*, Oxford: Oxford University Press, 257–277.

Haas, E. (1958) *The Uniting of Europe*, Stanford: Stanford University Press.

Haas, P. (1992) (ed.) 'Knowledge, power and international policy coordination', monographic issue, *International Organization*, 46(1), Winter.

Hager, G. (1996) 'Republicans throw in towel on seven-year deal', *Congressional Quarterly – Weekly Report*, 54(4), January 27: 213–216.

Hall, P. (1986) *Governing the Economy. The Politics of State Intervention in Britain and France*, Cambridge: Polity Press.

—— (1989) (ed.) *The Political Power of Economic Ideas. Keynesianism Across Nations*, Princeton: Princeton University Press.

—— (1993) 'Policy paradigms, social learning and the state. the case of economic policy-making in Britain', *Comparative Politics*, 25(3), April: 275–296.

Hall, R. E. and Rabushka, A. (1995) *The Flat Tax*, Stanford: Hoover Institution Press, second edition.

Hallerberg, M. (1996) 'Tax competition in Wilhelmine Germany and its implications for the European Union', *World Politics*, 48, April: 324–357.

—— and Basinger, S. (1997) 'Internationalization and changes in tax policy in OECD countries: the importance of domestic veto players', *Comparative Political Studies*, 30.

Hamada, K. (1966) 'Strategic aspects of taxation on foreign investment income', *Quarterly Journal of Economics*, 80: 361–375.

Hansen, S. (1983) *The Politics of Taxation*, New York: Praeger.

Harcourt, A. J. (1996) 'Regulating for media concentration: the emerging policy of the European Union', *Utilities Law Review*, 7 (5) : 202–210.

Hay, D., Horner, F. and Owens, J. (1994) 'Past and present work in the OECD on transfer pricing and selected issues', *Intertax*, 10: 423–432.

Hayward, J. and Klein, R. (1994) 'Grande Bretagne. De la gestion publique à la gestion privée du déclin économique', in B. Jobert (ed.) *Le tournant néo-libéral en Europe*, Paris: L'Harmattan, 87–121.

Heclo, H. (1972) 'Review article: policy analysis', *British Journal of Political Science*, 2: 83–108.

—— (1974) *Modern Social Politics in Britain and Sweden*, New Haven: Yale University Press.

—— (1978) 'Issue networks and the executive establishment', in A. King (ed.)

The New American Political System, Washington, DC: American Enterprise Institute: 87–124.

—— and Wildavsky, A. (1974) *The Private Government of Public Money*, Berkeley: University of California Press.

——, Heidenheimer, A. and Adams, T. (1990) *Comparative Public Policy*, New York: St Martin's Press, third edition.

Heiner, R. A. (1983) 'Origins of predictable behavior', *American Economic Review*, 73: 560–595.

Higson, C. and Elliott, J. (1993) 'Effective tax rates on UK and foreign income – the impact of the UK budget proposals, *British Tax Review*, 3: 330–339.

Hinnekens, L. (1994) 'Compatibility of bilateral tax treaties with European Community law. The rules', *EC Tax Review*, 4: 146–166.

Hirschman, A. O. (1970) *Exit, Voice, and Loyalty*, Cambridge, MA: Harvard University Press.

Hjern, B. and Hull, C. (1982) 'Implementation research as empirical constitutionalism', *European Journal of Political Research*, 10: 105–115.

Hocking, B. (1993) *Localizing Foreign Policy. Non-central Governments and Multi-layered Diplomacy*, London: St. Martin's Press.

Hodges, M. (1972) (ed.) *European Integration*, Harmondsworth: Penguin.

Hoffmann, S. (1966) 'Obstinate or obsolete? The fate of the nation-state and the case of Western Europe', *Daedalus*: 862–915.

—— (1982) 'Reflections on the nation-state in Western Europe today', *Journal of Common Market Studies*, 21(1–2): 21–37.

Hogwood, B. (1992) *Trends in British Public Policy*, Buckingham: Open University Press.

—— and Peters, G. B. (1983) *Policy Dynamics*, Brighton: Wheatsheaf.

Holzner, B. and Marx, J. H. (1979) *Knowledge Application. The Knowledge System in Society*, Boston: Allyn and Bacon.

Hood, C. (1994) *Explaining Economic Policy Reversals*, Buckingham: Open University Press.

Hooghe, L. (1996) (ed.) *Cohesion Policy and European Integration. Building Multi-Level Governance*, Oxford: Oxford University Press.

Hufbauer, G. C. (1992) *US Taxation of International Income: Blueprint for Reform*, Washington, DC: Institute for International Economics.

Ingram H. and Rathgeb-Smith, S. (1993) (eds) *Public Policy for Democracy*, Washington, DC: Brookings Institution.

—— and Schneider, A. (1993) 'Constructing citizenship: the subtle messages of policy design', in H. Ingram and S. Rathgeb-Smith (eds) *Public Policy for Democracy*, Washington, DC: Brookings Institution, 68–94.

Inland Revenue (1991) *EC Direct Tax Measures, A Consultative Document*, London: Inland Revenue.

—— (1992) *The New Inland Revenue*, London: Inland Revenue.

—— (1993) *Corporation Tax Surplus ACT. Proposals for Reform. A Consulative Document*, London: Inland Revenue.

Institute for Fiscal Studies (IFS) (1994) *Setting Savings Free. Proposals for the Taxation of Savings and Profits*, London: IFS.

International Bureau of Fiscal Documentation (IBFD) (1994) *The Taxation of Parent Royalties, Dividends, Interest in Europe*, Amsterdam: IBFD Publications.

—— (1995) *Survey of the Implementation of the EC Corporate Tax Directives*, Amsterdam: IBFD Publications.

—— (various years) *EC Corporate Tax Law. Commentary on the EC Direct Tax Measures and Member States Implementation*, Amsterdam: IBFD Publications, two loose-leaf volumes.

—— (various years) *The Tax Treatment of Transfer Pricing*, Amsterdam: IBFD Publications, four loose-leaf volumes.

International Chamber of Commerce (ICC) (1995) 'ICC comments on OECD transfer pricing guidelines for MNEs and tax administrations – Discussion draft part I', *Intertax*, 1: 39–42.

International Fiscal Association (IFA) (1994) *Harmonization of Corporate Taxes in the EC*, Deventer: Kluwer Law and Taxation Publishers.

Isaac, J. (1989) 'Corporate tax harmonisation', in M. Gammie and B. Robinson (eds) *Beyond 1992: A European Tax System*, London, IFS Commentary No. 13: 20–29.

Jacobsen, J. K. (1995) 'Much ado about ideas. The cognitive factor in economic policy', *World Politics*, 47, January: 283–310.

Janeba, E. (1995) 'Corporate income tax competition, double taxation treaties, and foreign direct investment', *Journal of Public Economics*, 56: 311–325.

Jenkins-Smith, H. C. and Sabatier, P. A. (1994) 'Evaluating the advocacy coalition framework', *Journal of Public Policy*, 14(2): 175–203.

Jobert, B. (1989) 'The normative frameworks of public policy', *Political Studies*, 37: 376–386.

Jordan, G. and Richardson, J. J. (1979) *Governing Under Pressure*, Oxford: Martin Robertson.

Kahneman, D. and Tversky, A. (1979) 'Prospect theory: an analysis of decision under risk', *Econometrica*, 47: 263–291.

—— (1982) 'The psychology of preferences', *Scientific American*, 246(1), January: 160–173.

Kaldor, N. (1955) *An Expenditure Tax*, London: Allen & Unwin.

Kaplan, P. T. (1993) 'Treaty shopping under the new US–Netherlands treaty', *Bulletin for International Fiscal Documentation*, 47, April: 175–180.

Kasten, R., Sammartino, F. and Toder, E. (1994) 'Trends in federal tax progressivity, 1980–1993', in J. Slemrod (ed.) *Tax Progressivity and Income Inequality*, Cambridge: Cambridge University Press, 9–50.

Kay, J. A. (1986) 'Tax reform in context: a strategy for the 1990s', *Fiscal Studies*, 7(4), November: 1–17.

Kellow A. (1988) 'Promoting elegance in policy theory: simplifying Lowi's arenas of power', *Policy Studies Journal*, 16(4), Summer: 713–724.

Keohane, R. (1986) (ed.) *Neorealism and its Critics*, New York: Columbia University Press.

—— and Nye, S. (1989) *Power and Interdependence*, Glenview: Scott, Foresman, second edition.

Keren, M. (1993) 'Economists and economic policy-making in Israel. The politics of expertise in the stabilization program', *Policy Sciences*, 26: 331–346.

King, A. (1973) 'Ideas, institutions and the policies of governments: a comparative analysis', *British Journal of Political Science*, 3: 291–313; 409–423.

King, E. (1994) *Transfer Pricing and Valuation in Corporate Taxation: Federal Legislation vs Administrative Practice*, Dordrecht: Kluwer.

King, M. A. and Fullerton, D. (1984) (eds) *The Taxation of Income from Capital. A Comparative Study of the United States, the UK, Sweden, and West Germany*, Chicago and London: The University of Chicago Press.

Kingdon, J. W. (1984) *Agendas, Alternatives and Public Policy*, Glenview: HarperCollins.

Kitterer, W. (1990) 'Comment on Alberto Giovannini', in H. Siebert (ed.) *Reforming Capital Income Taxation*, Tubingen: J. C. B. Mohr, 19–21.

Kleiboer, M. and Hart, P. (1995–1996) (eds) 'Coping with policy controversies', monographic issue of *Knowledge and Policy*, 8(4).

Knott, J. and Wildavsky, A. (1980) 'If dissemination is the solution, what is the problem?', *Knowledge*, 19(4): 537–578.

Kopits, G. (1992) 'Tax harmonization in the European Community: policy issues and analysis', Washington, DC: International Monetary Fund *Occasional Paper* No. 94.

Krugman, P. (1991) *Geography and Trade*, Cambridge, MA: MIT Press.

Kuhn, T. (1962) *The Structure of Scientific Revolutions*, Chicago: University of Chicago Press.

Kuiper, W. G. (1988) 'EC Commission proposes a directive on the harmonization of rules for the determination of taxable profits of enterprises', *European Taxation*, 28(10): 319–329.

Lakoff, G. (1987) *Women, Fire, and Dangerous Things: What Categories Reveal About the Mind*, Chicago: University of Chicago Press.

Lane, J. E. (1987) (ed.) *Bureaucracy and Public Choice*, London: Sage.

Lange, P. (1993) 'Maastricht and the social protocol: why did they do it?', *Politics & Society*, 21(1), March: 5–36.

Lawson, N. (1992) *The View From No.11. Memoirs of a Tory Radical*, London: Corgi Books.

Leape, J. I. (1993) 'Tax policies in the 1980s and 1990s: the case of the United Kingdom', in A. Knoester (ed.) *Taxation in the United States and Europe. Theory and Practice*, London: St Martin's Press, 276–311.

Liberatore, A. (1995) 'Arguments, assumptions and the choice of policy instruments', in B. Dente (ed.) *Environmental Policy in Search of New Instruments*, Dordrecht: Kluwer, 55–71.

Lindberg, L. (1963) *The Political Dynamics of European Economic Integration*, Stanford: Stanford University Press.

Lindblom, C. E. (1959) 'The science of muddling through', *Public Administration Review*, 19(1): 79–88.

—— (1965) *The Intelligence of Democracy*, New York: The Free Press.

—— (1975) 'The sociology of planning: thought and social interaction', in M. Bornstein (ed.) *Economic Planning, East and West*, Cambridge, MA: Ballinger, 23–67.

—— (1986) 'Who needs what social research for policymaking?', *Knowledge: Creation, Diffusion, Utilization*, 7: 345–366.

—— (1990) *Inquiry and Change. The Troubled Attempt to Understand and Shape Society*, New Haven: Yale University Press.

—— and Cohen, D. K. (1979) *Usable Knowledge*, New Haven: Yale University Press.

Lindquist, E. A. (1988) 'What do decision models tell us about information use?', *Knowledge in Society*, 1(2): 86–111.

—— (1990) 'The third community, policy inquiry, and social scientists', in S. Brooks and A. G. Gagnon (eds) *Social Scientists, Policy, and the State*, New York: Praeger, 21–51.

—— (1992) 'Public managers and policy communities: learning to meet new challenges', *Canadian Public Administration*, 35(2): 127–159.

Lodin, S. O. (1978) *Progressive Expenditure Tax: An Alternative?*, Stockholm: LieberForlag.

—— (1995) 'Is the American approach fair? Some critical views on the transfer pricing issues', *Intertax*, 5: 240–245.

Lowi, T. (1964) 'American business, public policy, case studies and political theory', *World Politics*, 16: 677–693.

—— (1972) 'Four systems of policy, politics and choice', *Public Administration Review*, 32(4): 298–310.

Lupi, R. (1996) *Le illusioni fiscali. Risanare gli apparati per riformare il fisco*, Bologna: Il Mulino.

McCloskey, D. (1985) *The Rhetoric of Economics*, Hemel Hempstead: Harvester and University of Wisconsin Press.

—— (1994) *Knowledge and Persuasion in Economics*, Cambridge: Cambridge University Press.

MacDougall, D. (1992) 'Economic and monetary union and the EC budget', *National Institute Economic Review*, 140, May: 64–68.

——(1994) *Knowledge and Persuasion in Economics*, Cambridge: Cambridge University Press.

McLure, C. E. (1986) 'Tax competition: is what's good for the private goose also good for the public gander?', *National Tax Journal*, 39(3), September: 341–348.

——(1989) 'European integration and taxation of corporate income at source: lessons from the US', in M. Gammie and B. Robinson (eds) *Beyond 1992: A European Tax System*, London, *IFS Commentary* No. 13: 39–51.

——(1992) 'The political economy of tax reform and their implications for interdependence: United States', in I. Takatoshi and A. O. Krueger (eds) *The Political Economy of Tax Reform*, Chicago: University of Chicago Press, 97–115.

—— and Zodrow, G. R. (1987) 'Treasury I and the tax reform act of 1986: the economics and politics of tax reform', *Economic Perspectives*, 1(1), Summer: 37–58.

—— (1994) 'The study and practice of income tax policy', in J. M. Quigley and E. Smolensky (eds) *Modern Public Finance*, Cambridge, MA: MIT Press, 165–209.

Macridis, R. (1961) 'Interest groups in comparative analysis', *Journal of Politics*, 23(1), February: 25–45.

Majone, G. D. (1989) *Evidence, Argument and Persuasion in the Policy Process*, New Haven and London: Yale University Press.

—— (1991) 'Market integration and regulation: Europe after 1992', *EUI Working Papers SPS* No.10, Florence.

—— (1992) 'Regulatory federalism in the European Community', *Environment and Planning C: Government and Policy*, 10: 299–316.

—— (1993a) 'The European Community between social policy and social regulation', *Journal of Common Market Studies*, 31(2), June: 153–170.

—— (1993b) 'Ideas, interests and policy change', in H. Redner (ed.) *An Heretical Heir of Enlightenment. Science, Politics and Policy in the Work of Charles Lindblom*, Boulder: Westview Press, 283–298.

—— (1993c) 'When does policy deliberation matter?', *EUI Working Papers*, Florence: European University Institute.

—— (1994a) 'The rise of the regulatory state in Europe', *West European Politics*, 17(3): 77–101.

—— (1994b) 'Comparing strategies of regulatory rapprochement', in OECD (1994) *Regulatory Co-operation for an Interdependent World*, Paris: OECD.

—— (1996) 'A European regulatory state?', in J. J. Richardson (ed.) *The European Union: Power and Policy-Making*, London: Routledge, 263–277.

Manera, M. (1995) 'Indeducibilità del disavanzo di fusione: una contraddizione nel sistema di imposzione fiscale delle imprese', *Rassegna Tributaria*, 38(1): 44–50.

Manganelli, A. (1993) 'Italy: tax treaty and anti-avoidance implications of the implementation of the parent–subsidiary directive', *European Taxation*, 33, October: 333–339.

Mansbridge, J. J. (1990) (ed.) *Beyond Self-Interest*, Chicago: University of Chicago Press.

March, J. C. (1966) 'The power of power', in D. Easton (ed.) *Varieties of Political Theory*, Englewood Cliffs: Prentice-Hall, 39–70.

—— and Olsen, J. P. (1989) *Rediscovering Institutions. The Organizational Basis of Political Life*, New York: The Free Press.

—— (1995) *Democratic Governance*, New York: The Free Press.

Marin, B. and Mayntz, R. (1991) (eds) *Policy Networks. Empirical Evidence and Theoretical Considerations*, Frankfurt am Main and Boulder: Campus and Westview Press.

Marino, G. (1993a) 'Profili fiscali delle riorganizzazioni di imprese con elementi di ultraterritorialità', *Diritto e Pratica Tributaria*, 64 (I): 2089–2119.

—— (1993b) 'Brevi note sul trasferimento di sede all'estero', *Diritto e pratica tributaria*, 64: 1028–1038.

Markoff, J. and Montecinos, V. (1993) 'The ubiquitous rise of economists', *Journal of Public Policy*, 13(1): 37–68.

Marks, G. (1992) 'Structural policy in the European Community', in A. Sbragia (ed.) *Europolitics. Institutions and Policy-Making in the 'New' European Community*, Washington, DC: Brookings Institution.

—— (1993) 'Structural policy and multi-level governance in the EC', in A. W. Cafruny and G. G. Rosenthal (eds) *The State of the European Community. Vol. 2: The Maastricht Debates and Beyond*, Boulder: Lynne Rienner Publishers, 391–410.

——, Scharpf, F.W., Schmitter, P. C. and Streeck, W. (1996) *Governance in the European Union*, London: Sage.

Marsh, D. and Rhodes, R. A. W. (1992) (eds) *Policy Networks in British Government*, Oxford: Clarendon Press.

May, P. J. (1992) 'Policy learning and failure', *Journal of Public Policy*, 12(4): 331–354.

Mayr, S (1995) 'Italy: refund of tax credit and equalization tax on dividends distributed to foreign shareholders resident in certain treaty countries', *Intertax*, 1: 35–38.

Mazey, S. and Richardson, J. J. (1993) (eds) *Lobbying in the European Community*, Oxford: Oxford University Press.

—— (1994) 'The Commission and the lobby', in G. Edwards and D. Spence (eds) *The European Commission*, London: Longman, 169–201.

—— (1995) 'Promiscuous policy-making: the European policy style?', in C. Rhodes and S. Mazey (eds) *The State of the European Union; Vol. 3: Building a European Polity*: 337–359.

—— (1996a) 'Influencing the EU's agenda: interest groups and the 1996 IGC', *Paper prepared for the twenty-fourth ECPR Joint Sessions*, Oslo, 29 March–3 April.

—— (1996b) 'The logic of organisation: interest groups', in J. J. Richardson (ed.) *European Union: Power and Policy-Making*, London: Routledge, 200–215.

Meade, J. E. (1978) *The Structure and Reform of Direct Taxation*, London: Allen & Unwin.

Messere, K. (1993a) *Tax Policy in OECD Countries*, Amsterdam: IBFD Publications.

—— (1993b) 'A personal view on certain aspects of the Ruding Committee report and the EC Commission's reaction to it', *European Taxation*, 33, January: 2–14.

Milward, A. S. (1992) *The European Rescue of the Nation State*, London: Routledge.

Milward, B. H. (1980) 'Policy entrepreneurship and bureaucratic demand creation', in H. M. Ingram and D. E. Man (eds) *Why Policies Succeed or Fail*, London: Sage, 255–277.

Minarik, J. J. (1989) 'How tax reform came about', in D. Colander and A.W. Coats (eds) *The Spread of Economic Ideas*, Cambridge: Cambridge University Press, 141–154.

Moore, R. M. (1992) 'United Kingdom', *European Taxation*, 32, April–May: 177–178.

Moravcsik, A. (1991) 'Negotiating the Single European Act: national interests and conventional statecraft in the European Community', *International Organization*, 45(1), Winter: 19–56.

—— (1993) 'Preferences and power in the European Community: a liberal intergovernmentalist approach', *Journal of Common Market Studies*, 31(4): 473–524

—— (1994) 'Why European integration strengthens the state', *Paper given to the Annual Convention of the American Political Science Association*, New York.

Mucciaroni, G. (1990) 'Public choice and the politics of comprehensive tax reform', *Governance*, 3(1), January: 1–32.

—— (1991) 'Unclogging the arteries: the defeat of client politics and the logic of collective action', *Policy Studies Journal*, 19(3–4): 474–494.

—— (1992) 'The garbage can model and the study of policy making: a critique', *Polity*, 24(3), Spring: 459–482.

—— (1995) *Reversals of Fortune. Public Policy and Private Interests*, Washington, DC: Brookings Institution.

—— (1996) 'What's new in public policy and American politics?', *Policy Studies Journal*, 24(2): 316–320.

Mundell, R. (1961) 'A theory of optimum currency areas', *American Economic Review*, 51: 657–665.

Musgrave, R. A. (1959) *The Theory of Public Finance. A Study in Public Economy*, New York: McGraw-Hill.

—— (1965) (ed.) *Essays in Fiscal Federalism*, Washington, DC: Brookings Institution.

—— (1983) 'Who should tax, where, and what?', in C. E. McLure (ed.) *Tax Assignment in Federal Countries*, Canberra: Australian National University Press.

—— and Musgrave, P. B. (1984) *Public Finance in Theory and Practice*, fourth edition, New York: McGraw-Hill.

Nelsen, B. F. and Stubb, A. (1994) (eds) *The EU: Readings on the Theory and Practice of European Integration*, Boulder: Lynne Rienner Publishers.

Nias, P. (1995) 'Harmonization by the back door?', *International Tax Review*, 6(9), October: 29–32.

Nugent, N. (1994) *The Government and Politics of the European Union*, third edition, London: Macmillan.

Oates, W. (1972) *Fiscal Federalism*, New York: Harcourt Brace.

—— (1994) 'Federalism and government finance', in J. M. Quigley and E. Smolensky (eds) *Modern Public Finance*, Cambridge, MA: Harvard University Press, 126–151.

Odling-Smee, J. and Lawton, D. (1990) 'Reforming capital income taxation: the UK experience', in H. Siebert (ed.) *Reforming Capital Income Taxation*, Tubingen: J. C. B. Mohr, 231–257.

OECD (1979) *Transfer Pricing and Multinational Enterprises*, Paris: OECD.

—— (1991) *Taxing Profits in a Global Economy. Domestic and International Issues*, Paris: OECD.

—— (1992) *Model Tax Convention on Income and on Capital*, Paris: OECD.

—— (1993) 'Intercompany transfer pricing regulations under US section 482 temporary and proposed regulations', *Bulletin for International Fiscal Documentation*, 47, November: 619–629.

—— (1994) *Tax Information Exchange between OECD Member Countries. A Survey of Current Practices*, Paris, OECD.

—— (1995) *Transfer Pricing Guidelines for Multinational Enterprises and Tax Administrations*, Paris: OECD.

—— (1996a) *OECD Economic Surveys: Italy*, Paris: OECD.

—— (1996b) *Controlled Foreign Company Legislation*, Paris: OECD.

O'Neill, M. (1996) (ed.) *The Politics of European Integration: A Reader*, London: Routledge.

Ostrom, E. (1986) 'An agenda for the study of institutions', *Public Choice*, 48: 3–25.

Ostrom, V. (1991) *The Meaning of American Federalism*, San Francisco: ICS Press.

Otsuka, I. (1994) 'Japan and US in transfer pricing war', *International Tax Review*, 5(7): 9–10.

Owens, J. (1993) 'Globalisation: the implications for tax policies', *Fiscal Studies*, 14(3): 21–44.

Pagan, J. C. and Wilkie, J. S. (1993) *Transfer Pricing Strategy in a Global Economy*, Amsterdam: IBFD Publications.

Palumbo, D. (1987) (ed.) *The Politics of Program Evaluation*, London: Sage.

Pearson, M. (1989) 'Corporate tax harmonisation in the European Community', in M. Gammie and B. Robinson (eds) *Beyond 1992: A European Tax System*, London, IFS Commentary, No.13: 90–96.

Pechman, J. A. (1989) (ed.) *The Role of the Economist in Government: An International Perspective*, Hemel Hempstead: Harvester.

Pedone, A. (1980) *Evasori e tartassati*, Bologna: Il Mulino.

—— (1989) (ed.) *La questione tributaria. Analisi e proposte*, Bologna: Il Mulino.

Peters, G. B. (1991) *The Politics of Taxation. A Comparative Perspective*, Cambridge, MA, and Oxford: Blackwell.

—— (1992a) 'The policy process: an institutionalist perspective', *Canadian Public Administration*, 35(2): 160–180.

—— (1992b) 'Bureaucratic politics and the institutions of the European Community', in A. M. Sbragia (ed.) *Europolitics: Institutions and Policy-Making in the 'New' European Community*, Washington, DC: Brookings Institution.

—— (1994) 'Agenda-setting in the European Community', *Journal of European Public Policy*, 1(1): 9–26.

—— and Barker (1993) (eds) *Advising West European Governments. Inquiries, Expertise and Public Policy*, Edinburgh: Edinburgh University Press.

Peterson, J. (1995) 'Decision-making in the European Union: towards a framework for analysis', *Journal of European Public Policy*, 2(1): 69–93.

Picciotto, S. (1992) *International Business Taxation. A Study in the Internationalization of Business Regulation*, London: Weidenfeld and Nicolson.

—— (1993) 'Transfer pricing and the antinomies of corporate regulation', in J. McCahery, S. Picciotto and C. Scott (eds) *Corporate Control and Accountability*, Oxford: Clarendon Press, 374–405.

Pierson, P. (1996) 'The path to European integration. A historical institutional analysis', *Comparative Political Studies*, 29(2), April: 123–163.

Pirie, M. (1988) *Micropolitics. The Creation of Successful Policy*, Aldershot: Wildwood House.

Pollack, M. A. (1994) 'Creeping competence: the expanding agenda of the EC', *Journal of Public Policy*, 14(2): 95–145.

—— (1997) 'Delegation, agency and agenda setting in the European Community', *International Organization*, 51(1) Winter: 99-134.

Powell, W. W. and DiMaggio, P. J. (1991) (eds) *The New Institutionalism in Organizational Analysis*, Chicago: University of Chicago Press.

Power, M. (1993) 'The politics of financial auditing', *Political Quarterly*, 64: 272–284.

Prud'homme, R. (1993) 'The potential role of the EC budget in the reduction of spatial disparities in a European economic and monetary union', in H. Reichenbach (ed.) *Stable Money, Sound Finances*, Brussels: Commission, DG for Economic and Financial Affairs, 317–351.

Puchala, D. (1972) 'Of blind men, elephants and international integration', *Journal of Common Market Studies*, 10(1): 267–284.

Putnam, R. (1988) 'Diplomacy and domestic politics: the logic of two-level games', *International Organization*, 42(2): 427–460.

Quigley, J. M. and Smolensky, E. (1994) (eds) *Modern Public Finance*, Cambridge, MA: Harvard University Press.

Quirk, P. J. (1989) 'The cooperative resolution of policy conflict', *American Political Science Review*, 83(3): 905–921.

—— (1990) 'Deregulation and the politics of ideas in Congress', in J. J. Mansbridge (ed.) *Beyond Self-Interest*, Chicago: University of Chicago Press, 183–199.

Radaelli, C. M. (1988) 'Europeanism, Italian way', *Relazioni Internazionali*, 52(4): 92–98.

—— and Dente, B. (1996) 'Evaluation strategies and the analysis of the policy process', *Evaluation*, 2(1): 51–66.

Rädler, A. J. (1993) 'Where does tax harmonization stand today?', *EC Tax Review*, 4: 198–199.

Razin, A. and Sadka, E. (1989) 'International tax competition and gains from tax harmonisation', *NBER Working Paper* No. 3152.

Regonini, G. and Giuliani, M. (1994) 'Italie: au delà d'une démocratie consensuelle?', in B. Jobert (ed.) *Le Tournant Néo-Libéral en Europe*, Paris: L'Harmattan, 123–199.

Reichenbach, H. (1993) (ed.) *Stable Money, Sound Finances*, Brussels: Commission, DG for Economic and Financial Affairs. Also published as monographic issue of *European Economy*, No. 53.

Rein, M. and Schön, D. (1991) 'Frame-reflective policy discourse', in P. Wagner, C. H. Weiss, B. Wittrock and H. Wollman (eds) *Social Sciences and Modern States. National Experiences and Theoretical Crossroads*, Cambridge: Cambridge University Press, 262–289.

—— (1996) 'Frame-critical policy analysis and frame-reflective policy practice', *Knowledge and Policy*, 9(1): 85–104.

Rich, R. F. and Oh, C. H. (1994) 'The utilization of policy research', in S. S. Nagel (ed.) *Encyclopedia of Policy Studies*, second edition, New York and Basel: Marcel Dekker, 69–92.

Richardson, J. J. (1982) (ed.) *Policy Styles in Western Europe*, London: Allen & Unwin.

—— (1995) 'EU water policy: uncertain agendas, shifting networks and complex coalitions', in H. Bressers, L. O'Toole and J. J. Richardson (eds) *Networks for Water Policy*, special issue of *Environmental Politics*, London: Frank Cass, 139–167.

—— (1996) 'Policy-making in the European Union. Interests, ideas and garbage-cans of primeval soup', in J. J. Richardson (ed.) *The European Union: Power and Policy-Making*, London: Routledge, 3–23.

—— and Jordan, G. (1979) *Governing under Pressure*, Oxford: Robertson.

——, Maloney, W. A. and Rudig, W. (1992) 'The dynamics of policy change: lobbying and water privatisation', *Public Administration*, 70: 157–175.

Risse-Kappen, T. (1996a) 'Explaining the nature of the beast. International relations theory and comparative policy analysis meet the European Union', *Journal of Common Market Studies*, 34(1): 53–80.

—— (1996b) 'Ideas, communicative processes, and domestic political change in Europe: a conceptual framework and some preliminary results', *Paper given to the Tenth Conference of Europeanists*, Chicago, March: 14–16.

Ritter, W. (1994) 'On a slippery slope', *Intertax*, 8–9: 312–313.

Robinson, A. and Sandford, C. (1983) *Tax Policy-Making in the United Kingdom. A Study of Rationality, Ideology and Politics*, London: Heinemann Books.

Rochefort, D. A. and Cobb, R. W. (1994) (eds) *The Politics of Problem Definition*, Lawrence: University Press of Kansas.

Rose, R. (1991) 'What is lesson-drawing?', *Journal of Public Policy*, 11: 3–30.

—— and Karran, T. (1987) *Taxation by Political Inertia*, London: Macmillan.

Rosen, S. (1973) (ed.) *Testing the Theory of the Military-Industrial Complex*, Lexington: Lexington Books.

Rosenau, P. (1993) 'Anticipating a post-modern policy current?', *Policy Currents*, 3(2), May: 1–4.

Russo, V. (1989) *Il Ministero delle Finanze*, Rome: La Nuova Italia Scientifica.

—— (1995) 'La riforma della amministrazione finanziaria', *Rassegna Tributaria*, 1: 96–98.

Sabatier, P. (1986) 'Top-down and bottom-up approaches to implementation research: a critical analysis and suggested synthesis', *Journal of Public Policy*, 6(1): 21–48.

—— (1988) 'An advocacy coalition framework of policy change and the role of policy-oriented learning therein', *Policy Sciences*, 21: 129–169.

—— (1993) 'Policy change over a decade or more', in P. A. Sabatier and H. C. Jenkins-Smith (eds) *Policy Change and Learning. An Advocacy Coalition Approach*, Boulder: Westview Press, 13–39.

—— and Jenkins-Smith, H.C. (1993) (eds) *Policy Change and Learning. An Advocacy Coalition Approach*, Boulder: Westview Press.

Sala-i-Martin, X. and Sachs, J. (1992) 'Fiscal federalism and optimum currency areas: evidence for Europe', in M. B. Canzoneri, V. Grilli and P. R. Masson (eds) *Establishing a Central Bank: Issues in Europe and Lessons from the US*, Cambridge: Cambridge University Press, 195–219.

Samuels, L. B. (1995) 'Remarks on revenue estimating and the OECD transfer pricing guidelines', *Intertax*, 2: 64–68.

Sandford, C. (1993) *Successful Tax Reform*, Bath: Fiscal Publications.

Sandholtz, W. (1993) 'Choosing union: monetary politics and Maastricht', *International Organization*, 47(1): 1–39.

Sandler, D. (1994) *Pushing the Boundaries*, London: Institute of Taxation and IFS.

Santos, P. (1993) 'The spatial implications of economic and monetary union', in H. Reichenbach (ed.) *Stable Money, Sound Finances*, Brussels: Commission, DG for Economic and Financial Affairs, 353–367.

Sartori, G. (1970) 'Concept misformation in comparative politics', *American Political Science Review*, 54: 1033–1053.

Sbragia, A. (1992) (ed.) *Europolitics. Institutions and Policy-Making in the 'New' European Community*, Washington, DC: Brookings Institution.

Scharpf, F. W. (1988) 'The joint-decision trap: lessons from German federalism', *Public Administration*, 66(3): 239–278.

—— (1989) 'Decision rules, decision styles, and policy choices', *Journal of Theoretical Politics*, 1: 149–176.

—— (1990) 'Games real actors could play: the problem of mutual predictability', *Rationality and Society*, 3(2): 471–494.

—— (1991) 'Games real actors could play: the challenge of complexity', *Journal of Theoretical Politics*, 3(3): 277–304.

—— (1994a) 'Games real actors could play: positive and negative co-ordination in embedded negotiations', *Journal of Theoretical Politics*, 6(1): 27–53.

—— (1994b) 'Community and autonomy. Multi-level policy-making in the European Union', *Journal of European Public Policy*, 1(2): 219–242.

—— (1996a) 'Europeanization and democratic governance', *Paper given to the Conference on the Europeanisation of Public Policies*, Paris, 20–21 June.

—— (1996b) 'Negative and positive integration in the political economy of European welfare states', in G. Marks, F. W. Scharpf, P. Schmitter and W. Streeck, *Governance in the European Union*, London: Sage, 15–39.

—— (1997) 'Economic integration, democracy and the welfare state', *Journal of European Public Policy*, 4(1): 18–36.

Schelpe, D. (1995) 'The arbitration convention: its origin, its opportunities and its weaknesses', *EC Tax Review*, 2: 68–77.

Schmitter, P. C. (1974) 'Still the century of corporatism?', *The Review of Politics*, 36: 85–131.

—— (1996) 'Examining the present Euro-polity with the help of past theories', in G. Marks, F. W. Scharpf, P. C. Schmitter and W. Streeck (eds) *Governance in the European Union*, London: Sage, 1–14.

Schneider, A. and Ingram, H. (1993) 'Social construction of target populations: implications for politics and policy', *American Political Science Review*, 87(2): 334–347.

Schön, D. A. (1979) 'Generative metaphor. A perspective on problem-setting in social policy', in A. Ortony (ed.) *Metaphor and Thought*, Cambridge: Cambridge University Press, 254–283.

—— and Rein, M. (1994) *Frame Reflection*, New York: Basic Books.

Schultze, C. L. (1995) 'The balanced budget: needed? Effective? Efficient?', *National Tax Journal*, 48(3), September: 317–328.

Scrivener, C. (1990a) 'Harmonization of tax law within the Community', *European Taxation*, 30, December: 355–358.

—— (1990b) 'Corporate taxation in Europe and the single market', *Intertax*, 4: 207–208.

Shadish, W., Cook, T. and Leviton, L. (1992) *Foundations of Program Evaluation. Theories of Practice*, London: Sage.

Simon, H. (1957) *Models of Man*, New York: Wiley.

Sinn, H. W. (1990) 'Tax harmonisation and tax competition in Europe', *European Economic Review*, 34: 489–504.

Slemrod, J. B. (1990) 'The economic impact of the tax reform act of 1986', in J. Slemrod (ed.) *Do Taxes Matter? The Impact of the Tax Reform Act of 1986*, Cambridge, MA: MIT Press, 1–12.

—— (1995) 'Free trade taxation and protectionist taxation', *International Tax and Public Finance*, 2: 471–89.

Smith, J. A. (1991) *The Idea Brokers. Think Tanks and the Rise of a New Policy Elite*, New York: The Free Press.

Sorensen, P. B. (1994) 'From the global income tax to the dual income tax: recent tax reforms in the Nordic countries', *International Tax and Public Finance*, 1(1): 57–79.

Special Committee of Tax Law Consultative Bodies (1993) *Recommendations on Tax Development of Tax Legislation*, London: The Law Society.

Spector, P. H. (1993) 'Triangular problem settled in US–Netherlands treaty protocol', *Bulletin for International Fiscal Documentation*, 47, December: 698–700.

Steinmo, S. (1993) *Taxation and Democracy*, New Haven: Yale University Press.

Stigler G. (1971) 'The theory of economic regulation', *The Bell Journal of Economics and Management Science*, 2: 3–21.

Stone, D. (1996) *Capturing the Political Imagination. Think Tanks and the Policy Process*, Ilford: Frank Cass.

Stone, D. A. (1988) *Policy Paradox and Political Reason*, Glenview: Scott, Foresman.

—— (1989) 'Casual stories and the formation of policy agendas', *Political Science Quarterly*, 104(2): 281–300.

Strange, S. (1994a) 'The power gap: member states and the world economy', in F. Brouwer, V. Linter and M. Newman (eds) *Economic Policy-Making and the European Union*, London: Federal Trust, 19–26.

—— (1994b) *States and Markets*, London: Pinter, second edition.

Struening, E. L. and Brewer, M. B. (1983) (eds) *Handbook of Evaluation Research*, London: Sage.

Tanzi, V. (1993) (ed.) *Transition to Market. Studies in Fiscal Reform*, Washington, DC: International Monetary Fund.

—— (1995) *Taxation in an Integrating World*, Washington, DC: Brookings Institution.

—— and Bovenberg, A. L. (1990) 'Is there a need for harmonising capital income taxes within EC countries?', in H. Siebert (ed.) *Reforming Capital Income Taxation*, Tubingen: J. C. B. Mohr, 171–196.

Tax Law Review Committee (1995), *First Interim Report*, London: Institute for Fiscal Studies.

Thalmann, P. (1992) 'Tax coordination and competiton in Switzerland', in Commission (1992) *Report of the Committee of Independent Experts on Company Taxation* (Ruding Report), Luxembourg: Office for Official Publications, 397–416.

Thommes (1990) 'The European dimension in international tax law', *Intertax*, 10: 464–476.

Thompson, G. (1990) *The Political Economy of the New Right*, Boston and London: Twayne Publishers.

Thompson, M., Ellis, R. and Wildavsky, A. (1990) *Cultural Theory*, Boulder: Westview Press.

Tiebout, C. (1956) 'A pure theory of local expenditures', *Journal of Political Economy*, 64: 416–424.

Tranholm-Mikkelsen, J. (1991) 'Neo-functionalism: obstinate or obsolete? A reappraisal in the light of the new dynamism of the EC', *Millennium*, 20: 1–22.

Tremonti, G. (1993) 'Il futuro del fisco', in F. Galgano, S. Cassese, G. Tremonti and T. Treu (eds) *Nazioni senza ricchezza, ricchezze senza nazioni*, Bologna: Il Mulino, 49–91.

—— and Vitaletti, G. (1986) *Le cento tasse degli italiani*, Bologna: Il Mulino.

—— (1991) *La fiera delle tasse*, Bologna: Il Mulino.

—— (1994) *Il federalismo fiscale. Autonomia municipale e solidarietà sociale*, Rome-Bari: Laterza.

Tsebelis, G. (1990) *Nested Games. Rational Choice in Comparative Politcs*, Berkeley: University of California Press.

—— (1994) 'The power of the European Parliament as a conditional agenda-setter', *American Political Science Review*, 88(1): 128–142.

—— (1995) 'Decision-making in political systems: veto players in presidentialism, parliamentarism, multicameralism and multipartyism', *British Journal of Political Science*, 25: 289–325.

Turro, J. (1995) 'Treasury official reiterates US support for arm's length principle, urges finalization of OECD transfer pricing report', *Tax Notes International*, 10(4), January 24: 297–298

Uckmar, V. (1993) 'L'operatività della amministrazione e la legislazione: la formazione delle leggi', in CNEL (ed.) *Il difficile decollo dell'amministrazione finanziaria*, Rome: CNEL, 63–67.

United Nations (1980) *United Nations Model Double Taxation Convention Between Developed and Developing Countries*, New York: UN Publications.

Vanistendael, F. (1992) 'The Ruding Committee Report: A Personal View', *Fiscal Studies*, 13(2): 85–95.

—— (1993) 'Some basic problems on the road to tax harmonization', *European Taxation*, 33, January: 22–24.

—— (1994) 'Quo vadis European taxation?', *EC Tax Review*, 4: 144–145.

Varazi, F. (1995) 'Reddito di impresa e trasferimento di sede all'estero', *Rassegna Tributaria*, 38(4): 687–694.

Verdun, A. (1996) 'The democratic deficit of EMU: who governs the domestic economy?', *Paper prepared for the First ECSA–Canada biennal conference*, St Catherine's, Ontario, 31 May–1 June.

Visco, V. (1986) 'Un prelievo equo, ragionevole, efficace', *MicroMega*, 2: 247–269.

—— (1991) 'Alcune osservazioni sulla formazione delle decisioni legislative in materia di politica fiscale', *Rivista di Diritto Finanziario e Scienza delle Finanze*, 50(2): 261–287.

—— (1995) 'Alcune note sulla legislazione fiscale in materia di redditi da capitale', in G. Muraro and N. Sartor (eds) *La tassazione delle attività finanziarie*, Milan: Angeli, 50–69.

Vogel, D. (1989) *Fluctuating Fortunes. The Political Power of Business in America*, New York: Basic Books.

—— (1995) *Trading Up. Consumer and Environmental Regulation in a Global Economy*, Cambridge, MA, and London: Harvard University Press.

Wagner, P., Weiss, C. H., Wittrock, B. and Wollman, H. (1991) (eds) *Social Sciences and Modern States. National Experiences and Theoretical Crossroads*, Cambridge: Cambridge University Press.

Wallace, H. (1996) 'Politics and policy in the EU: the challenge of governance', in H. Wallace and W. Wallace (eds) *Policy-Making in the European Union*, Oxford: Oxford University Press, 3–36.

—— and Wallace, W. (1996) (eds) *Policy-Making in the European Union*, Oxford: Oxford University Press.

——, Wallace, W. and Webb, C. (1987) (eds) *Policy-making in the EC*, Chichester: Wiley, third edition.

Wallace, W. (1983) 'Less than a federation, more than a regime', in H. Wallace,

W. Wallace and C. Webb (eds) *Policy-making in the European Community*, Chichester: Wiley, second edition.

—— (1996) 'Government without statehood: the unstable equilibrium', in H. Wallace and W. Wallace (eds) *Policy-Making in the European Union*, Oxford: Oxford University Press, 439–460.

Walsh, C. (1993) 'Fiscal federalism: an overview of issues and a discussion of their relevance to the European Community', *European Economy*, 5: 25–61.

Ward, G. (1993) 'Reforming the public sector: privatisation and the role of advisers', *Political Quarterly*, 64: 298–305.

Ward, I. (1995) 'Identity and difference: the European Union and post-modernism', in J. Shaw and G. More (eds) *New Legal Dynamics of European Union*, Oxford: Clarendon, 15–28.

Weiner, J. E. (1992) 'Tax coordination and competition in the USA', in Commission (1992) *Report of the Committee of Independent Experts on Company Taxation* (Ruding Report), Luxembourg: Office for Official Publications, 417–438.

Weingast, B. (1979) 'A rational choice perspective on Congressional norms', *American Journal of Political Science*, 23: 245–262.

Weir, M. and Skocpol, T. (1985) 'State structures and the possibilities for "Keynesian" responses to the Great Depression in Sweden, Britain and the United States', in P. D. Evans, D. Rueschemeyer and T. Skocpol (1985) (eds) *Bringing the State Back In*, Cambridge: Cambridge University Press, 107–163.

Weiss, C. H. (1979) 'The many meanings of research utilization', *Public Administration Review*, 39(5): 426–431.

—— (1980) 'Knowledge creep and decision accretion', *Knowledge: Creation, Diffusion, Utilization*, 1(3), March: 381–404.

—— (1986) 'Research and policy-making: a limited partnership', in F. Heller (ed.) *The Use and Abuse of Social Science*, Beverly Hills and London: Sage, 214–235.

—— (1987) 'When politics and evaluation meet' (with a postscript), in D. Palumbo (ed.) *The Politics of Program Evaluation*, Beverly Hills and London: Sage, 45–70.

—— (1990) 'Policy research: data, ideas, or arguments', in P. Wagner, C. H. Weiss, B. Wittrock and H. Wollman (eds) *Social Sciences and Modern States. National Experiences and Theoretical Crossroads*, Cambridge: Cambridge University Press, 307–332.

Weizman, L. (1995) 'Basic principles for a democratic treaty-making process', *Tax Notes International*, 10(3), January 16: 255–259.

Wendt, A. E. (1987) 'The agent-structure problem in international relations theory', *International Organization*, 41(3): 335–370.

Whalley, J. (1990) 'Foreign responses to US tax reform', in J. Slemrod (ed.) *Tax Progressivity and Income Inequality*, Cambridge: Cambridge University Press, 286–313.

Wildavsky, A. (1979) *The Art and Craft of Policy Analysis*, London: Macmillan.

Williams, D. (1991) 'The British reaction to the French package', *Intertax*, 11: 560–565.

Wilson, J. Q. (1980) *The Politics of Regulation*, New York: Basic Books.

Wincott, D. (1993) 'The Treaty of Maastricht: an adequate "constitution" for the European Union?', *EPPI Occasional Papers*, European Public Policy Institute, University of Warwick, No. 6, June.

—— (1995a) 'Institutional interaction and European integration: towards an everyday critique of liberal intergovernmentalism, *Journal of Common Market Studies*, 33(4): 597–609.

—— (1995b) 'The European Court of Justice in a policy perspective', *Paper prepared for the Fourth ECSA Conference*, Charleston: May.

Witte, J. F. (1985) *The Politics and Development of the Federal Income Tax*, Madison: University of Wisconsin Press.

Wittrock, B. (1982) 'Social knowledge, public policy and social betterment. A review of current research on knowledge utilization in policy-making', *European Journal of Political Research*, 10: 83–89.

Wright Mills, C. (1956) *The Power Elite*, New York: Oxford University Press.

Yee, A. S. (1996) 'The casual effect of ideas on policies', *International Organization*, 50(1): 69–108.

Yin, R. K. (1994) *Case Study Research*, London: Sage, second edition.

Zodrow, G. R. (1991) 'On the "traditional" and "new" views of dividend taxation', *National Tax Journal*, 44: 497–509.

Index